D1326052

BE YOUR OWN
LANDSCAPE
DETECTIVE

BE YOUR OWN
LANDSCAPE
DETECTIVE

INVESTIGATING WHERE YOU ARE

RICHARD MUIR

SUTTON PUBLISHING

First published in 2007 by
Sutton Publishing, an imprint of NPI Media
Cirencester Road · Chalford · Stroud · Gloucestershire · GL6 8PE

Reprinted 2007

British Library Cataloguing in Publication Data
A catalogue record for this book is available from the British Library.

Hardback ISBN 978-0-7509-4333-8
Paperback ISBN 978-0-7509-4334-5

Photographs and maps by Richard Muir

Typeset in Garamond.
Typesetting and origination by
Sutton Publishing Limited.
Printed and bound in England.

Contents

To the true enthusiasts.
May you reclaim your heritage.

Introduction

This is a Do-It-Yourself book. I have attempted not just to give you some insights into the ways that our rural landscapes have formed, but also to help you to become your own local landscape detective. You will not begin writing learned articles for journals like *Landscape History* just as soon as a reading of the book is complete. But you *should* begin to look at your countryside in a more quizzical, penetrating and informed manner and you *will* be aware of the main events, movements and ideas that have guided its evolution.

Amateur enthusiasts are neglected and undervalued. When I began writing books for ordinary people about the discovery of landscape over twenty-five years ago, the prospects seemed bright. I expected that hundreds of thousands, indeed, millions of people would find delight and stimulation in exploring our homeland. This has not quite happened. I think television has been partly to blame, since the historic landscape is so often presented as the realm of celebrities and all the rest of us watch them from armchairs rather than getting out and about in the real thing. Just a few of these celebrities have real expertise and awareness – for example Julian Richards and his excellent *Blood of the British* series, where the historic people, the sites and the technologies are never upstaged by the presenter. Too often, however, egos promoted by the backstage work of under-credited researchers command the stage and the serious viewer's historic landscape study involves craning to see what is happening in the real scenes behind the posturing and gesticulating presenter.

In the course of all this, it is easy to forget that the foundations of learning about our setting were not put in place by celebrities or even by professors, but by amateur enthusiasts. These were often people driven to amazing lengths of endurance and sacrifice by the urge to discover and understand. Country doctors might halt their traps beside a quarry to enquire if the quarrymen had found any fossils to sell. Village schoolteachers might brave the tides to hammer geological samples from sea cliffs. Vicars might scour the woods for botanical specimens and realise that different insects or snails were found in different habitats. Governesses escaped their charges to spend a quiet hour sketching butterflies in the herb garden. It always amazes me to realise that the age I have just described is not some intellectual Stone Age. The essential concepts of field archaeology were not really put in place until the 1930s and amateur diggers and pilots made important contributions then. Geography at Oxford, the first British university to teach it, is little more than a century old and was established at a time when the subject was built around the efforts of mainly self-appointed scholars who relied upon personal wealth to fund their studies.

Today's amateur enthusiasts should be proud of their status and lineage and be complimented on the work they have achieved, but their position at the heart of heritage and environmental study has been usurped by the managerial culture of the great quangos and the bureaucratic culture that they generate. Where enthusiasts are involved it may be only to fill in questionnaires appraising the latest institutional initiative. I can think of nothing more infuriating than hearing, as I do, of local scholars who have had their work rebuffed by being told that a computer survey had already produced all the answers concerned – and knowing full well that the GIS programme involved is founded on worthless trivia. While footpaths have been blocked and grand old trees felled for lack of protection, a fortune has been spent on sham research that is not worth its space in the archives. I cannot count the times when the institutional networkers have brought me close to despair. But I can say with certainty that I have never left a local history society, an archaeological field group or a meeting in a village hall without feeling reinvigorated by the members' enthusiasm. Also, I have always left knowing something about the locality that I did not know before.

We all need our mentors. I hope that this book can fill a special niche, as there are not many mentors around. People who are desperately keen to learn about the historic environment will have to be self-taught. I was lucky to be born at a time when older men could pass on their knowledge about places to kids without facing suspicions about their motives. Three such men introduced me to my corner of the Yorkshire Dales. An ex-RFC pilot showed me the paths and lanes and where they led and thus provided the directions for countless walks; a slow-talking naturalist who passed his days as a plumber and his nights outdoors introduced me to the local wildlife; and 'Uncle' George would bounce in unexpectedly and announce that we were all going for a nature walk. None of these men knew very much about landscape history, but they did show me that rambling was a very acceptable pastime and that all the different components in the scene were there for good reasons.

Today's universities have been drawn into the managerial morass and all concerned know very well that the throughput of students and the output of research are the things by which they will be judged. Often side-tracked or undervalued, extramural departments rarely offer as much as they once did to potential enthusiasts; qualifications are 'in' but learning is not. Not all that long ago they provided mentors of great vision and courage. In my native Yorkshire Dales the influence of Dr Arthur Raistrick was immense. He was a man of impressive courage and integrity who, as a Quaker, suffered internment for his pacifist beliefs. He died in 1991, just four years short of his 100th birthday, though one may still meet his surviving disciples at work on the history of this landscape. William Hoskins may not quite have been the founder of landscape history, but he was its foremost exponent. He came from a fairly modest Devon background, and despite being dependent on his university posts was not afraid to rage in print about the bureaucratic culture abroad in postwar Britain or what he saw as warmongering in the early nuclear age. Maurice Beresford, his most influential successor and the co-founder of the excavations at Wharram Percy, never concealed his pacifist views and the former students and volunteers that he inspired are numerous in the Broad Acres. Sadly, today the age of the giants seems over and enthusiasts must keep their love of the setting alive till a better day dawns. We have much to pass on.

Study of our historic countryside is not just a work-out for our minds and I will tell you why. In the 1960s, when work as a young local reporter had made me bored with my native dale for the first and only time in my life, I was incredibly lucky to be offered a place at Aberdeen University. On leaving the train I was surprised to find that the townspeople were speaking a language totally unlike the Scots I had heard on *Dr Finlay's Casebook*, and I could scarcely understand them. In the weeks that followed my ear became attuned to the Doric dialect and I noticed that the people of North East Scotland shared a quality that I had seen eroding away in the Yorkshire Dales. *They knew exactly who they were – and they were much stronger as a result.* They did so because they were strongly bonded to places, and these places were ones where their families had lived for quite some time. Meanwhile, as the English became more footloose and were wafted from place to place by the lures and vagaries of employment, they were becoming more insecure and more temperamental, and a new term, 'identity crisis', was gaining common currency. Over the years I have come to realise that a strong bonding with one's home-place helps to buttress one's sense of identity, and hence one's strength and sense of well-being. Many of us are strangers in the lands of others, but a growing engagement with that setting can greatly help the establishment of new roots. Like a nourishing nerve tonic, our locale is absorbed into our personality. I like to imagine that it enters through the soles of the fell boots. Then, if the locals regard you as an outsider, watch their faces when you reel off a string of facts about the history of the lanes, dwellings and woods of *their* locality that they do not know!

Let me say again that there is more involved than intellectual curiosity. The countryside is in turmoil, attacked from many sides with all manner of gimcrack proposals. Does that new planning notice on the telegraph pole in your street herald a proposal to stick a wind turbine over your back fence, a housing estate in the grove or a mink farm in the orchard? The enthusiast's passion for the rural landscape adds great power to the conservational cause, while a knowledge of the history of the locality can provide vital factual evidence for opposing destructive schemes.

I have mentioned the weakness of the amateur enthusiast's cause and how the worthy contributors to understanding and civilised life have been sidelined. But what of the strengths? In modern times the word 'amateur' has taken on connotations of inferiority to 'professional'. The amateur, however, has several superior facets. The amateur can indulge his or her enthusiasms to the full and enjoy each moment invested. I have had two spells of university work of nine years each, involving lecturing, research and research supervision in environmental fields, and about a similar length of time in authorship, landscape photography and cartography for amateur enthusiasts – though often the fields have overlapped. I do what I enjoy, but I have to do it to deadlines, send out invoices and try not to lose receipts – I even go to meetings and all the rest of the paraphernalia of professional life. I truly believe that the times when I did the *least* geography were those when I was employed as a senior lecturer in the subject. Once I get my boots on and leave the office behind I am as excited by the landscape as I ever was, but were I an amateur I could savour the pleasures of landscape detection without bothering about the rest. I could do it whenever I wanted and for as long as I wished. And I could lose the receipts.

Here we come to the superiority of the enthusiast. Amateurs have the greatest of research resources: time. One may not recognise answers as quickly as some paid experts, but often these answers have to be teased out over weeks, months or even years. Nobody will pay one to ramble for hours deep in thought, to revisit a site for the twentieth time to see what it looks like with dawn's dew on the grass. The ability to reflect and then to change one's mind, to explore a new direction of enquiry and then to change one's mind again is beyond price.

In the chapters that follow I have given guides to the interpretation of the main components of landscape: lanes, fields, hamlets and so on. Here are some more general hints that should be borne in mind.

- Do not jump to conclusions; stalk them slowly. The face of the countryside changes with the hour, the season, the weather and the transit of the sun. Land that seems devoid of features in some conditions will, in others, display relics that stand out like chapel hat pegs (as we say up here).

- If you want to specialise on a topic, like villages or routeways, do not be blind to the other components in the landscape. The key to the course of an old road might be contained in a field hedgerow or a holloway on a common. Cast your net wide, for the clues may be thinly spread.

- Do not be overawed by professionals – of whom the wisest are those prepared to say 'I don't know'. Remember, time is on your side and persistence will reveal answers that a genius in a rush could never find.

- The eye is a most remarkable instrument. In harness with the brain, it *learns* to recognise little aspects and facets of the scene that seemed invisible before. See half a dozen different medieval house sites and thereafter you will begin to recognise them in scores of places. Your eyes should train themselves: just show them a few examples of relevant things to get them started.

- Books (like this!) are excellent, but remember that the illustrators and editors will obviously seek to print very clearly pronounced examples of things like lost village sites or medieval fish ponds. The ones that you see may not be clearly pronounced at all and may not even be typical of their genre.

- When you have worked hard and produced good results you will recognise it. And if it is good, it deserves to be preserved. Remember that this is by far the greatest era of outdoor heritage destruction that has ever been known. In a few decades the place where you worked may have been utterly obliterated. Your notebooks, write-up, sketches and photographs may be the only surviving records. They will help future local historians/archaeologists and might even assist a partial reconstruction of the site in more civilised times to come.

- On the whole I think local librarians tend to be more sympathetic and encouraging to such projects, with the managers of environmental institutions tending to have their eyes on the promotion of their quango and of themselves. You do not want your research folder to vanish in some managerial shake-up so the archives of the local library may be the safest haven. But you should remember that various forms of digital storage have already become redundant and that much 'preserved' information is likely to vanish along with the obsolete technological recording media. Archivists seem to agree that old-fashioned paper is still the safest option.

ONE

Trees and Woods

Woods are fascinating places and they are packed with clues concerning the history of their locality. They are also among the most misunderstood of the facets of the landscape.

1. SOME IDEAS ABOUT WOODS

'Woods are the last relics of the ancient wildwood that once covered all of the country' WRONG
'Woods were wild places that lay outside the world of villages and working countryside' WRONG
'You will not find many traces of human activity in a wood' WRONG
'Woods were maintained for untold centuries to produce fuel and many other materials essential to human life' RIGHT
'Most woods seen today display the results of modern neglect of traditional woodland management techniques' RIGHT

2. IS IT A WOOD?

If your 'wood' has straight boundaries and is packed with evergreen spruce, pine or fir trees all of the same age or in stands of the same age, this is probably not a wood but a **plantation**. In plantations timber is grown commercially, just like a crop of wheat or sweetcorn. Such softwood plantations were commonly established on nineteenth-century estates or on poorer ground after the First World War, when Britain's strategic shortages in timber had been exposed. They often exist as monocultures of just one alien evergreen species, like sitka spruce or lodgepole pine.

However, in Victorian and Edwardian times, and on some more recent estates, deciduous woods, many of them ancient, were felled and replanted. In the earlier examples, larch and Scots pine were often planted to produce softwood timber for boards and posts for fencing, gate-making and other uses around the

Until now trees have generally been studied as specimens, like this one – Britain's largest wild cherry at Studley Royal, near Ripon – rather than as components of the human-made landscape.

Hayley Wood in Cambridgeshire is a medieval wood with a rich ground flora of bluebells and oxlips.

estate. Sometimes, they were mixed with beech, which shaded out undergrowth, and rhododendrons, which sheltered pheasant to create settings for the fashionable pheasant shoots. Woods of this kind have undergone **coniferisation**. Their old, irregular shapes tend to survive, and often a few old pollarded trees and woodland shrubs like hazel still stand along their borders.

Thus, three main types of wood may be encountered (see Table 1.1).

3. BOUNDARIES

At the edge of the wood look carefully at the junction with the roadside or fieldscape. In the Middle Ages woods were usually bounded by **woodbanks** and ditches, though in northern districts a dry-stone wall often sufficed. The woodbank provided a reminder that the wood was a valuable resource, and sometimes the importance of the boundary was emphasised by pollards aligned along its crest. Since these banks were built centuries ago, any pollards may

Table 1.1. *Three main types of wood*

	Old or ancient	Coniferised	Plantation
Shape	irregular	irregular	often geometric
Boundaries	often an old wood-bank, dry-stone walls in north	often stone wall or woodbank	often fence or wire, deer fence in Highlands
Species	native deciduous trees, like oak, ash and horn-beam, and under-storey shrubs, like hazel and bird cherry	often early introduced conifers – Scots pine or larch – plus beech and rhododendron. The last named may now be rampant	alien conifers, some-times with landscaping, for example with cherry trees around the margins

have gone and soil will have eroded from the bank into the ditch. So the old woodbank need not be a prominent feature today. Where stone was abundant, as in the Yorkshire Dales, the outer face of the bank might be faced or *revetted* with stones or cobbles and in many stone-rich northern localities the wood was ringed by a dry-stone wall.

Woods could sometimes advance or retreat, so the absence of a woodbank does not prove that your wood is not very old. Woods could expand beyond their old woodbanks, but any earthwork banks found running across the woodland floor need not necessarily be former woodbanks. They might be the lesser banks that partitioned old coppice woods into compartments, known as **haggs** or **panels**. These compartments were cut in rotation.

4. WHAT WERE WOODS FOR?

Medieval woods were part of the working countryside and they had several important uses (see also Chapter Eight). These included:

- **Pannage** and **mast**: The pasturing of herds of swine on fallen acorns and beech nuts respectively.
- **Agistment**: Taking a rent from outsiders to allow them to graze livestock in the woods alongside the beasts of the lord and his tenants.
- **Hunting**: The lord often purchased from the Crown the right of *free warren* to hunt small game on his own estates.

- **Honey**: In ancient and medieval times there were no artificial sweeteners and honey from wild bees was eagerly devoured by people who tasted nothing else so sweet.
- **Browse**: Oak, ash and elm yielded leafy fodder that could be lopped in summer and fed to cattle or deer.
- **Winter fodder**: See **hollins**, below.
- **Timber and fuel**: See *How trees were managed*, below
- **Woodland craft industries**: See page 10.

5. HOLLY GROVES OR HOLLINS

In the Middle Ages there were no refrigerators or canneries to store meat and the supplies of hay for winter fodder were often too small. The need to slaughter valuable livestock in autumn could be avoided by keeping the hungry animals alive by feeding them holly. The leaves on the higher boughs lacked thorns as the trees did not 'expect' browsing at this height. Holly was cultivated in groves known as **hollins**. Branches of holly were lopped in late autumn and stored in little barns, and this fodder could be crucial in keeping a farming community going through the depths of winter.

Detection: Any grove containing holly might have been a hollins. The decisive evidence comes from place-names, like Hollins Hall, Hollins Lane, Low Hollins, etc. In the northern dales, these are remarkably numerous.

6. HOW TREES WERE MANAGED

Trees were managed in different ways in order to produce the types of timber needed for diverse tasks. Medieval and earlier woods were *working* woods, and you would seldom find trees within them growing in their natural forms. Rather, they displayed the signs of varying management techniques.

Common ways of managing trees

- **Wood pasture**: Here the production of poles and browse was combined with grazing. The pollarded trees, often oak or ash, were sufficiently widely spaced to admit light and allow grass to carpet the space between the trees.
- **Pollarding**: This allowed trees to be combined with cattle, horses and deer. They were 'beheaded' above the reach of browsing (around 8ft, or 2.4m).

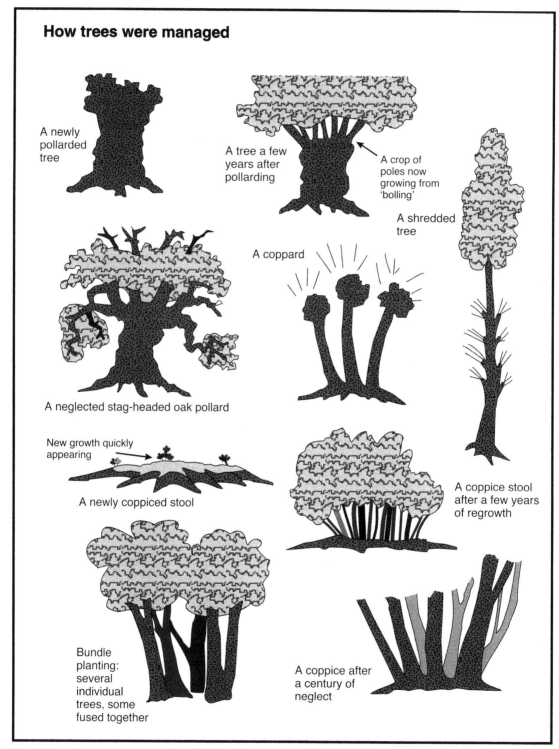

Fig. 1. How trees were managed: pollards and coppices.

Poles would then grow from the **bolling** and could be lopped when young for browse or cut after a few years for fuel. Pollarded trees were common in deer parks (see Chapter Eight), where leafy fronds from the oak and elm trees were tossed to the ground for deer or cattle to find.

- **Coppice**: Here trees were felled at ground level, after which thickets of rods/poles would spring from the old **coppice stool**. Coppices had to be fenced against wild animals and domestic livestock but they produced masses of light timber for fuel, wattle and many other uses. When the underwood was coppiced, light could flood in and there would be a colourful eruption of ground flora.

- **Coppice with standards**: In this popular and widespread system the underwood was coppiced and large timber trees were allowed to grow above the coppice as 'maidens' or standards. The underwood was cut on a short coppice cycle while the standards towering above might live through about five coppice cycles. Then they were felled to provide heavy timber for house construction, shipbuilding, mill wheels and other major structures.

A tiny fragment of once-extensive upland wood pasture surviving in the Yorkshire Dales. Being on rather high and exposed ground, the oaks are rather stunted, though they are very old. Formerly part of the Fountains Abbey estates, this wood pasture was later incorporated in a deer park.

Less common ways of managing trees

- **Shredding**: This involved removing the side branches of a tree till only a plume of foliage remained at the top. The loppings must have been fed to animals. Examples are not easy to find today, but shredded trees in hedgerows can be seen in the early landscape paintings of the seventeenth to eighteenth centuries.
- **Coppards**: These were trees first coppiced and then the several trunks or stems rising up from the stool were pollarded. Hornbeams growing in Epping Forest were managed in this way to produce fuel for London's hearths.
- **Bundle planting**: This has only recently been recognised. Some 'trees' with multiple trunks are really composed of several individual trees, originally planted together in a bundle in the hope that at least one seedling would survive.

7. HOW DID THE WOODS EVOLVE?

As the centuries have rolled by woods have passed through different stages of management and evolution.

At the time of Domesday Book (1086) wood pasture was very widespread in England. Much of the tree-studded pastureland existed as commons where members of the local community enjoyed rights to graze their beasts and lop fronds or poles. As the population grew and societies became more technologically and commercially 'advanced', higher levels of timber production were demanded. Meanwhile, the privatisation of much common land put further pressures on the ancient wood pastures. In the course of the Middle Ages the emphasis shifted from wood pasture towards woods producing masses of coppiced timber. These woods were divided into different compartments so that blocks of woodland could be cut in rotation to give a regular flow of production.

In the north of England particularly coppice-with-standards woodland underwent massive expansion at the end of the Middle Ages. In the Sheffield region the coppice components were cut every 20–25 years, mainly for charcoal and white coal (see below). The standards towering above were graded according to the number of coppice cycles imposed on the surrounding underwood. A 'waver' had seen one cycle, a 'black bark' two and a 'lording' three.

In the seventeenth and eighteenth centuries considerable ornamental planting was associated with landscape parks (see Chapter Eight). The trees involved

The medieval technique of managing woodland as coppice beneath standard trees has been revived in this Suffolk wood, where the coppiced underwood gives shelter to birds.

were important commercially, and timber sales might be prominent in the accounts of the stately home and its landscape park. Meanwhile, gnarled old trees were being removed from most of the remaining vestiges of wood pasture, which became open grazing land or ploughland.

As North American and Scandinavian timber began to be imported and landowners started to think in shorter commercial terms, the traditions of woodmanship in the home-grown deciduous woods gradually fell into decline. Some old woods were coniferised and others modified for estate pheasant shooting. By the end of the First World War the old crafts of coppicing and pollarding were almost extinct. Typically the deciduous woods seen today display the deformed products of decades of neglect of coppicing and pollarding. Pollards bear massive boughs that are increasingly likely to break under their own weight, while trunks as thick as pythons rear from the old coppice stools.

In the Scottish uplands Scots pine is indigenous (though in England and Wales it is probably only native in the Lake District). Scots pine, like other conifers, does not respond to the management techniques applied to native hardwoods, but pine timber was valued for shipbuilding, construction, flooring and many other uses.

A myth has developed that Scotland was covered in a great Caledonian pine forest. In fact, depletion of native woods was apparent in many places during the Middle Ages and softwood timber from Scandinavia was shipped into Scottish east coast ports. Later the further depletion of resources, often wasteful, for smelters, ships' masts and other demands all took their toll. Grouse moors were also advanced at the expense of the trees, but the pines are now effectively re-advancing in many places.

In the Scottish uplands look out for oak woods containing trees all of a similar, fairly young age. These are likely to have been planted to produce bark that yields tannin for the leather tanning industry.

8. THE USES OF TIMBER

Country folk acquired a wealth of understanding about the best types of timber to use for particular tasks. Oak was the most valuable timber and its hard, weather-resistant character allowed its use in the building of houses and ships. Other trees that produced structural timber were ash and elm and the now-rare black poplar.

9. WOODLAND INDUSTRIES

Many old industries operated in woods, attracted by their fuel supplies, water resources and the easier access to minerals. It is often surprising to find how few traces remain of woodland industries that were significant until quite modern times. Table 1.3 shows some of the main old woodland industries and the evidence that they may have left in your woods.

Summary

The woods have swiftly concealed most traces of once-important industries. Look out for place-names like 'Baile Hill', 'Forge Wood', 'Kiln Wood' or 'Bark House'. Soil containing slag and cinders or stained with charcoal can tell a story, while circular hollows may mark old charcoal-burning sites.

10. WHAT DO WE SEE IN WOODS TODAY?

The typical wood today displays examples of trees managed in the old ways but neglected for around one or two centuries.

Pollards: Eventually (more than 200 years ago in many places), country people ceased to lop poles and browse from the woodland and hedgerow pollards.

Table 1.2. *Trees and their uses*

Alder	Coppiced to yield the best gunpowder and clog wood. The timber produced a dye.
Ash	Springy timber for tool handles, cart bodies and spokes, coppice products, barrel hoops.
Beech	Beech mast for swine; hard white timber for firewood and turning, cheap turned chair components.
Birch	Stove fuel; timber for the backs of bushes and cotton reels; rope from the 'bast' and a hair dye from the twigs.
Black poplar	Structural timber for cottage building.
Dogwood	Rods or 'dags' used for skewers.
Elm	Weatherboarding; wood for the cartwright; wheel hubs; coppice timber, bows, chair seats and many other uses.
Field maple	Turned drinking vessels and musical instruments.
Hazel	Coppice timber much used for faggots; rods for spars and sways to peg down thatch; pea sticks; long rods used in 'heathering' woven into top of hedges; wattle and nuts.
Holly	Foliage for winter fodder; white timber for the craftsman.
Hornbeam	Said to produce the best firewood; its extreme hardness favoured its use for cogwheels in mills.
Lime	Once used for shields; coppice timber for turning.
Oak	Heavy, weatherproof structural timber; planks; studwork for buildings; barrel staves; posts; cartwright timbers; tannin for dyes; cleft posts for palings.
Scots pine	Planking; masts; decking; fuel.
Spindle tree	Fine-grained wood used for spindles.
Sweet chestnut	Coppiced timber split for durable fence posts; workable furniture-making material resembling oak.
Sycamore	May not be native. Fine-grained wood for carving.
Wild cherry, pear and crab apple	Fruit; high-quality fruitwood timber for musical instruments and inlays.
Yew	Long-living churchyard trees whose evergreen foliage symbolised eternal life. Extremely hard red and white timber used for longbows; berries contain deadly poison.

Table 1.3. *Woodland industries*

Industry	Remains
Iron forging/smelting Charcoal from the woods and ore from wooded commons attracted the iron industries. Where there were streams to dam, ponds might be made to power bellows for blast-furnaces or forge hammers.	Hummocky ground where pits were dug for ore. Glassy slag and cinders in mounds beneath the leaf mould. Earthworks of industrial ponds, or ponds still surviving. Hills, sometimes named 'Baile Hill', where smelters and blast-furnaces were placed on the hilltop to catch the wind.
Hurdle-making This used wattle from the coppices. Wattle was woven through rods held upright in the ground to form 'sails'.	'Sails' or hurdles of wattle were used for movable fencing and were made in their thousands in the woods. The craft had few if any structures and has gone without trace.
Wood turning Pole-lathes taking power from bent saplings were set up in the coppices over many centuries. Medieval woods attracted turners who produced the vast quantities of cheap platters and drinking vessels needed in those times. Later craftsmen mass-producing turned parts for Windsor chairs would buy up stands of beech in the Chilterns, often living in huts in the woods while they worked.	Like the hurdle-makers, their craft is marked only by the presence of neglected coppices. Their huts have blown down and rotted and the masses of shavings from their lathes have moulded under the leaf litter on the woodland floor. The coppices where they worked may now be abandoned and full of distorted trunks.
Barking Bark, particularly oak bark, produced tannin that was used to tan leather.	Apart from the survival, particularly in Scotland, of the managed oak woods concerned, there are few remaining traces. 'Bark House' place-names sometimes found on old maps denote the shacks where the gathered bark was stored and dried.
Charcoal burning This industry produced the fuel for other industries, like iron working. It was one of the last to vanish, for some burning continued to produce ingredients for gunpowder and fuel for the braziers in the trenches of the First World War. Timber was cut into billets which were stacked tightly in great clamps and covered in turf to burn very slowly, converting the timber into charcoal.	The coppices worked by the charcoal burners or 'colliers' are now neglected. Sometimes saucer-shaped depressions about 10–25ft (3–7.5m) across mark the sites of the old clamps, and occasionally the wreckage of the steel kilns used in the last days of burning can still be found in the woods. Any abandoned drums decaying in the woods may have been used in distilling methylated spirits.

Industry	Remains
Kiln-dried timber Through into the Industrial Age, kiln-dried timber or 'white coal' was mixed in furnaces with charcoal, which also came from the local coppices.	White coal kilns have the appearance of shallow hollows with traces of a 'spout' at one end. In some woods around the old industrial areas of northern England they can be very numerous.

Instead of resembling lollipops, with a fuzzy ball of leaves, rods and poles crowning their stocky trunks, the pollards began to bear boughs that, unlopped, grew heavier and heavier, all fanning out from the old level of pollarding. As these boughs thickened and became more contorted, they assumed the Gothic forms portrayed by Rackham in his illustrations to fairy tales. Ultimately some of these boughs break under their own weight, while ancient oaks acquire a **stag-headed** appearance when foliage in the dwindling canopy retreats from their uppermost branches. Such trees may still have centuries of life ahead.

Coppices: In the working coppice wood the stools were coppiced every 12–25 years. As the light flooded into the newly cleared site, plants would flower on the woodland floor, while for a few years **dead hedges** would need to be set around the coppiced area to keep swine and other beasts away from the soft buds and shoots. After regular coppicing was abandoned, rods from the stools became poles which grew into up-reaching trunks thicker than a man's thigh. Clusters of abandoned stools with gross stems reaching out like tentacles from a giant squid are commonplace in the woods.

Standards: The abandonment of old traditions has allowed many old trees to grow far larger than they would have done in days gone by. Some have become 'landmark trees', although the old records show that there were always trees around of great size and celebrity. Many marked the courses of old boundaries.

11. WHAT CAN WE LEARN FROM PLACE-NAMES?

A great deal! Place-names indicate areas of open countryside that were previously wooded and they tell us about the ways in which many woods were used. Most localities contain a selection of the names listed in Table 1.4 (see page 14) indicating the presence of woodland.

Table 1.4. *Names recording woods*

Name or element	Language of origin	Original meaning
Abhall	Scots Gaelic	Orchard, apple
Coed	Welsh	A wood
Coille	Scots Gaelic	A wood
Crann	Scots Gaelic	A tree
Daroch	Scots Gaelic	An oak
Den, dene	Old English	A wood where swine pastured
Grove	Old English	A small wood
Field	Old English	Farmland close to a wood
Fiodh	Scots Gaelic	A wood
Frith	Old English	A wood (these woods are often very old)
Hanger	Old English	A wooded slope
Hollins	Old English	A grove where holly was cut
Holt	Old English	A small wood or thicket
Hurst	Old English	A wooded hill
Giuthas	Scots Gaelic	A tree
Ley, lea	Old English	Trees or a clearing
Lund	Old Norse	A wood (these woods are often very old)
Shaw	Old English	A wood
Storth	Old Norse	Brushwood or a plantation
With, worth	Old Norse	A wood
Wood	Old English	A wood

12. WOODLAND ANCESTORS

In the Middle Ages ordinary people frequently took their names from the places where they lived or from their occupations. The profusion of old wood-related surnames show how largely woods featured in their lives.

An ancient and long-neglected beech coppice in Epping Forest.

- **People who lived in or beside a wood**: Atwood, Frith, Greenwood, Grove, Hartley, Leigh, Lund, Shaw, Spring, Wood, Woodgate, Woodhouse.
- **People who worked in a wood**: Ashburner, Barker, Carpenter, Collyer, Cooper, Forester, Parker, Sawyer, Turner, Woodward.
- **People who cleared wood or lived on recently cleared land**: Hey, Ridding, -royd (e.g. Acroyd, meaning oak clearing), Sart, Stocks, Stubbs, Stubbings.
- To these we should add many Smiths, for smithies and forges were often sited among the sources of charcoal.

13. YOU ARE THE DETECTIVE

Each locality is different: how much can you discover about yours? Here are some ideas.

- Obtain an identification guide and discover which trees and underwood shrubs flourish in your locality. Oak and chestnut like acid soils, while ash prefers a little lime. Old woods have several main species and they come in various groupings, like the hornbeam-plus-oak woods of south-east England or the oak-plus-lime woods on the acid soils of the Midlands and

Table 1.5. *Names describing coppiced woods*

Name or element	Language of origin	Original meaning
Copy, copse, coppice	Middle English	A coppiced wood
Fall	Middle English	A coppiced wood
Hagg, panel	Old Norse	A coppice or division of one
Spring	Old English	Rarely a stream, normally refers to a coppice that 'springs forth' from the coppiced stool. A very common woodland place-name.

Table 1.6. *Names describing land cleared of trees long ago*

Name or element	Language of origin	Original meaning
Hay	Old English	Hedge or small wood, often in cleared land
Ridding, ridden	Old English	Land rid of woodland
Rode, royd	Old English	Cleared land
Sart	Old French	Land cleared for cultivation
Stocks, stocking	Old English	Land cleared of tree stumps
Stubbs, stubbing	Old English	Ground covered in tree stumps
Thwaite	Old Norse	Clearing/meadow

Wales. Catalogue your assemblages of trees and shrubs and discover your local woodland character.

- Look at a fairly large-scale map of your locality (the old 6in to a mile maps kept in local libraries and county record offices are very revealing). Scour the map for woodland names and see what they can tell you about the retreat of woods. You may find Saxon 'Lund' and 'Frith' names far from any surviving woods, while the 'Ridding' and 'Stocks' names show where land was being cleared in the Middle Ages. Do not just focus on individual place-names but look for the broader picture that the names reveal.

- Look for names that tell you about how your local woods were managed. 'Spring' names denoting old coppice woods are very common.
- Look at the shape of the wood and explore its boundaries. Clusters of little woods, like islands in an archipelago, often result from the fragmentation of a once large and continuous wood. Look for the woodbanks associated with old woods. There may also be internal banks that divided the different haggs or coppice compartments.
- Woods can colonise new land as well as retreating. If you look closely you may find traces of old hedgerows or 'ridge-and-furrow' ploughland that have been taken over by the wood. There may also be little platforms or low, overgrown walls marking the dwellings of the woodland people of long ago. Woodland ponds may have been hammer ponds powering mill wheels driving the hammers at forges or the bellows at furnaces.

14. WHERE DO TREES COME FROM?

- Some trees were deliberately planted, while others have germinated and grown naturally.
- Trees in the old woods were hardly ever planted.
- When the old standards were felled their stumps would naturally produce new stems and these stumps must frequently have become coppice stools.
- The tall standards in a wood would come from the natural germination of acorns, ash keys and so on. Which ones survived would depend on competition from other trees and the choices of the woodsmen about which species were most valuable.
- The trees seen in plantations and coniferised woods have all been planted and usually they belong to alien species that could not naturally germinate and grow in the locations concerned.
- Trees in parkland are often a mixture of native trees that pre-date the park and deliberate plantings. Often the latter were chosen to fill in the gaps in the 'inherited' tree patterns. Sometimes the trees chosen seem to mimic the native species, in the way that pollarded sweet chestnuts from a distance resemble gnarled old pollarded oaks. The faster-growing species, like beech and sweet chestnut, were favoured for parkland plantings.
- Hedgerow trees were planted, often with seedlings dug from nearby woods.
- Isolated trees in fields are often thought to have been planted as specimens and in order to provide shade and rubbing posts for cattle. Actually a very high proportion of these trees can be shown to have originated in former

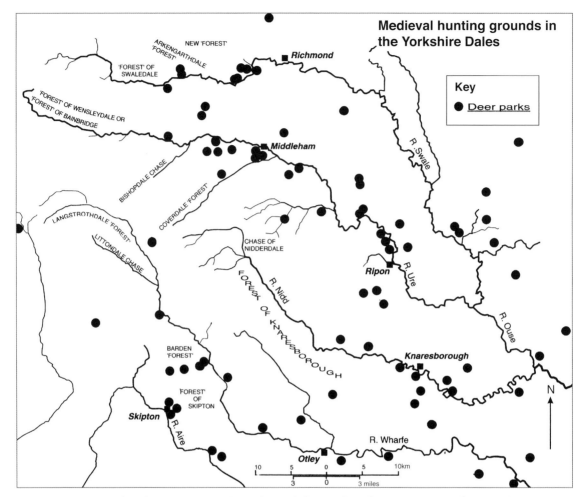

Fig. 2. Medieval hunting grounds in the Yorkshire Dales, showing Forests, 'forests', deer parks and chases (not all contemporaneous). Many places referred to as 'Forests' were actually chases belonging to the nobility.

hedgerows: after the hedge shrubs have died or been removed, one or more old hedgerow trees may be left standing.

- Special plantings were made for a host of purposes, such as the sycamore groups that often shelter upland farmsteads in the Pennines or the Scots pine shelter belts seen throughout Britain from the south-west up to the Scottish Highlands. Sometimes trees or woods were planted to commemorate particular people or events and specimen trees might mark anything from the grave of a pet to an anniversary.

15. LANDMARK TREES

- In North America today trees that are particularly valued by their town or state communities may be designated as 'landmark' trees.

- Special trees were always valued for their role as landmarks within their setting.

- In Saxon times trees very frequently served as boundary marks. Thorn trees were especially favoured, perhaps because the early flowering of the blackthorn and hawthorn symbolised rebirth to pagan societies and the death and resurrection of Christ to Christian ones.

- Trees that were important landmarks on boundaries continued to be significant in medieval and even later times. They may be discovered in old maps and other documents with names like 'Great Mark Oak' or 'Shire Oak', both of which words denote boundaries. The 'Three Shire Oak' stood at a junction of county boundaries and was said to shade parts of Yorkshire, Derbyshire and Nottinghamshire and to drip over 777sq yd (650sq m); it was thought to have died around 1800.

- Landmark trees or 'head trees', often on or near boundaries, frequently marked the places where local courts were held. The courts of the medieval bishops of St Albans were held under an ash tree growing in the middle court of the abbey. Oaks, so imposing and long-lived, were the most popular choices, though in Germany, where the tradition also existed, limes were more favoured.

- Trees with more sinister connotations were those employed as gallows, where wrongdoers were hanged, and as gibbets, where the corpses of execution victims were suspended in iron cages. Sometimes artificial gallows were erected on prehistoric barrows, but often trees standing at crossroads were used, so that the ghosts of the victims might be confused and thus could not return to haunt their native settlements. Suicides were also buried at remote roadsides and crossroads. In early times stakes might be driven through their hearts to transfix the spirit, and various roadside trees were reputed, surely erroneously, to have grown from these stakes.

- Some trees are associated with particular historical events. The Royal Oak at Boscobel in Shropshire, where Charles II hid after the royalist defeat at Worcester in 1651, became so famous that it was plagued by souvenir hunters and had to be protected by a wall. As with several other landmark trees, like the Glastonbury Thorn and the Three Shire Oak, after it died its name was inherited by a successor tree. Two landmark trees, a holm oak and

Queen Mary's Thorn, grow in the courtyard of St Mary's College at St Andrews; the latter is said to have been planted by the queen in 1563.

16. FINDING LANDMARK TREES

A few landmark trees, like the Major Oak in Sherwood Forest and the (latest) Glastonbury Thorn, still exist. Discovering former landmark trees can follow a variety of directions and there are no particular avenues that are bound to lead to success.

Old maps, like the large-scale estate maps of Elizabethan times, can be very rewarding. I found both 'Priests Oke' and 'Ambush Oke' on a 1591 map of Feckenham in Worcestershire. The Ambush Oke stood isolated on a common, not far from a track, and it seemed a most likely place for ambushers to lie in wait.

Old documents of all ages can be helpful. Saxon charters, available in good libraries in bound and translated collections, are full of references to trees used as boundary marks. For example, a charter granted by King Aethelred in 1012 of lands at Wetmore in Staffordshire to Burton Abbey mentions a boundary thorn, a tree stump, a wooded hillside, a boundary elm and a gallows site by the Trent where thieves were hanged. In addition, references to landmark trees can turn up in unexpected places: I found a list of then-celebrated landmark trees in the 1874 correspondence of a tree sleuth, one Louise Charlotte Frampton.

Because trees were so frequently used as boundary marks, any charters or legal documents relating to estates, recorded perambulations of Forest boundaries; maps attached to legal documents and so on are likely to note landmark trees. The question then to pursue is where are those trees now? An oak that was a prominent 250-year-old boundary mark at the end of the Middle Ages might possibly still be alive today.

Wherever we have old trees of proven age, the closer we come to establishing a growth curve for a particular region, allowing ages to be estimated for other trees of that species in the area.

Of all the sources available to tree detectives, the first editions of the British Ordnance Survey 6in to a mile maps, appearing for different localities at differing dates around 1850, are the most helpful. This is because they plot every tree that the surveyors found in the mid-nineteenth century; sometimes they apparently surveyed each tree in, while in other places they probably sketched them in. In either case the results are sufficiently accurate to allow each surviving tree to be identified today. Sadly, in cases where I have worked only around one in eight of those trees still stands.

17. CONSERVING THE LEGACY

The wonderful heritage of historic trees will only be conserved if enthusiasts argue their case with passion and determination. Unfortunately this is a litigious age and public authorities and private owners generally prefer to fell veteran trees rather than to risk litigation, even from trespassers. Transport authorities are both powerful and frequently unsympathetic to the case for preserving landmark roadside trees. It is not always recognised that in long-lived trees like the oak, hollowness is part of the growth process, not a sign of degeneration. In fact, hollow trees have structural advantages in resisting gales.

The pattern of applying tree preservation orders is very uneven. Some authorities aim for a blanket preservation of countryside trees of any standing, though some borough authorities give priority to 'parks and gardens' interest and show less concern with the surrounding rural landscapes. Wildlife is adapted to native tree species, and the alien specimen plantings in urban parks have far less value. Unless conservation cases are promoted, many authorities will sanction the felling of healthy trees rather than taking up a case for preservation with property owners and their tree 'surgeons'.

Any tree enthusiasts seeking to improve tree conservation in their localities will be far more convincing if they are well-versed in the heritage of trees. Those who know more about the local resource of ancient trees and woodland than do the authorities become the guardians of a valuable resource of information – and this can open doors and lead to consultations.

Lastly, beware of official claims to have 'done it all'. Work on recording, say, ancient woodland done by consultants and/or crude computer programs is often incomplete and sometimes worthless. There is no substitute for the diligent, time-little-object researches of the dedicated amateur enthusiast. A team of five consultants working for a day on a local tree project would charge well over £1,000. Enthusiasts, if properly grounded, could do the same task more thoroughly for nothing.

TWO

Fieldscapes

1. SOME IDEAS ABOUT FIELDS AND FIELD PATTERNS

'A field is a field is a field. They all look the same don't they?' WRONG

'Fields first appeared when the Anglo-Saxons cut back the forests in the Middle Ages' WRONG

'You can tell the age of a hedgerow by counting the different tree and shrub species growing in a 50m length' WRONG

'Our field network has been gaining (and losing) fields and evolving from prehistoric times right through to the modern period' RIGHT

'Exploring fields and their patterns in a locality is all about discovering *shapes* and *sizes*: every era of field creation produced its own distinctive field packages and each one had its characteristic field shapes and patterns' RIGHT

'In most localities in Britain the landscape is built around the fieldscape and the exploration of fields, and their story is something that the amateur enthusiast can tackle with high hopes of success' RIGHT

2. MEETING FIELDS

Fields are as old as farming and the first ones in Britain appeared when the farmers of the New Stone Age (Neolithic period) cleared land for cultivation perhaps 6,000 years ago. Today, field patterns tend to be taken for granted, but in England commonly and in Scotland and Wales to some degree they are the most prominent component of the traditional landscapes. We should also remember that although fields and their tracery patterns of hedgerows and walls form the essence of our national scenery, they were created for functional rather than scenic reasons, and from the outset they have performed the following tasks:

- **Dividing a landholding** into smaller packages for more convenient working.

The outlines of a rather rectangular prehistoric field system are displayed as earthworks in the Valley of Stones, Dorset.

- **Providing protection** for cereal, hay and legume crops against trespassing wild animals and farm livestock. These might otherwise invade via lanes or neighbouring land. In the days of open field farming, when livestock tended to roam, special **pinfolds** served by officials known as 'pinders' were used to impound any trespassing animals (see below).
- Helping to **mark the boundaries** between adjacent properties.
- Giving a plain **visual demarcation** between different types of shared land and between commons and private holdings.

The fields that you find in your locality are unlikely to be the first ones to have been there, for as farming circumstances changed one pattern of fields would be replaced by another, while this in turn might later give way to yet another.

Fields were wholly functional, and few people, if any, in the past were much concerned about the prettiness of the hedgerow network or the patterns of emerald and gold in the fieldscape. The fields that people set out reflected the farming technology and demands of their day. In the earliest times of criss-cross ploughing with pointed boughs hauled by small oxen, the fields were very small and compact. More efficient early medieval ploughs with iron-shod cutting blades (coulters), mould-boards to turn the sod and strings of beefy oxen to haul them allowed strips, 'lands' or 'selions' some 200 or more metres long to be ploughed. When horses were harnessed to the plough later in the Middle Ages, even longer strips could be ploughed without the animals needing to pause for breath.

On the whole, readjustment was preferred to the wholesale removal of a set of fields. Any field pattern that is seen is quite likely to reflect earlier rather than modern situations, though countless miles of hedgerows and dry-stone walls have been dragged out to merge fields into vast arenas where the huge farm machines can manoeuvre.

3. THE MOST ANCIENT FIELDS

Fields from the prehistoric period (i.e. between about 4000 BC and the Roman landings in AD 43) come in a variety of shapes and sizes, depending upon what they were used for and the scale of the area that was being enclosed by fields. They also differ according to whether we encounter them as 'fossils' or as parts of the living, working countryside. If you discover some possibly ancient fields the following questions can be posed to get a clearer picture:

How do we know these fields are prehistoric?

- Are they 'respected' by features like prehistoric tombs, lanes, boundaries or tracks that we know to be ancient? Do the fields mesh with the ancient patterns – look at the ancient fields and prehistoric settlements on the map of west Cornwall, see Fig. 3.
- Are they crossed by any Roman roads which, by cutting off corners to form inconvenient little triangular fields, show that our fields were already in existence when the Romans arrived?
- If the fields in question are still 'living', can we see the pattern vanishing into any upland moors or commons or into lowland heaths?
- Does the pattern exist as earthworks or tumbledown walls in an area of ancient common? If it does, then the fossil fieldscape must be older than the common, and most commons were well established by the dawn of the Middle Ages.
- In many places this question will be a difficult one to answer without recourse to detailed survey. Many of the fields fringing Dartmoor that form the still-living countryside look, and probably are, prehistoric and field patterns of essentially prehistoric form remained in use throughout the Roman occupation and on into the Saxon and medieval periods, and sometimes beyond.

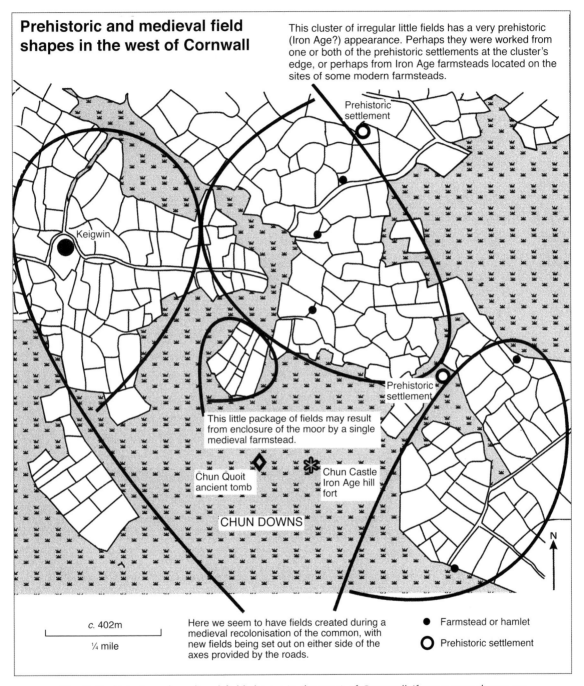

Prehistoric and medieval field shapes in the west of Cornwall

This cluster of irregular little fields has a very prehistoric (Iron Age?) appearance. Perhaps they were worked from one or both of the prehistoric settlements at the cluster's edge, or perhaps from Iron Age farmsteads located on the sites of some modern farmsteads.

Prehistoric settlement

Keigwin

Prehistoric settlement

This little package of fields may result from enclosure of the moor by a single medieval farmstead.

Chun Quoit ancient tomb

Chun Castle Iron Age hill fort

CHUN DOWNS

N

c. 402m

¼ mile

Here we seem to have fields created during a medieval recolonisation of the common, with new fields being set out on either side of the axes provided by the roads.

● Farmstead or hamlet

O Prehistoric settlement

Fig. 3. Prehistoric and medieval field shapes in the west of Cornwall (from a map drawn up in the 1870s).

What do prehistoric fields look like?

A variety of different shapes and sizes can be formed, though the individual fields concerned are usually quite small and compact, ranging from about the size of a football or hockey pitch down to that of a cricket square or even a couple of tennis courts. Sometimes they form networks like brickwork, or elsewhere grids or irregular patterns. The following types are most likely to be seen:

- **Small fields with rather irregular or 'sub-rectangular' shapes forming patterns like the cells in wire netting or frogspawn**. These can sometimes be linked to a particular prehistoric farmstead and appear to represent the holding of enclosed land that surrounded it. The patterns are often associated with the uplands in the south-west of England and elsewhere that were deserted when the climate deteriorated during the Bronze Age. On the margins of Dartmoor the fossil prehistoric wall lines can sometimes be seen running down from the moor to form elements of the still-living fieldscape of working walled pastures. Such fields might be 3,000 or even 4,000 years old!
- **Field networks formed by scarp-like banks in the Downs**. Before ploughing devastated the ancient field patterns on the southern chalk downlands in the 1960s, 1970s and 1980s, the evocative traces of prehistoric farming enhanced the old sheep pastures. Most of the ancient field banks or **lynchets** have been levelled, although now, when freshly ploughed, the Downs of Wessex, Sussex and Kent still reveal the blurred shapes of ancient fields outlined as soil marks. The fields of the sloping Downs were gradually defined as the **ards** (simple ploughs) bit into the slopes horizontally to create more level platforms for cultivation. As the fields developed, the shelves became backed by steepened steps leading up to the next level. As with most ancient field patterns, the fields were probably enclosed by hedgerows that would have crowned the plough-cut banks that bounded them. In places where excavations have removed the soil and subsoil from ancient fields in the downlands, shallow, criss-cross patterns grooved into the chalk bedrock by the tips of the ards have been seen.
- **Co-axial field patterns**. For no good reason people tend to imagine prehistoric communities as being 'primitive' and disorganised. To those who hold such views, it will come as a surprise to learn that, from at least the Bronze Age onwards, countrysides could be carpeted in carefully designed

networks of fields that could extend across dozens and dozens of square miles. **Co-axial field networks** consist of such fields, which all have the same orientation, and the extent of fields all sharing a common axis, shows that the networks must have been imposed across great swathes of countryside as manifestations of a single grand idea. They show planning and they show the great powers to command that were wielded by their creators. Whether they were the work of tyrants or committees we do not know, but plainly an individual or a group had the power to dictate the working of the countryside across a broad area. Such networks have been recognised in places as far apart as Dartmoor, where they are known as **reaves**, Norfolk and Swaledale.

Encountering ancient fields

Prehistoric fields are encountered in all manner of states and conditions.

Some are still at work on the lower flanks of a south-western moor or on some rocky Irish tableland, their dry-stone walls patched on countless occasions to contain the livestock. Look for walls of the **orthostat** type, which have massive boulders gathered during the original land clearance built into their footings. But bear in mind that such walls were also built during, and even after, the Middle Ages. In the lowlands hedged fragments of prehistoric field networks still survive in the living fieldscape. Only a shared orientation, running across many square miles and several parishes, may suggest their antiquity.

The old commons on the poorer ground that escaped ploughing during the historical era provides the safest refuges for ancient field walls. In areas of rough grazing look out for traces of small fields surviving as earthworks and displaying lynchet-like boundaries like the old downland fields. One may see slight ridges, perhaps with some out-cropping stones marking the course of former dry-stone walls and litters of rubble scattered around the former wall courses. All these features are well displayed on the old common above Grassington in Wharfedale.

Moors abandoned by cultivators in the Bronze Age tend to be very rich in the relics of field walls (many of which carried thorn hedges when still functioning). Look for the characteristic low banks and outcropping boulder rubble marking the courses of the prehistoric field walls. However, earthwork features are extremely difficult to recognise in heather moorland – areas often rich in the remains of Bronze Age farming and settlement – and the coarse, bushy plants can mask quite substantial remains. The first inkling of an ancient field wall may come when one feels it underfoot, though it is still invisible beneath the heather.

Co-axial field networks are usually more easily recognised on large-scale maps, like the Ordnance Survey 6in to a mile series, than on the ground. They may not be obvious at first glance, some sections having been abandoned and then developed in different ways, and all parts being coloured by the addition of later landscape features. Many ancient examples are yet to be discovered. But it is worth noting not only that such networks continued to be put in place after the prehistoric period was over, in Roman and even later times, but also that the great privatisation of common land in the eighteenth and nineteenth centuries also created geometric field networks. These, however, still look 'fresh', with their geometry still perfect, and they don't export a common orientation across a large area. Old co-axial networks have had time to blur. Hedges drift sideways, corners become rounded, gaps appear in the pattern where land has 'dropped-out' of cultivation, and lines that may once have been straight wander slightly as walls are patched and hedges spread.

4. FIELDS OF ROMAN TIMES AND THE DARK AGES

The Romans were very interested in exploiting British farm production, but on the whole they were content to leave farmers to work in the traditional ways. In a few places they introduced the system of **centuriation**, which involved dividing-up an expanse of land into a precisely geometrical grid of rectangular fields. Networks of co-axial fields are sometimes located beside Roman roads, the orientations of which they shared, and these must have been set out either by the Romans or by their successors.

Such field networks, like those flanking the Old North (Roman) Road south of Catterick or the Ilkley–Aldborough Roman road, can survive as field groups or as fragments leaving a series of 'fossil field corners' of right-angled bends marked by lanes and property boundaries, to give the countryside a 'rectangular' character. In any event the Roman roads can be seen to form their axes and the fields must have been marked out on the landscape from them.

For the first centuries of the Dark Ages the old field patterns either persisted or fell into decay during the severe crises that followed the withdrawal of the Roman legion about AD 410. The awful traumas of the fifth and sixth centuries must have seen the abandonment of farming life in many places.

Despite what the old textbooks claim, there is no evidence that the Anglo-Saxon settlers introduced new forms of fields and farming in the fifth century. It was not until the eighth or ninth century that the open strip fields, familiar to most of us from the history classrooms, began to be established.

5. OPEN FIELD FARMING

During the reigns of the later Saxon kings and right through the Norman era farming in England, some Welsh lowlands and southern Scotland was reorganised in a revolutionary way. Since the transformations often took place against a background of turmoil, such as civil wars between Saxon dynasties and the Viking raids, they could scarcely have been imposed by monarchs. That would have required stable government and more settled times. Rather, the innovations seem to have spread from estate to estate by a process of imitation. They were not, as the school books often tell, introduced by Anglo-Saxons, for no such system existed in the English homelands in southern Denmark, the Frisian Isles and northern Germany. The local thegns and other large landowners must have been responsible for copying and imposing what they saw happening on neighbouring estates.

The introduction/imposition of the revolutionary system of farming occurred during the course of other rural revolutions, which provided a host of parish or estate churches and saw the establishment of thousands of new villages, in which the rural populations were concentrated. *All these changes must, somehow, have been related.*

The reasons for such a thoroughgoing reorganisation probably lay in the preceding few centuries of population growth, so that the extra mouths needing to be fed put pressure on the environmental resources. There could have been a shortage of good pasture land (while hay was always in short supply) and a more efficient use of the ploughland ('arable') would have released some land as extra grazing. **Open field farming** is difficult to understand and extremely complicated to operate. Each member of the farming community had certain obligations and each was bound to other members by scores of regulations and arrangements to combine labour and share draught animals. Open field farming produced very distinctive landscapes and relics of this long-lived system of farming are all around us. These were its characteristic features:

- The ploughland of the estate or township was organised into several immense **fields**. These were often three in number, but two, four, five or more might be found. If there were three of them, then one would generally be fallowed each year – i.e. it would not be ploughed and cropped. After the harvest the village livestock would graze on the grass and weeds of the 'aftermath', at night being folded on the fallow field to enrich the soils exhausted by two or more years of cultivation. (In some cases the fallowing cycle seems to have operated on the 'furlongs' rather than the fields).

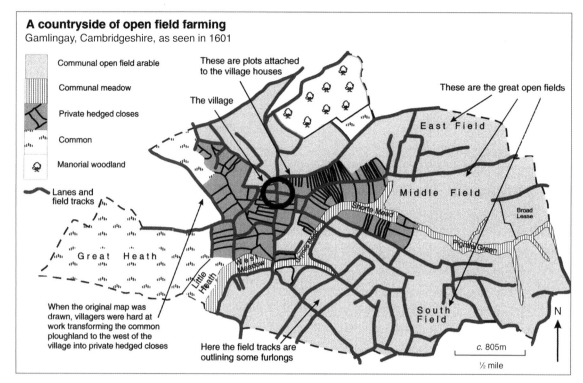

A countryside of open field farming
Gamlingay, Cambridgeshire, as seen in 1601

Communal open field arable

Communal meadow

Private hedged closes

Common

Manorial woodland

Lanes and field tracks

These are plots attached to the village houses

The village

These are the great open fields

East Field

Middle Field

Broad Lease

Great Heath

Shotte Mead

Pightle Green

Little Heath

When the original map was drawn, villagers were hard at work transforming the common ploughland to the west of the village into private hedged closes

Here the field tracks are outlining some furlongs

South Field

N

c. 805m

½ mile

Fig. 4. A countryside of open field farming: Gamlingay, Cambridgeshire, 1601. This is about as close a 'real world' example to the so-called Three Field System of the schoolbooks as one may find. Many parishes in the English Midlands had this sort of appearance in the Middle Ages. Note how the great open fields of ploughland dominate the landscape and how little is left for meadow and private and common pasture. The designation of land beside the stream as meadow was typical. Individual strips cannot be shown at this scale, though some furlong strip-blocks are outlined by field tracks.

- Each arable field would be sub-divided into **furlongs**: block-like divisions varying greatly in size but, say, very roughly, like a group of four football pitches. In the north of England the furlongs were variously known as 'cultures', 'shots' or 'flatts'.
- The furlongs were sub-divided into numerous narrow ribbons of land, packed side by side like sardines in a can or pencils in a case. These were the **strips**, also known as 'selions', 'loons' and 'lands'. They varied in width around a rough average 16ft (5m), and varied very much in length around the standard of a 'furrow long' or furlong of 220yd (200m). They were not straight like pencils, but curved slightly to give the shape of a reversed 'S' or else a reversed 'C' (or sometimes, a normal 'C'). This was because they

were ploughed by oxen strung out in a line and so the team had to be swung early into its turn as the **headland** at the end of the furrow was approached. Each feudal villager tenanted a collection of strips from his (sometimes, her) lord: around fifteen strips for the smaller tenants and thirty or so for the larger ones. These were scattered throughout the fields and so everyone had some 'dormant' strips in whichever great field was fallowing. Originally, the holdings may have been arranged so that tenants had the same neighbours working beside them in the fields as they did when at home, but over the years the patterns became blurred.

- As the team hauled the plough with its cutting blade or 'coulter', a snowplough-like board behind the blade turned the severed sod 'inwards'. As each strip was ploughed, this casting of the sod inwards had the effect of building it up into the form of a shallowly domed ridge, meanwhile giving the furlong a ridged texture like corduroy. The ridges and the furrows between the ridges are known as **ridge and furrow**. This ridging-up of the ploughland was probably mainly done to assist the run-off of surplus rainwater. Ridge and furrow is still quite often seen – but beware, the light and dark banding produced by the recent passage of a farm roller or harrow can give the illusion of ridge and furrow when seen from a distance!

- The medieval villagers needed an immense readiness to cooperate and an encyclopaedic knowledge of their local fields in order to make open field farming work. They had a multitude of words, now forgotten, to describe every bit and type of land, like 'slang', a small snaking field, 'pike', a pointed bit of ground, 'shoot', a projecting corner, 'gore', a strip that tapered to a point before reaching the headland, and scores more.

- To support the plough beasts and other livestock through the winter, the community needed hay (dried grass). This was grown in **meads** or **meadows** cut initially around mid-summer, with a second crop being taken at summer's end in favourable seasons. The meadows were generally on low, damp land, often beside flood-prone rivers. The wetness encouraged grass growth but hindered arable cultivation. Like the ploughland, the common meadows were divided into strips, 'doles' or 'dales', though they were not ridged. 'Mere stones' often marked the boundaries between the doles, and cases concerning the stealing of land by shifting the stones were frequently heard by the manor courts. The common place-name 'Lammas Land' related to meadow that was thrown open to the village livestock at Lammastide, after the mowers had taken the crop and had moved on to the harvest fields.

- **Pasture** came from several sources. There were the ancient wood pastures (see Chapter One), where the livestock grazed among the pollarded trees. Then there were the extensive commons, undivided and shared by the stock of the villagers and their lord. These commons, ever liable to encroachments, generally occupied the least valuable land, which might be upland, wood pasture or salt marsh. Extra pastures (and ploughland) might be obtained by reducing woods. There were often privately tenanted pastures forming a zone near the village homesteads, with their detailed hedge networks contrasting with the great sweeps of common ploughland.
- The village needed access to **woodland**. Some woods were held in common, but normally the villagers had rights to take essential timber for their fencing, house-building and ploughs from their lord's wood.
- Small plots, which might be elongated **tofts** or compact little **closes**, were normally attached to each village dwelling. They were used for growing herbs or vegetables, pig-keeping, housing chickens or small-scale cropping. They were often hedged.
- Quarries, marlpits, resources for animal bedding, turf for burning, heather, turf, reed and other thatching materials were found on the **commons**.

6. RELICS OF THE OPEN FIELDS

In some places open field farming lasted for a thousand years. Wherever it existed, it has tended to leave a strong impression on the landscape, even if none of the medieval farming practices have survived. The fossils of open field farming may date from the Middle Ages or from as recently as the nineteenth century. To recognise them, you need to have a mental picture of the operation as a living system of farming that involved whole villages in carefully synchronised activities. Countryside relics of open field farming include:

- **Ridge and furrow**: It tended to be the better land that was worked as ridged ploughland. The greater part of this remained in arable cultivation *after* the open fields were swept away, so that the ridges and furrows were soon levelled by later ploughing. The snaking ridges survive on land that was converted into permanent pasture and parkland. The height of the ridges varies. Where arable cultivation was almost continuous, as on the heavier soils of Midland counties, the ridges are high, like the backs of basking whales. In parts of the north, where very marginal land was only worked when starvation threatened, the growth of the ridges could be so

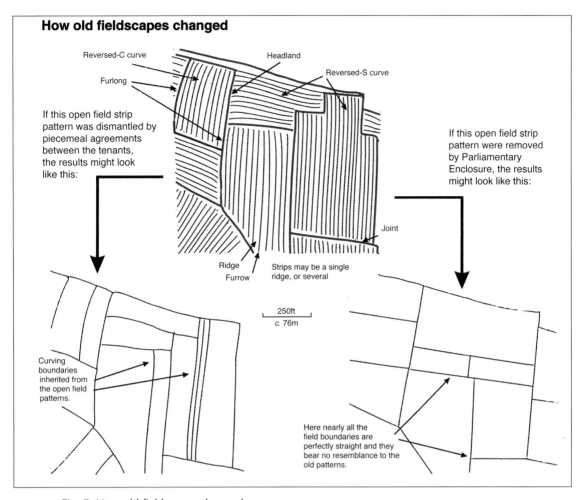

How old fieldscapes changed

Reversed-C curve

Headland

Reversed-S curve

Furlong

If this open field strip pattern was dismantled by piecemeal agreements between the tenants, the results might look like this:

If this open field strip pattern were removed by Parliamentary Enclosure, the results might look like this:

Joint

Ridge
Furrow

Strips may be a single ridge, or several

250ft
c. 76m

Curving boundaries inherited from the open field patterns.

Here nearly all the field boundaries are perfectly straight and they bear no resemblance to the old patterns.

Fig. 5. How old fieldscapes changed.

slight as to be obvious only when snow has just melted from the ridges but lingers in the faint dips between them. The width of the ridges varies from place to place and through time. In the Yorkshire Dales about 15ft (4.5m) between furrows is normal, but further south the ridges tend to be both higher and broader. Do not be deceived by the best textbook examples – the ridges can be so slight as to be only seen under shallowly slanting sunlight or light snow. *Beware!* Early in the Industrial Age land was still being ridged by ploughs hauled back and forth between steam engines. However, **steam ploughing** always produced *straight*, rather narrow, ridge and furrow.

- **Strips**: The masses of strips that once covered the vales like shoaling minnows have gone. However, as the old system was gradually dismantled, groups of strips would often be blocked together to form new, compact fields. The reversed S or C outline of the outermost strips in the package would be retained and would mark the new field boundary (see Fig. 5). Therefore we often find strip-edge outlines preserved by the hedgerows or walls that mark field boundaries. Look down the wall or hedgerow: does it swing slightly in the way described? If so, you are discovering the course ploughed by untold generations of medieval ploughmen. Sometimes a strip coincided with a plough ridge, but sometimes there were two or more adjacent ridges making up the strip.

- **Furlongs**: Often the old furlong patterns were demolished when time ran out for an open field system. In a minority of cases the furlongs were simply converted into new fields, as they had the convenient rectangular shape already. Indeed, in some places, and perhaps commonly, the furlongs seem to have been based on the field pattern that existed *before* open fields were introduced. Where this happened, the open field would consist of several existing fields, converted into furlongs and divided into strips. The evidence for furlongs in today's countryside may not be obvious. Some were converted (back?) into fields so look for traces of headlands (see below) at opposite ends of a package of former strips and field sides that curve slightly in strip-like manner.

- **Headlands and joints**: When he turned the plough on the headland at the end of each ridge, the ploughman was likely to take a stick and scrape the cloying mud from the blade and board. Over many years a rise or swell of ground would build up from the scrapings and the headlands so formed can sometimes be recognised, even though they are sometimes fairly slight. Headlands formed where two furlong-packages of strips met at roughly right angles. Where the two packages of strips had the same orientation, the swell at their junction was a double headland or **joint**.

- **Fields**: Though the largest components in the system, these can be the hardest to rediscover. The furlongs and their corrugations of old plough ridges may show very clearly, but it can be hard to deduce how many great fields were operated around the village and which furlongs belonged to which field. Continuous, slightly curving walls or hedgerows could mark old open field boundaries, but deer park boundaries are also possible when these are found.

- **Names**: The old way of farming had an immense vocabulary to describe all the nuances of the farmed landscape. Land, loon, acre, acreland, selion, shot, furlong, dale, dole, hades, head, gore and goar are among the many names inherited from open field farming, and where they are found centuries of open field farming are implied (see section 14, below).

7. VARIATIONS AND ABSENCES

The full-blooded open field system of farming did not occur everywhere. It was restricted to some but not all of the lowlands, especially places with strongly developed villages, which served as the dormitories for feudal labour, and with extensive areas of good arable land. The English Midlands became the heartland of open field farming, but borrowings and adaptations were found in the surrounding regions. In some places greatly modified variants of the strip field model were used, while in others it was completely absent.

In regions as far apart as Devon, Essex, Kent and the Welsh Marches there were lowland localities that never had fully fledged open field systems or the big villages that went with them. Perhaps the old estates had become too fragmented to allow the new methods to be accommodated. In these places the

In many places old enclosures, like these hedged fields in the Black Mountains on the Welsh Borders, escaped the advance of open field farming.

The old infield at Wasdale Head in Cumbria, patterned with field walls and great clearance cairns made of stones cleared from the land.

new patterns remained absent or else *very small common strip fields* worked by just a few tenants appeared.

In poorer localities, with sour, sandy soils or on the fringes of the uplands, a form of farming with just one great field was adopted. This is sometimes called the **infield-outfield system**. The infield formed the centre of the little farming world and got no respite from cropping, but it received all the muck from the byres, and sheep and cattle were folded on it after the harvest. Surrounding it were the pastures of the outfield, where enclosures would periodically be made and ploughed until they were exhausted. Then they were allowed to revert to pasture for many years as they slowly recovered fertility. This was a form of farming adjusted to less bountiful lands, like the Brecklands of the Norfolk/Suffolk border or the thin, stony soils of the Lake District, where there were fewer people to be supported and where flocks and cattle had more important roles to play.

A somewhat similar system was practised in the rolling lands of the Scottish banks (slopes), plateaux and 'straths' (valleys). **Runrig farming** was associated with areas lacking tightly organised feudal villages; instead tenants were arranged in hierarchies and lived in hamlets, known in English-speaking areas as **fermtouns** and in the Gaelic lands as **clachans**. The system resembled the infield system and usually had one great arable field spanning the best land – normally the ground between the upland moors and the wet, peaty 'mosses' of the lower hollows. As in the Midlands, the ground was divided and carved up into strips and ridges. It was often worked as a **group farm** or multiple tenancy by the joint efforts of the people of the hamlet(s) at its edge. The infield received all the muck of the locality and was often divided into **breaks** where oats, barley, rye and legumes were grown, its soil being too poor for wheat to flourish. Between the infield and the common moor were the pastures and temporary enclosures of the outfield. Runrig meant the dispersal of riggs, ridges or strips, and these strips were ploughed to produce massive ridges, with hand spades being used to ridge up the land in impoverished places. Terms of tenancy from the laird, the clan chief or his subsidiary tacksmen were very harsh and the insecurity of one-year leases was widespread. Where modern ploughing has not taken over, the remains of the riggs or plough ridges can be very pronounced. Generally, however, everything has surrendered to the changes of the **Improvements** of the eighteenth and nineteenth centuries.

8. MEDIEVAL FIELDS IN ADVANCE AND RETREAT

In the areas beyond and between the great open fields of the Middle Ages there was great field-making activity in the earlier medieval centuries. However, the arrival of the Black Death in 1348–9 brought the expansion to an end and in some places fields fell out of use for a while. The great expansion had been brought about by population growth, which was encouraged by the warm, dry conditions of the period leading up to the decline of the climate that began around 1300. Surplus population and surplus energy spilled out from the crowded villages, and had various impacts on the countryside. They included the following.

The assault on woodlands

Woodland products were essential to medieval life, but the shortage of farmland saw successive bites being taken from the woodland margins, so that the woods retreated and sometimes disappeared altogether.

This felling drive was known as **assarting**, from an Old French word for cutting. It was not just the starving poor who were involved, for yeomen and free peasants also played a large part, while lords and churchmen sometimes masterminded substantial assaults on the woods and a few men made a profession out of woodland clearance. In some cases of large-scale assarting, sizeable blocks of fields resulted. Peasant clearances generally produced piecemeal patterns of smallish, roughly rectangular fields, with each one representing a new transgression of the woodland boundary.

Sometimes the pioneers would take up residence in the newly cleared area, and though assarting could be used to expand the open fields, perhaps by adding an extra strip field or furlongs to the system, assarts tended to be privately tenanted. Lords who disliked the erosion of their woods and commons found themselves unable to resist the great tide and would legalise illegal clearances by taking rents from the squatters on the felled ground.

Very frequently medieval assarts can be recognised from their surviving place-names. *Sart* derives from the word assart; *Rudding(s)*, *Ridding* and *Ridden* denote land rid of trees; *-royd* is a very common assart word in northern England; *Stubbs* and *Stubbings* refer to land with tree stumps; *Stock* and *Stocking* describe land where tree stumps have been cleared, and *Steppings* is a clearing. In contrast, *Cut* names refer to land with drainage ditches or deep furrows.

Terracing of slopes

Desperation caused by over-population drove the churls to cultivate slopes that would normally have been left as grazing land. By ploughing parallel to the contours (*across* rather than *down* the slope) and letting the plough bite into the hillside, more level areas for ploughing could be created, with the slope taking on a staircase-like profile of 'risers' and 'treads'. Crops like barley, oats and rye could be grown on the flattened ground, with animals being tethered to graze on the 'risers' between.

Scholars have given these medieval cultivation terraces the characteristically unexciting name of **strip lynchets**. In the north of England they were known by the dialect name of *ranes* (in Lowland Scots a *rane* or *rand* is a border, stripe or strip of cloth or leather).

The terraces can still be seen on the flanks of the moors of south-west England, on the chalky slopes of the southern Downs (where they have generally been degraded by modern ploughing) and on the limestone 'banks' (hillsides) in the Yorkshire Dales, where Wensleydale and Wharfedale have particularly striking **flights** of ranes. The best collection that I know of is in Wharfedale, around Linton.

Many or most of these terraces must have been abandoned after the Black Death put an end to the population problem.

Coastal reclamation

Medieval people exhibited great ingenuity, but the problems of draining swamps, moors and salt marshes proved to be more intractable than most other challenges (see also Chapter Nine).

A flight of medieval cultivation terraces or strip lynchets preserved in the park at Studley Royal.

However, various schemes for draining land behind new sea banks were exploited by villagers and by monastic communities. A favoured method of winning new land from the sea involved **warping**, the building of barriers of posts, brushwood and stones, etc., to trap sediments and exclude the tides.

Both the sea and the tides of change would advance and retreat, and while salt marshes might be reclaimed in some places, villages, hamlets and farmland could be overwhelmed by drifting sand dunes elsewhere along the coast. When the climate turned stormy in the fourteenth century a long process of violent erosion began, which was particularly severe on the low clay coast of East Yorkshire.

The demesne

This was the 'home farm' of the lord of the manor. As the Middle Ages progressed, unrest and instability began to take hold in the feudal villages, lords often sought to withdraw their demesne strips from the tangle of the open fields.

Traditionally feudal tenants were expected to perform **boonworks** on the lord's land as a demonstration of their affection for him/her. In fact, they were obligated to provide labour services and these interfered with the working of their own holdings and were greatly resented.

The substitution of cash rents for the labour services painfully extracted from a resentful tenantry had advantages for both parties. It made the lord better able to employ professional, wage-earning labourers and tradesmen instead of chasing sullen tenants through the manor court, and it allowed tenants to attend to their own holdings without interference.

By extracting his strips from the open fields and reorganising them into compact fields beside the manor house the lord gained a greater freedom of action. He/she was not locked into the village farming system, for example by having a portion of strips in the fallowing field and by having to observe intricate methods of communal management. He/she could engage in ventures, say horse breeding, that did not fit in with the open field norms. However, in order to extract his strips from the common pool the lord would normally have to produce a series of complicated agreements about land exchanges in order to obtain the desired home farm of compacted fields.

In Scotland the very common name **Mains** denotes the home farm of an estate or lordship.

9. FIELDS AT THE END OF THE MIDDLE AGES

The feudal system did not vanish in some great explosion of freedom. Instead, it was gradually eroded over several centuries, with the first appearance of the Black Death signalling the beginning of a protracted end. On the land and in the villages the bondsmen or churls, who had formerly been obliged to render heavy labour services on the home farm or 'demesne' of their lord, became rent-paying tenants, then copyholders, whose entitlements were enshrined in the manor rolls. Slowly, the erstwhile bondsmen emerged as little entrepreneurs who were keen to extract their holdings from the common ploughland and meadows. Slowly too, all the safeguards and regulations enshrined in the intricate customs associated with operating common fields were seen as impediments to ambition and the onus shifted from the *community* to the *individual*. The decay of feudalism gave birth to a range of new and quite different fieldscapes. These included:

• **The conversion of some deer parks**: Deer parks had always accom-modated a variety of uses (see Chapter Eight). Now some were being converted entirely to farming. In 1529, at the end of the Middle Ages, the abbot of Fountains Abbey in Yorkshire set out terms for his parker at Brimham Park. Though the parker still lived in the old park lodge, there was no mention of any deer or other game, just the tending of the abbot's cattle and sheep. Today the interior of the park is seen to have been divided into fields, and these may well date from this time (see Fig. 6). Dates for the 'disparking' of parks can often be found, so that the field pattern inside them (usually a grid of fields with very slightly wavy boundaries) can be dated.

- **The enclosure of common ploughland and meadow**: As the feudal structures of the village fell apart, tenants could seldom wait to swap, sell and buy land in order to convert their numerous widely scattered strips into a few consolidated and compact fields. Packages of adjacent strips were acquired by wheeling, dealing, marriage and gifts to create the new privately held fields (see Fig. 5). If the land was lofty and rock-strewn these new fields would be bounded by dry-stone walls. More usually they were hedged around, with numerous young trees packing the hedgerows. Since these new fields were composed of groups of plough strips, their edges preserve the curving S- and C-strip plan, allowing these fields to be distinguished from, say, assarts. Meadows were also partitioned and privatised. Former common meadow is less easily distinguished, though sometimes names that reflect communal uses, such as Maypole Mead, Dancers' Meadow, Dancers' Plain or Lammas Land, may survive.

- **Intakes**: These are new fields that were taken-in by households from the **waste** or **common**, sometimes legally, but often at the expense of the community that shared the common. **Intaking** took place in the Middle Ages and continued through the following centuries. Paupers squatting on the common edge were particularly numerous as the population recovered strongly in the seventeenth and eighteenth centuries. Almost every hill-farm in the Yorkshire Dales and in Cumbria seems to have an intake component. Intakes can be recognised as rather irregular field patterns arranged around the lower edges of upland commons. By charting the extent of the intakes one can get a picture of the former open fell pasture or moorland of the old common before its edges were nibbled away.

- **The spread of water meadows**: The flooding of grassland at the end of winter stimulates the grass into growth and gives the sheep an 'early bite', relieving pressure in winter fodder. Rivers, streams and becks will flood naturally to inundate their flood plains, but the use of dams and sluices in the Middle Ages made the process surer and longer. More elaborate ways of drowning these 'floated meadows' were developed in the three centuries following the close of the medieval period. They were based on damming a watercourse and diverting water into a leat or **head main**, which then

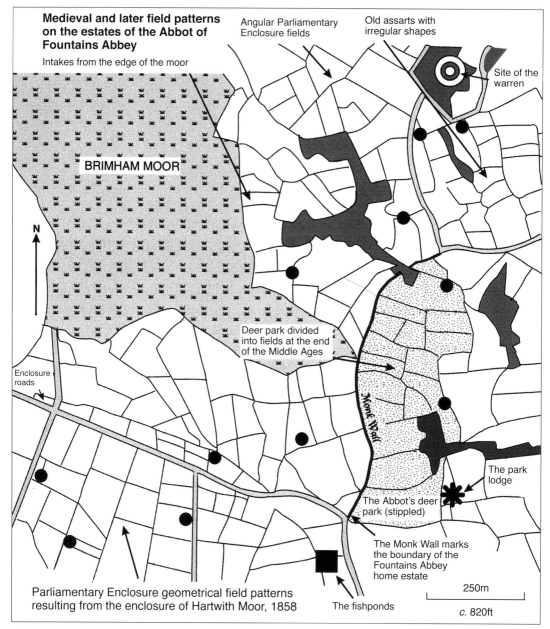

Medieval and later field patterns on the estates of the Abbot of Fountains Abbey

Intakes from the edge of the moor

Angular Parliamentary Enclosure fields

Old assarts with irregular shapes

Site of the warren

BRIMHAM MOOR

N

Deer park divided into fields at the end of the Middle Ages

Enclosure roads

Monk Wall

The park lodge

The Abbot's deer park (stippled)

The Monk Wall marks the boundary of the Fountains Abbey home estate

Parliamentary Enclosure geometrical field patterns resulting from the enclosure of Hartwith Moor, 1858

The fishponds

250m

c. 820ft

Fig. 6. Medieval and later field patterns on the estates of the Abbot of Fountains Abbey. Here, as in most places, the fieldscape is composed of fields of different types and ages. The oldest fields that we can recognise are the small irregular assarts resulting from clearance of woodland and moor in the Middle Ages. The oldest boundary is the Monk Wall, which marks the limit of the Fountains Abbey home estate and must date from soon after the abbey's foundation in the 1130s. The abbot's deer park and the warren and fishponds can still be recognised. Irregular fields around the edge of the moor are intakes, each one representing an enclosure of land from the open moor. Other areas of common moorland surrendered to Parliamentary Enclosure, which produced the geometrical patterns. Remaining woods are shown in dark shading and the black dots mark farmsteads.

fed **carriers** running along artificial ridges, sometimes arranged herringbone fashion, before spilling down on to the meadow and running back into the dammed river or stream. Springs issuing from a hillside could similarly be gathered at the foot of a slope and the water distributed. Water meadows were largely found in the southern half of England and were particularly common in Wessex. Valley bottoms and flood-plain edges with the earthworks of head mains and the ridge patterns of carriers can fairly easily be recognised as old water meadows once one knows what to look for. Sometimes one can trace the whole system of dam, sluices, mains and carriers and work out how it all fitted together.

10. FIELD MAKING'S LAST GREAT FLOURISH

While the peasants of the countryside were eagerly dismantling the old medieval farming patterns that had sustained their forebears for centuries, the big landowners were becoming increasingly resentful of the old traditions, checks and balances. The ogre of population pressure was again rising and the impoverished landless masses who huddled on the commons and in the declining Forests were sources of fear to the better-off. People of property realised that they might gain substantially by privatising the remaining countryside commons, and soon discovered that their selfish assaults on custom and the poor could be cloaked in the garb of progress. In the eighteenth century the cause of progressive farming found a patron in the king himself, with George III (r. 1760–1820), one of the more agreeable of monarchs, being fascinated by the new farming fashions.

Parliamentary Enclosure provided the means by which the land could be privatised. It had the advantage of *seeming* to be fair, though its consequences included a mass exodus of the rural poor. Like its great contemporary, the turnpike movement, Parliamentary Enclosure was discovered largely by accident. The first Act was passed in 1604, but the really serious adoption of the system did not come till more than a century later. The period 1750–1850 was the heyday of Parliamentary Enclosure, and when it finally petered out in 1914 about 22 per cent of England had been affected. The social and the scenic impacts were profound.

Parliamentary Enclosure worked on a parish-by-parish basis. In any parish the leading landowners could petition Parliament for an Act to enclose their commons (including remaining strip fields, dole meadows and even the village green). Once the Act was passed, commissioners – local dignitaries – and

A landscape of Parliamentary Enclosure in Nidderdale, North Yorkshire.

surveyors were appointed to produce the **award**. Because the system operated on a parish basis, any award would terminate at the parish boundary. Adjacent parishes might have their respective awards separated by decades, or even more than a century.

The appointed officials would map the situation as it existed before Enclosure (these pre-Enclosure maps often survive and provide fascinating portraits of old village England). Then a map would be drafted showing the transformations. Each landholder would receive an award of compacted land that was notionally equivalent to his or her stake in the parish commons before Enclosure.

In reality, the poor suffered so badly that they were generally obliged to abandon farming and find work as farm-hands, seek factory work in the new industrial towns or else board a vessel bound for the New World. With the common land gone, they had nowhere to graze a few cows or sheep, nowhere to gather bedding and nowhere to cut turf for fuel. They were also faced with a massive fencing bill, for the immediate fencing or walling of the new holdings was obligatory.

The poor generally knew what was in store for them and rowdy public meetings or even riots often accompanied the petition for an Act. Some affluent people sympathised with them, but this was another case where greed and injustice skulked behind the guise of progress.

A panorama of Parliamentary Enclosure countryside seen from Dolebury Warren, in Avon.

11. THE LANDSCAPES OF PARLIAMENTARY ENCLOSURE

Nothing quite like the Parliamentary Enclosure countryside had been seen in England before. Indeed, nothing remotely like it had been seen since the Roman exercises in centuriation.

The conditions stipulated that at the end of the day the recipients of awards should receive holdings equivalent to those they held before Enclosure, but now in compacted units. The officials responsible for producing the award could not have been expected to cope with the complexities of calculating areas with curving boundaries. Therefore they dealt in straight-line geometry. The Enclosure map that displayed their allocations was covered in straight lines and the fields drafted on the map were then superimposed on the real landscape as ink and paper became grass and hedgerows.

Only the common lands were affected. In almost every place there were old, privately held enclosures, some fields that were medieval or older and other fields formed from the piecemeal disintegration of open field farming. The straight-edged enclosure fields filled the gaps between the old fields with their kinked or wavy edges. They are not hard to spot.

Arbiters of taste, who had loved the great sweeps and undivided expanses of the old commons, derided the new Enclosure countrysides, with their angular walls of freshly hewn stone or their cross-banding of hedgerows. Now, of course, the patterns have mellowed and Enclosure countrysides seem distinctive and, in their way, quite attractive. Certainly the hedge- and wall-nesting birds would have welcomed their arrival.

Parliamentary Enclosure countryside can scarcely be mistaken, but when looking at it in detail, you should note the following:

- How one set or network of walls/hedges suddenly terminates at the parish boundary. When the parish next door was also subjected to an Act, another geometrical field network would take over, but it would not mesh with that of its neighbour.

- How a new little network of straight **Enclosure roads** was often provided to expedite local movements – though these roads, too, will tend to end at the parish boundary (see Chapter Three).

- How the countryside will often be sprinkled with farmsteads of almost exactly the same date as the new fields and roads. These tended to be the homes built by those who had done rather well from enclosure and who in many cases had forsaken the old village or hamlet to settle among their compacted fields.

- How the voids between the geometrical field patterns are normally filled with older fields – intakes, assarts and other enclosures. Most Parliamentary Enclosure countrysides have older countryside patterns embedded in them.

At roughly the same time that Parliamentary Enclosure was transforming many parishes in England and Wales, a similar movement, known as the **Improvements**, was changing many Scottish countrysides. Land was cleared of stones, numerous estate tree plantations were established and the patterns of fields and tenancies were 'rationalised' in such a way that countless small tenants were evicted, to be replaced by far fewer but more affluent farmers who could afford commercial rents. In many cases enlightened landlords attempted to establish fishing or manufacturing industries on their estates in purpose-built villages to provide alternative employment, though these seldom flourished.

12. FEATURES IN FIELDS

Farming required buildings and structures as well as fields. The following are some of the things that might be encountered in a ramble through the fieldscape.

A Scottish landscape of the Improvements in Strathdon.

Windmills

Windmills were invented in Asia and the first examples had upright sails radiating from a vertical shaft. Legend claims that Crusaders brought the use of wind power back to Britain, but in fact windmills seem to have been well established here by the late twelfth century.

In countless townships and parishes people with grain to be ground might take it to a watermill down by a river or to a windmill high on the watershed, while some could choose between the two forms of milling. In any event the lord of the manor and his miller would take their dues — or rather more — and the monopoly was a source of great resentment. Households grinding grain at home between the stones of **hand querns** could expect to be fined.

A post mill at Stevington in Bedfordshire.

The earliest windmills were little **post mill**s, where the whole mill pivoted around a stout central post to face the blowing wind. **Smock mills** developed when the sails were fixed to a revolving cap above a fixed timber body that contained the milling equipment. During the fifteenth century **tower mills** appeared, in which the timber body of the smock mill was converted into brick and stone. The post mill at Bourn in Cambridgeshire, dating from 1636, is thought to be the oldest surviving windmill.

Steam milling engines were introduced in the 1780s and by 1946 only about fifty of the several thousand previously operational windmills remained. Not all were used for grinding grain. In the wetlands they were used to raise water into drains and sometimes windmills were even used to lift brine into pans at saltworks (see Chapter Nine).

Windmills were sited to catch the strongest winds and their traces are usually associated with windy plateaux and hilltops. 'Windmill Hill' names are quite common, while sometimes the little artificial mounds on which the mills stood can be recognised – in a few cases even the cross-shaped indentation left by the crosstree base of the mill may be detected.

Dovecotes

Fat squabs might excite few appetites today, but in the past they were a reliable source of meat and the fledgling doves were produced in great numbers in specially built dovecotes. Since the adult birds caused great nuisance in the nearby grain and vegetable fields, the keeping of doves was the prerogative of the feudal lord. Later dovecotes were mainly associated with the chief estate farms (the Mains in Scotland, where the houses are **doocots** or **dow-cots**).

The late-medieval dovecotes tended to be cylindrical. Their interior walls were lined with nesting niches which were reached from a ladder fixed to a revolving pole. Such buildings remained popular until the decline of pigeon breeding in the nineteenth century.

The most impressive surviving dovecote is the great lectern-shaped example built at Willington in Bedfordshire from materials pillaged from monastic houses and dating from 1540. Much smaller lectern-shaped dovecotes are associated with many Mains farms in eastern Scotland: East Fife has numerous examples.

The interior of a dovecote at Bruton in Somerset, showing the nesting niches.

An imposing dovecote at Willington in Bedfordshire.

Fishponds

These were normally operated to meet the needs of the lord and his guests at the manor house and are described in Chapter Seven. Fishponds are often in or close to old deer parks. Look out for areas of rectangular or trapezoidal shape defined by low, water-retaining banks, or rectangular or oval scoops. Sizes range from several tennis courts to less than half a bowling green. The ponds were always placed above the limits of flooding and could be perched on valley sides with the water trapped by retaining banks on their downslope side. Ideally the river where the wild fish for stocking the pond were caught would not be far away. Often **stew ponds** are found in sets of different sizes, some being for the young fish. Some ponds were periodically drained, with crops being planted in their very rich silts.

Warrens

Rabbits disappeared from Britain before the last Ice Age but the Normans re-introduced them from southern Europe after the Conquest. It took the animals a long time to acclimatise to the cool, damp British climate. For most of the medieval period the rabbit was carefully nurtured as a delicacy, until a more robust British strain developed and the animals gradually spread and became vermin. Some signs of rabbit-keeping remain in the landscape.

The remains of a medieval fishpond at Landbeach in Cambridgeshire.

Rabbits were provided with artificial warrens or 'conigers', sometimes surrounded by hedges to become **coneygarths**. The warrens often consisted of a number of artificial mounds, often of an elongated cigar-shaped form, now known as **pillow mounds**. These provided ease of burrowing, though sometimes artificial runs and nesting spots were created inside the pillow mounds.

Each warren was carefully guarded against poachers and predators, sometimes with a warrener being placed in charge. Medieval illustrations show the netting of rabbits, and ladies of noble birth using ferrets (domesticated polecats) to catch rabbits in pillow mounds.

Pillow mounds are quite common survivals on upland plateaux and sandy areas, though their function was only rediscovered around the middle of the last century. Long-abandoned hillforts, with their defensive perimeters and artificial banks, were sometimes adapted for the purpose, and Dolebury in Avon is an Iron Age hillfort that is packed with pillow mounds. Old warrens are very often preserved as place- and field-names, such as Warren Farm, Warren Lodge, Coneygar, Coney Corner and so on. Any 'bunny' or 'rabbit' names will not relate to medieval warrens, where adult rabbits were known as coneys.

Pinfolds

Pinfolds or pounds were used to impound trespassing livestock and were common in the days of open field farming, when there was less partitioning of the landscape and footloose animals could cause considerable damage if they got into the common meadows or cropland.

Only a very few village pinfolds have survived, but they were usually small enclosures, much smaller than a bowling green, often with stone walls and a gate. This gate could be locked to prevent irate owners, who would be fined for the depredations of their animals, from reclaiming them illegally. Pound-breaking was a common crime in the old villages, and certainly one of the easier ones to solve.

The pinfolds were generally located within a village and sometimes beside an adjacent green, though more isolated examples were known. Medieval examples would have been densely hedged or have wattle and paling fences, although some stone-walled pounds were built at various periods. Several brick-built examples were in service in the nineteenth century.

Pounds or pinfolds and the *pinders* who manned them may survive in field names, such as Pinfold Croft, Pound Close and Pinderfield, though in cider-making country a **Poundhouse** name will refer not to a pinfold but to a building housing a donkey-powered apple-crushing engine.

13. FIELD PROJECT

It is best to study the fields in your locality both on the map and on the ground. As one rambles around, helpful little details are likely to catch the eye but it is less easy to judge the shape of a given field or the patterns formed by groups of fields. This is where the plan view of the map comes in. Perhaps more than in any other area of landscape detection, shape is the key that unlocks the answers.

Perhaps the most useful map to use is the Ordnance Survey 6in to a mile. The first edition, dating from about 150 years ago, will show parts of the fieldscape lost through modernisation. The scale is sufficiently detailed for most purposes, but small enough to allow the broad pattern to emerge. Fields are also shown on the 4cm to 1km or 2½in to a mile map at a scale of 1:25,000, but at this scale most fields appear smaller than a little fingernail. Your local reference library should hold a copy of the local 6in map.

With the aid of the map and stout walking boots, you can now interrogate the fieldscape just as a detective would examine a witness. You might work along the following guidelines:

- *Do the field boundaries form geometrical patterns with angular corners? Are the walls or hedgerows dead straight? Do the patterns end at the parish boundary?*

If the geometrical patterns are crisp and 'fresh', this must be a Parliamentary Enclosure fieldscape.

- *Are there geometrical grid-work field patterns that seem rather smudged and blurred?*

Over time, hedges migrate slightly and countless episodes of patching will cause walls to drift a little out of line. In this case, you might have fields that are elements in an ancient co-axial system.

If this is a possibility, look across the map for other collections of fields sharing the same orientation as those in your study area. If such fields and field tracks and lanes occur again and again across the region, you may have found sets of 'living' fields that have existed since prehistoric or Roman times. The acid test for a prehistoric network is to see if any Roman road slices through the pattern. If the blurred but grid-like set of fields is only localised, it might result from the carving up of an older passage of landscape, like a deer park, or perhaps the consolidation of the lord's demesne.

- *Are the field boundaries curving or slightly wavy?*

Look carefully at the map and look along the line of walls/hedgerows in the field. Do some at least of the boundaries show smoothly curving reversed S or C sweeps? If they do, then the fields were formed by the dismantling of old open strip fields. They could be as early as the fifteenth century or as late as the eighteenth/nineteenth. The oldest trees in their hedges may give some more clues to the age of the pattern, for they could have gone in with the first hedge.

- *Are the fields smallish and irregular but without the frequent gentle S and C sweeps?*

If so, they could have begun as assarts during medieval woodland clearance. Check the local place-name evidence to see if any typical assart names like Stubbs, Ridding and -royd are to be found.

- *Are the fields irregular and sometimes angular, and are they arranged in 'layers' around fell pasture or moorland?*

If so, they are likely to be intakes from the upland common. It is quite likely that you can link them to the farmstead whose household 'pinched' the land from the common.

- *Are the fields small and squarish or irregular; are they bounded by hedge banks or very dense hedgerows; are there traces of hedges that were removed to enlarge the fields; and can the boundaries sometimes be traced running into the adjacent upland?*

Such fields, seen especially in the south-west of England and the upland margins of Wales, have the characteristics of prehistoric fields and, indeed, this is what they must often be. (For the other characteristics of prehistoric fields, check section 3, see page 24 et seq.)

- *What can the field names tell you?*

Use the information below to develop your project.

14. THE MIRACLE OF FIELD NAMES

It is not widely known that every field had a name. These names can be found on large-scale maps from the nineteenth century and earlier and often they can be discovered by talking to the farmers in your locality. Some may still use them, while others will remember them. They were descriptive, so they can tell us about the fields and their setting in former times. The names can be of varying ages, ranging from the medieval period to Georgian and later times and they could change, for example when a new tenant took over a holding. Names and the sort of evidence they can give are summarised in Table 2.1.

For more comprehensive listings ask your library to obtain John Field's excellent *English Field Names, a Dictionary* (David & Charles, 1972).

Table 2.1. *Field names and what they reveal about the setting*

Type of name	Examples
For bad land	Bare Bones, Hungry Hill, Poison Piddle, Twistgut
For good land	Paradise, Honey Field, Providence
For former industry	Kiln Field, Potters Field, Saw Pit Close
For former vegetation	Wych (elm) Ground, Sale (willow) Meadow, Nettlebed, Plum Tree Close, Judas Tree (elder) Flatt
For wet land	Plash Field, Carr Holme, Slade Meadow, Mirey Hill, Moss Field, Lumb Field
For assarts	Stubbs, Stocking, Croft, Riddens, Sarts
For nearby woods	Storth Field, Frith Field, Spring Close, Copse Close, Hurst Furlong
For charity land	Queen Anne's Bounty, Poor Piece, The Windows, Labourers, Lamplands (strips providing income for church candles)
For sites of games or dancing	Plaster ('plaistow') Green, Fiddlers Green, Maypole Bank, Football Garth, May Field.
For land supporting a shrine to the Virgin Mary	Lady Meadow (those like Lady Day Close had rents due to fall on Lady Day, 25 March), Lady Lands

Type of name	Examples
For land from open fields	Longlands, The Riggs, Severals (land enclosed within the open fields), Shot Field, The Flatt, Head Lands, Balk Close, Everyone's Mead
For pasture	Lease, Leasow, Slaight, Park Field, Parrock Close, The Green
For meadow land	The Holmes, Ing Mead, Lammas Mead
For little bits of land	Pig Hill (from 'pightel'), Hoppett Close
For nooks of land	Wray Close, Hale Close, Hern, Patch, Plat Close, Pleck Ground
For pointed corners	Gore Close, The Pike, Pilch Leasow
For empty land	Jacks Croft, Jack Ridding
For local wildlife	Monkey Field, Puss Field (both these refer to hares rather than the animals named), Brock Leasow, Adder Bank
For land distant from the farm	Jericho, Tasmania, Sebastopol
For the size of the field	Twentyacre, Five Day Work (for the lord of the manor)
For the shape of the field	Doublet Field, Leg of Mutton, Swallowtail, Shovel

15. FIELD BOUNDARIES

In prehistoric times, as clearings expanded, merged and became more permanent, farmers must have explored different types of boundary barriers. At first these may have been needed mainly to exclude deer, wild cattle and wild horses and to stake out territories., but later on the value of partitioning land into handily sized enclosures for confining stock and dividing crop land would have been recognised.

- The repertoire of barrier-makers was quite large. Banks and ditches were beginning to be used to define sacred areas within the ritual landscape, although the lines of pits (**pit alignments**) that seem to have marked out communal territories would have been less effective if exported to the farmland.

- Clearing land for cultivation must have led to the collection of stones and boulders from the surface. These might be heaped up in great mounds or **clearance cairns**, but they would have been much more useful when carefully piled up to form a **dry-stone** (i.e. without mortar) **wall**. **Dead hedges** could be made from loppings of boughs and bundles of thorns that would be woven around posts to create a prickly barrier. Dead hedges had the advantage that they could be erected and removed at will, though they did not endure for very long as the dead materials in them decayed.

How living or *quick hedgerows* came to be used must remain a mystery, but it seems likely that people noticed how shrubs were germinating in the lee of dead hedges or colonising boundary banks, and drew the necessary conclusions.

To begin with, when woodland was being cleared for farming and timber was abundant, post and rail fences may have been used, with fibrous bindings used instead of nails. Certainly during the colonisation of North America fences that were hugely wasteful of timber were employed. Later, however, such fences would have been rather rare. In the Middle Ages **palings**, often made from cleft oak posts, were sometimes used to fence deer parks, while a few 'pale', 'palings' and 'rails' field names indicate the use of fencing.

16. THE AGES OF WALLS AND HEDGEROWS

In recent years some progress has been made in recognising how wall building methods changed over the years, but the study of countryside history is still confused by the persistence of the notion that hedges can be dated by counting the number of species that they contain. This is a fallacy. **The ages of hedges cannot be gauged by species counting**. A few of the reasons why they cannot are listed below:

- Records show that, rather than being planted with just one species, old countryside hedges were planted with various seedlings and saplings gathered in the woods.
- Old rural communities did not want single-species hedgerows. Hedge-makers would include thorns, which gave a barrier effect, useful fruits, like bramble, gooseberry, crab apple, gean, bullace and so on, and timber trees, like oak, ash and elm, normally grown as closely spaced pollards.
- Ecologists know that all plants exist in very competitive conditions. The plant that is best suited to a given situation can be expected to expand at

the expense of its neighbours. Thus elm, blackthorn, holly, bird cherry and various other shrubs will spread along hedgerows, eventually turning them into monocultures in the course of their invasion.

- In some parts of the country there are far more potential hedgerow colonists than in others. In the southern downlands wayfaring tree, spindle tree, purging buckthorn and various other species will all colonise hedgerows, while in the Lake District, for example, the trees and shrubs that are sufficiently well adapted to colonise hedges in the cool, wet and windy settings are far fewer.

- Who or what would tell the next plant in line that a new century was about to dawn and it should prepare to enter a hedge? Who or what could bar it from doing so earlier?

The invasion of a Yorkshire hedgerow by elm.

- The more species a hedgerow contains, then the smaller the number of potential colonists becomes. Therefore it should become progressively harder for each successive entrant from the dwindling pool of new species to gain a foothold in a hedge. The 'one per hundred years' rule defies logic.

- Even if the method worked in part, we could never recognise a Roman or early Saxon hedge because there is insufficient room in any 50m-long section of hedgerow to accommodate all the different trees and shrubs necessary to produce the result, even if such variety were present in the locality.

- The results claimed for hedgerow dating are hugely inconsistent, with different counters counting different things: some count all roses as one, some count two or three or more rose species; some count twining plants, like honeysuckle and old man's beard and some do not; and some count all the *prunus* or plum-like trees as one and some count them separately.

The best way of attempting to date hedgerows involves relating the hedge to the field types described above. If a hedgerow has a 'backwards-S' plan it is likely to date from the carve-up of open fields, quite possibly in Tudor/ Elizabethan times. This hunch would be confirmed if large old pollards around five centuries old are seen growing in the hedgerow.

We *can* distinguish between the Parliamentary Enclosure hedgerows, which were generally, though not always, planted with nursery-grown hawthorn (occasionally with oak standards or some other trees included), and the older hedgerows. Plants like oak, hazel, holly and field maple do seem to signify older hedges, just as sycamore, ash, elder and wild rose among the hawthorn tend to signify younger ones. As a hedge develops, it excludes as well as includes.

Never look at just a single stretch of hedgerow. Farmers were likely at any time to grub up and replant a gappy and failing hedge. So within any length of old hedge you are likely to encounter replanted stretches in which hawthorn will dominate, in the company of those plants mentioned above.

Walls can, to some extent, be dated by their appearance. However, the warning about refurbishment applies even more in the case of walls. Field walls are prone to being blown down in gales or to suffer less severe damage when careless ramblers scrabble over them. In the past every farmer in hill and stone-rich country could make a workmanlike job of walling (the key to gaining speed is the ability swiftly to recognise which stone to pick up to fill which gap). Any old wall encountered in a ramble is quite likely to have been patched on more than one occasion by a farmer or professional waller employing the skills and

A fieldscape of old fields and hedgerows near Pumpsaint in Wales. Prehistoric and medieval woodland clearance produced countryside like this.

fashions of their age. Eventually a wall will become all patching and its original character will vanish. In exploring walls the following clues may be helpful:

- Prehistoric field walls employed orthostats – boulders that must have been dragged from the land in advance of cultivation. The orthostats were set out in lines that formed the bases of the walls, while in some cases the whole wall was built of such boulders. Examples of partly tumble-down orthostat walling can be seen at various sites where prehistoric fieldscapes survive – the field walls near the prehistoric settlement of Kestor in Devon are good examples. It is very likely that many prehistoric walls were really **Cornish hedges**, consisting of low walls containing a packing of earth in which hedging shrubs grew. Long after their abandonment, only the stone and boulder litter will remain.

- Though orthostat walls are generally spoken of as being prehistoric, in fact the building of such walls continued well into the Middle Ages in some locations. Medieval walls were sometimes built on footings of larger rocks. In contrast to the very professional walling styles employed in the eighteenth and nineteenth centuries, medieval field walls have a rather less methodical 'stone-piled-on-stone' appearance. However, we should take

Prehistoric walls with massive moorstone orthostats at Kestor in Devon.

account of the stresses that such a wall must have undergone and also wonder how much of what we see results from successive patchings.

- After the Middle Ages more craftsman-like walls began to be built, with double skins of walling culminating in a single row of **topstones**.

- The improvement in the craft of walling was encouraged by Parliamentary Enclosure, for the awards normally included stringent stipulations concerning the required height of the wall and even the frequency with which **through stones** should be built into the courses to provide strengthening bridges between the two faces, keying them together. In these walls the courses in the two faces were laid with an inward slope or **batter**, so that they had the cross-section of an attenuated A. The gap between the two faces was filled with chippings, known as **fillings** or **heartings**, which had been hammered free in shaping the stones to fill their niches. This core of chippings helped to ventilate the wall and made frost damage less likely. When the wall had almost reached its full height, the batter of the two faces caused them to converge, and topstones were then set across the whole width of the wall. In typical dry-stone walls, the topstones were the only ones mortared into place, this being necessary to protect the wall top against damage by leaping livestock and scrabbling ramblers.

- Roughly similar walling techniques were employed by Scottish landowners in the course of the parallel process of Improvements. However, the super-abundance of rocks left by the glaciers in some localities led to the building

Very well-built walls, like this Cumbrian example, appeared after the Middle Ages, but with all such old walls it is very hard to tell how much patching has taken place.

of **consumption dykes** – massive walls constructed partly to dispose of the field stones. These could be up to 25ft (7.6m) in width. Very rarely, older examples of thickened walls and clearance cairns can be seen elsewhere, most remarkably near Wasdale Head in Cumbria.

A great diversity of hybrid hedge, bank and wall types exists. **Cornish hedges** are walls supporting hedges, often orthostat walls, that include a packing of earth in which grow the shrubs that crown the walls. A Lowland Scottish **backit dyke** is an earth bank that is faced or revetted in stone. Similar examples can be seen in the northern Dales, where the bank sometimes carries a hedgerow. In the south-western half of England hedges were often planted on earthen banks, which would be carefully maintained and returfed. All hedges are likely to develop their own banks as drifting or washing soil is trapped in the rank vegetation at the foot of the hedge. The character of a hedge reflects the farming patterns of its location: the cattle farmer needed a tall, robust, bullock-proof barrier, while the sheep farmer was not so bothered about height but needed a very dense base to his hedge so that lambs could not wriggle through and be separated from their mothers.

An unusual wall of stone flags, reminiscent of a stegosaurus, on Orkney.

17. CHARTING THE DECAY OF WALLS AND HEDGES

The widespread grubbing-up of hedgerows as part of the broader losses of old countryside to mechanised, subsidy-driven farming has received much comment. It is less widely appreciated that neglect can be more destructive than the bulldozer, for hedgerows require regular maintenance, not only the annual trimming and ditch-clearing, but also a thorough-going laying every 15–25 years. Hedges were elements of a countryside in which labour was cheap and abundant. These conditions no longer apply and most hedges now receive a brutal annual slashing by a mechanical cutter and no laying whatsoever. Meanwhile, in the uplands and stony country, field walls are being dismantled to create larger pastures or their stones are carted away on trailers to become garden and roadside walls in increasingly gentrified settings. The relics of walls and hedgerows are as abundant as those of the surviving boundaries. These clues may help you to unlock the story:

- In traditional systems of laying the main trunks among the hedgerow shrubs would have their side growths trimmed off to become **pleachers**. At their bases the pleachers would be chopped through with a billhook until just a narrow sliver of living tissue attached them to their roots. Posts would be hammered in on either side of the hedgerow, a pace or less apart. The pleachers would then be tipped over to rest at acute angles between the posts. Finally pliable wands of hazel or willow would be woven around the tops of the posts to form a protective top to the hedge, known as **heathering**.

- Bushy growth would be left on the tips of the pleachers and new growth would be swift to burst forth, but for the first three years or so after laying the hedge would be very vulnerable to browsers. Then it would emerge as a rejuvenated and revitalised barrier, with plenty of dense and vigorous young growth to repel and contain animals. After another dozen or so years gaps would begin to appear, and the hedge would require a new round of laying. There will be many hedges that had gone through well over fifty laying cycles before the modern era of neglect arrived.

- Some hedges are still being laid using traditional methods by different conservation bodies, though they represent only a tiny fraction of the

The roadside hedge of an abandoned medieval right of way that has become 'gappy' for want of maintenance.

The base of a typical old hedge showing the 'elbows' left from the last laying a century or more ago.

hedgerow resource. You can discover the evidence for laying in the past by inspecting the base of any Victorian or older hedge. The main stems coming up from the ground will be seen to bend sharply, to create a series of elbows. These elbows are the relics of the last row of pleachers to be bent over before laying was abandoned.

• Thousands of hedgerows are gradually dying for want of laying and one can recognise the sequence of decay. First, the hedge ceases to be stock-proof and farmers fill the gaps with fence boards, bedsteads or barbed wire. Next the gaps widen further, until the hedge is just a row of thorn shrubs and old hedgerow trees separated by gaps large enough to walk through. The last of the hedgerow trees may die before the thorn shrubs, leaving just a row of widely separated thorns. In some cases the old pollards may outlive the shrubs, so that one is left with broken alignment of elderly trees.

Finally, a few solitary trees remain, but a close inspection of the ground will show that any surviving trees are standing on the slight swell of the old hedge-line. Sometimes, the faint dip of the old hedge-foot ditch can also be spotted.

- Countless trees that are assumed to have been planted in isolation, perhaps to shade livestock or beautify the scene, are really former hedgerow trees: the last witnesses to the lost world of a hedgerow.

- Much less has been written about the removal of old field walls in the uplands. Many of them were the products of the private enclosure of commons and it is ironic that when the commons were divided up by walls, many arbiters of scenic taste thought this deplorable. Subsequently the walls mellowed and darkened and became objects of affection. Since they were erected only in very shallow trenches, these walls leave very few traces once the stones have been taken away. Soon we will have to rely entirely on the maps of the nineteenth and twentieth centuries to tell us where the walls were.

THREE

Tracks, Lanes and Routeways

1. SOME IDEAS ABOUT TRACKS, LANES AND ROUTEWAYS

'There were no routeways in Britain before the Romans came' WRONG

'The road network that the Romans built, though falling deep into neglect, was the best transport there was until the era of the turnpikes in the eighteenth century' TRUE

'Roads all look the same, so it is impossible to try to deduce their history' WRONG

'Roads of different ages may look quite similar, but when all the landscape and historical evidence is considered, a history of roads in a locality can be pieced together' RIGHT

'In almost any area the evidence of abandoned roads and lanes is likely to be as vital to the historical picture as the evidence of those routes that have endured' RIGHT

2. TYPES OF ROUTEWAY

Enquiries into the roads, lanes and tracks of a locality are likely to involve landscape history detective work of a harder kind. However, I believe that in any local study the old patterns of commerce and communication should be studied right at the start. The alignments and destinations of the routeways form a skeleton around which the work that follows can be built. Superficial glances at the roads and lanes in an area will not produce many answers: for example, at first glance straight sections of minor Roman roads that are still in use look rather like the straight Parliamentary Enclosure roads of the eighteenth and nineteenth centuries. Yet with careful attention to detail, a fairly comprehensive identification of routes of different ages can be gained. The main types involved are as follows:

- **Prehistoric roads**: These might be long-distance trackways or ceremonial routes, or else local lanes and field tracks may survive but which are now indistinguishable from other members of the tangle of lanes.
- **Roman roads**: These were carefully surveyed and engineered routes. The major examples, like Watling Street, are well known, but there were also more local Roman roads as well as upgraded native tracks that were adopted by the Romans.
- **Roads of the Dark Ages**: In England, Saxon and Danish societies seldom engaged in serious road-building. They inherited prehistoric and Roman routeways and simply modified the network in a pragmatic way, to connect new villages and towns or to serve the rising pilgrimage trade.
- **Saltways**: developed for the distribution of salt from diggings in Cheshire and from coastal saltings, were often used for long-distance travel, and some salt roads were already ancient by the Dark Ages.
- **Medieval roads**: The growing medieval population relied heavily on the ageing Roman system of national and regional roads and on waterways, some of them also Roman in age. New roads tended to be produced simply by trampling out a route, while existing roads were poorly maintained.
- **Drove roads**: The droving trade must surely date back to prehistoric times, and it continued until the railways provided a more efficient form of transport than moving cattle on the hoof. Many of the old roads in the Scottish Highlands and Islands were, at least in part, drove roads.
- **Pack-horse roads**: This form of trading must similarly have existed for thousands of years and was associated particularly with uplands, where the road systems were too poor to allow the use of wheeled vehicles.
- **Military roads**: In the Scottish Highlands and Islands the first coherent and well-engineered road system was the one provided, with military considerations to the fore, by British occupying forces.
- **Turnpikes**: These toll roads multiplied in the late eighteenth century and provided the first really significant improvement to the now rundown Roman system.
- **Enclosure roads**: These little local roads, mainly straight, were produced as part of the Parliamentary Enclosure of the old commons (see Chapter Two), mainly in the 1750–1850 period.
- **Waterways**: The ditches and 'lodes' used by narrow craft in the medieval period were scarcely less important to the national economy than the famous canals of the dawning Industrial Age.

3. PREHISTORIC ROADS

Prehistoric communities engaged in trade in a small range of essential commodities and goods. In roughly consecutive order these were flint for tool-making; roughed-out flint and other stone axes; pottery; salt; copper; gold; tin; bronze goods; iron and iron goods. In some cases distribution seems to have been accomplished partly by coastal shipping, though there were some long-distance routeways that traversed the different clan and tribal territories.

These routeways did not exist as broad, surfaced tracks, like modern motor roads. Instead they were broad zones of movement containing lots of branching tracks that would merge or split as travellers sought the easiest ground. Sometimes they followed ridge tops, but such lofty **ridgeways** need not have been the norm, but rather the sort of tracks that survived after the lower stretches of routeway were abandoned and ploughed up. Some form of diplomatic conventions must have existed to protect travellers as they passed from one tribal homeland to another.

In some wetlands, like the Somerset Levels, **trackways** of wattle and brushwood were built from quite early prehistoric times, while elsewhere some short, straight tracks were produced in the Iron Age. However, the pre-Roman societies lacked the national vision as well as the organisation needed to create an all-British transport system.

Wayland's Smithy, a prehistoric chambered tomb, is positioned right beside the Dorset Ridgeway, adding support to the prehistoric date of the routeway.

Many ridgeway long-distance routeways have been proposed, but to be credible candidates should be associated with concentrations of ancient finds, such as stone or bronze axes, and with prehistoric monuments, such as chambered tombs. Only a few candidates, for example the Dorset Ridgeway, satisfy the criteria.

There were also routeways of a ceremonial nature, used for ritual processions. Such tracks and avenues are associated with important monument groupings or **ritual landscapes**, such as the West Kennet Avenue near Avebury.

As well as the long-distance routeways and the ritual avenues, there must have been a close network of field tracks, local routeways and regional connections. Many of these surely survive as winding country lanes, but we will never recognise more than a small fraction of them.

Excavations of local roads or lanes at later prehistoric sites have occasionally exposed ancient wheel ruts, showing the use of small carts as well as the inevitable pack-horses and backpacks for the smaller-scale movement of goods.

4. ROMAN ROADS

Most Roman roads were military roads that were constructed early in the occupation to facilitate the movement of armies in the subjugation of Britain. In time these roads also attracted commerce, while still being useful for patrolling the tribal territories.

The key to the success of the roads was not so much their straightness as the efforts that were made to make a well-drained roadbed. Roads typically had the form of a continuous ridge or **agger**, built of rammed materials with good drainage qualities, like gravel and sand, and flanked by drainage ditches. As well as being well engineered, the roads were also well surveyed; sightings were taken from vantage points like hilltops using a simple cross-headed staff to establish alignments. The work was all done by serving soldiers.

The type of surface depended upon the status of the road and the materials that were locally available. Rammed gravel, river cobbles or paving slabs were variously used. Often the roads were clasped by heavy stone kerbs, which helped to prevent the roadbed from spreading outwards.

The roads were only straight where topography and good sense allowed this. Where they dipped down to river crossings, ascended valley flanks or avoided steep hills (like the man-made mount of Silbury Hill) their courses would deviate. Where existing trackways were adopted, the alignments would be more curving and responsive to the topography. However, more than 1,500 years after

The Wheeldale Roman road in the North York Moors, thought to be a military route associated with coastal signalling stations.

The Blackstone Edge Roman road in the Pennines. The central groove is thought to have been provided for the pole used for braking vehicles.

they were set out, some Roman alignments are still in use, though they have tended to fragment into straight sections now linked by bits of later road bridging the gaps.

The Roman roads were associated with various structures: places where horse teams could be changed, rest stations, perhaps checkpoints for documents and so on; these have of course gone, but some **milestones** remain, usually on abandoned roads where they could not later be tossed into the foundations to patch up the crumbling roadbed.

5. DARK AGE ROADS

The beginning of the period was a time of decline, when many roads that had bustled with commerce in the time of the Roman Empire fell into decay. Little road maintenance or road-building took place in the years leading up to the Norman Conquest. However, the fact that kings and warlords were able to shift their forces quite quickly across the country, at least in the summer campaigning period, suggests that a basic infrastructure of roads had survived. The roads known as **harepaths** were associated with military movements, though they were probably normal roads that troops sometimes found useful.

The old **salt roads** must have remained in use but the emergence of an early interest in pilgrimage, for example to the shrine of St Wilfrid in Ripon, also gave rise to the use of **pilgrim ways** in anticipation of the immense tourist trade that developed after the Conquest.

The mention of boundary landmarks in Saxon charters demonstrates the existence of a tight network of unmade local lanes and paths that served their rural communities. Any farming community needed a dense little network of field tracks, particularly where open field farming was practised and each household had its strips scattered across the village lands. When trade quickened, **market roads** were forged by linking convenient paths and field tracks together.

6. MEDIEVAL ROADS

The negligence of transport needs continued, largely because the authorities could not create institutions larger than the manor that could create and maintain new roads suitable for regional and national traffic and commerce. Consequently new routes were developed in *ad hoc* ways, with the interests of travellers being subordinated to the indifference of the communities controlling

Ancient tracks can dissolve into the landscape or linger as droves and farm tracks. This example at Killinghall in North Yorkshire seems to have been a branch from an old saltway to the river crossing over the Nidd, see photograph on page 74.

The glories of vernacular architecture did not come from attempts to beautify buildings but from the poverty of the roads, making it essential to build with what was readily to hand, like the timber, mud and thatch in these cottages at Cropthorne, near Worcester.

The medieval bridge on the Nidd at Killinghall has been widened, so that the telltale medieval ribbed arches are only seen on half of the bridge.

the localities through which they passed. Even so, this was a time of intensifying movement. The lanes and highways were used by lords, ever circulating between their manors, by kings and their retinues, who were forever on the move, by forces of masons shifting from one project to another, by pilgrims and by many others. Some people were frequently on the move and even villagers could aspire to go on pilgrimage.

The pattern of settlement was unstable; villages appeared and others were abandoned; some towns decayed, while new trading centres were set out; and farm and hamlet populations were still being drawn into larger villages. Consequently the transport networks were quite fluid, and even as new roads were being established, others were lapsing back into the fieldscape.

Medieval roads were numerous but were seldom maintained in a purposeful manner. Manor courts were forever fining tenants for failing to clear roadside ditches, letting their hedgerows grow out into the trackways or even digging cesspits in the highways. Consequently lanes and roads that could be used by wheeled transport were relatively few and, unless gradients were gentle, commerce relied heavily upon pack-horses. River boats offered the only possibility for bulk transport in many places.

Corpse roads were used by communities living in the more remote upland areas that lacked churches. Such roads might have been used when families made the long and probably occasional journey to worship at their appointed church, but they were also used by bearers carrying corpses in light wicker coffins for burial. Some such parties sometimes perished in swollen rivers or blizzards on the way, encouraging the authorities to provide chapels of ease.

Many roads used in medieval times were inherited from earlier ages. Ones that *originated* in the Middle Ages can be difficult to identify unless they were connected to a new town or village, or else were recorded in old charters as rights of way, like many roads used by the monks and lay brethren.

7. DROVE ROADS

Roads have been used for the movement of livestock since the Stone Age. **Drove roads** were doubtless used by non-drovers, too, but where large-scale movements of cattle on the hoof were concerned there was a threat to farmland by the wayside and so the roads tended to follow the high and thinly settled areas. Thus confrontations with angry farmers were avoided, while open pasture could

Hubberholme church in the Yorkshire Dales began life as a chapel of ease that was licensed for burials in the late fifteenth century after a burial party lost its corpse in the River Wharfe while heading for Arncliffe church.

Abandoned roads slowly sink back into the countryside. The trees from the roadside hedges of this monastic right of way for Fountains Abbey still trace its course.

be found and cattle could feed at **stances** along the way. Eventually drove roads had to descend from the high ridges and enter the lowland countryside, where they shared the old village market roads with other users.

The intensity of droving varied greatly according to external conditions. In times of relative peace in the Scottish Borders, there was a heavy trade of Scottish cattle to markets in England. The routes that the herds followed can be traced. From the upland pastures of the Highlands and the Inner Hebrides, the cattle were taken first to the great cattle markets or **trysts** in Scottish towns, like Falkirk, and then moved south in vast herds. At places like Malham in the Yorkshire Dales the drovers sold on their cattle, and then returned to Scotland, while the cattle continued their journey southwards, eventually ending up at the great meat markets, notably Smithfield in London.

One problem with marketing livestock 'on the hoof' was that they would walk off much of their value, arriving at market very lean, and so animals would be sold on for fattening en route. In preparation for the arduous trek across the high passes of the Southern Uplands and northern Pennines, cattle were shod with iron shoes. Iron plates were also fitted to the feet of Welsh hill cattle bound for market at places like Shrewsbury. A blacksmith in Tregaron is said to have shod masses of cattle before they set off for the border. Similarly East Anglian geese destined for London via many cobbled streets and stony lanes had their feet dipped in hot tar and sharp sand to give them some form of protective footgear. Turkeys were furnished with little leather bootees, while pigs are said sometimes to have been walked to market in woollen stockings with leather soles.

Droving on the hoof had a remarkably long history and the long-distance Scottish trade persisted from early in the Middle Ages to well into the nineteenth century, when the railways provided a more efficient means of transporting livestock.

8. PACK-HORSE ROADS

Pack-horse traders must have been very active in prehistoric times (for example on the saltways) and the survival into the late nineteenth century of the commercial trading of goods transported in panniers slung across the backs of pack-ponies is a testimony to the enduring inadequacy of the road system. Pack-horses provided the only effective means of bulk transport in areas of steep and broken country, where the narrow, uneven and rutted lanes could not cope with carts or wagons. Pack-horse trading was fairly ubiquitous in medieval Britain, but later on it was more a feature of the uplands of the northern and western areas.

No roads were exclusively reserved for pack-horses. In many localities the strings of ponies shared lanes and market roads with a variety of other users and their horses, users like the **badgers** who moved from farm to farm to buy produce to sell on. However, pack-horse traders must often have been the main users of the long-distance trackways that linked towns, pits and mills across the higher watersheds.

The basis of the trading was well organised. Every market or industrial town, particularly those in the northern and western counties, housed contractors who would undertake to transport different commodities (wool, yarn, coal, iron goods, etc.) at a fixed rate per mile. Teams of ponies controlled by a **jagger** (named after a favoured type of German pony) followed in a string behind a lead horse and, with their polished harness and jingling bells, they must have made a colourful sight.

The days of pack-horse trading are remembered mainly for the legacy of arched **pack-horse** bridges. These were not necessarily used mainly by the traders, though their low parapets always assisted the passage of ponies bearing

Rosthwaite packhorse bridge in the Lake District.

panniers. The trade disappeared in the closing decades of the nineteenth century as a result of improvements in large-scale transport systems, particularly the turnpikes, the canals and the railways.

9. MILITARY ROADS

The ancient examples of the Roman roads and the less clearly defined **Here-paeth** or harepath Dark Age military tracks were followed by the British in Scotland in the eighteenth century and, to some extent, in the establishment of railways in Victorian Ireland. As with the Roman roads, routes that began as means for the rapid deployment of troops soon became valuable for commerce and day-to-day contacts.

In Scotland, where an Act of Union between England/Wales and Scotland had been agreed in 1707, uprisings in the clan territories of the Scottish Highlands in 1715 and 1719 prompted the construction of military roads. Work began in 1725, was revived in the years around the great uprising that ended in the Jacobite defeat at Culloden in 1746, and continued during the subjugation of the Highlands and the harsh suppression of clan culture.

The engineering of the routes was undertaken by competent military engineers, most notably the Irish general George Wade. His programme included the building of Fort Augustus and Fort George, which would combine with Fort William to form a barrier across the Highlands, and their garrisons and those of other barracks provided bases for redcoats patrolling the region on the new roads.

Many fine stretches of military road survive in Scotland, complete with their bridges. A notable ruin of the era is the Bernera Barracks in Glenelg, completed in 1723 in response to the 1715 rising. It was one of four barracks built to control the crossing to Kylerhea on Skye. One of the many military bridges built can be seen in Glenshiel, while on the other side of the Highlands there is an example in Glengairn. One of the most dramatic stretches of road crosses the Corrieyairack Pass and links Laggan Bridge and Fort Augustus.

The bridge on the military road in Glenshiel.

10. TURNPIKES

A solution to the problem of chronically inadequate roads was stumbled upon in 1663 in an Act that empowered Justices of the Peace in three counties in the Midlands to charge tolls for the upkeep of their sections of the Great North Road. It was only at the end of the century that the true potential of this system began to be recognised and the proliferation of **turnpikes** became an achievement of the eighteenth century.

The system allowed investors to improve specified sections of local/regional highway and then to recoup their outlay and, they hoped, make some profit by levying charges on users of the new or improved route. The tolls were collected at ticket windows in roadside **toll houses**, which were generally built to distinctive designs. Some sections of road were barred by gates or pivoting poles, hence the term turnpike.

In the uplands particularly the effects of turnpiking were dramatic, with carriages and wagons appearing in market towns that had hitherto been accessible only to pack-horses. However, the turnpiking era coincided with the early phases of the Industrial Revolution and the existing roads did not always connect up the areas of new industry. Sometimes replacement routes were needed, like the one built to link up the young mill villages shown in Fig. 7, page 89.

The quality of the road-building depended on the funds available, the terrain and the condition of any older route being improved. In general the turnpikes were of a decent quality and very much better than the roads they replaced. There was a reborn appreciation of the importance of providing free drainage and Thomas Telford, who engineered the Holyhead road in Wales, was a noted road-builder.

Turnpikes would not yield their full income if travellers and merchants were able to circumvent the tollbooths. Therefore local lanes that might have provided useful diversions were often closed, like the two lanes shown in Fig. 7.

11. ENCLOSURE ROADS

The Parliamentary Enclosure of ancient common land, as described in Chapter Two, very often involved a reorganisation of roads and lanes in the parish concerned. Sometimes the old rambling lane patterns survived, though in many cases jinking and winding lanes were replaced by ones that ran arrow-straight. However, the usefulness of such improvements was greatly reduced by the fact

A typical little Enclosure road at Low Bishopside, Nidderdale.

that they only affected a particular parish. Therefore the new roads, however helpful they might be, would end abruptly at the parish boundary. The Enclosure of the adjacent parish might happen decades before or after one set of rationalised roads had been created. The results were often disjointed sets of lanes that did not link together very well.

Enclosure roads tended to have a width between their hedgerows of 30 or 40ft (9.1 or 12.2m), though some with widths of 60ft (18.3m) were built. Part of the width consisted of verges, that were especially useful for grazing livestock moving 'on the hoof'. Normally being dead straight, the Enclosure roads can resemble Roman roads when their termination at a nearby parish boundary is not apparent. They are always welcomed by rural motorists who know nothing of their origins as the straight tracks often provide eagerly awaited opportunities for overtaking tractors.

12. WATERWAYS

Waterways tend to be less attractive to traders because they do not necessarily go in the directions of trade. Customising waterways involves a great deal of expense and demands the ability to measure levels along the route and provide locks if necessary. However, the poverty of the road network made water transport essential to medieval commerce, particularly where bulky cargoes and long-distant movements were involved. The Romans had the capability to provide urban water supplies via precisely levelled **aqueducts**, while medieval people built quite elaborate systems of channels, ponds and sluices in association with their moats and fishponds.

Prehistoric communities are known to have used the rivers of Britain, and the distribution of distinctive goods like Lakeland stone axes suggests coastal shipping also took place. Under the Romans the intensity of transport increased and bulk transport must have been needed to extract hides, lead ore and slaves from the colony and to bring food supplies up to the huge military bases in northern England. Roads and rivers would not have been sufficient and various

The helmet-shaped peak in the Langdales is Pike o' Stickle. It was quarried in the Stone Age for volcanic tufa, greatly favoured for axe making. Some of the output seems to have been taken to the coast and exported by coastal shipping.

The Car Dyke, a Roman canal probably used to transport East Anglian farm produce to the northern garrisons. Like other Roman waterways, it remained in use during the Middle Ages.

canals were apparently cut across the lowlands of eastern England. The Car Dyke and at least three of the narrow canals or **lodes** in this area are believed to be of Roman origins, notably Reach lode that terminates in Reach village, Cambridgeshire.

In the Middle Ages navigable rivers, cuts and ditches were essential for tasks like shifting barge-loads of dressed stone to church building sites or importing exotic goods destined for the great fair networks. However, local interests often caused problems, as when **fish weirs** interfered with navigation or when millers closed sluices to pond-back a head of water, thus barring navigation (occasionally this was helpful, particularly in cases where a mill dam could also function like a **flash lock** and a boat could burst through on the rush of water when a gap was opened.) Towns could stagnate (like Hedon) or perish utterly (like Torksey in Lincolnshire) when their watery lifeline became choked and impassable.

Mainly because of the smallness of the craft used, different river systems tended to have heads of navigation that lie far inland, in places that we would never imagine to have been river ports. Low modern river levels caused by excessive diversions and extractions of water or crop watering may produce shallows and rapids in places that were once navigable (or could be bypassed by short portages when levels were low). Any riverside village merits consideration as a possible medieval river port.

The canal age at the dawn of the Industrial Revolution produced its own landscape of artificial waterways. These canals were far more ambitious than those that had gone before, with systems for maintaining their levels and reducing seepage, tunnels and dramatic flights of locks.

13. BRIDGES

Bridges of many different ages will be seen in the course of any cross-country journey in Britain. Each one has a story to tell. The greatest mistake people make when they try to read these stories is assuming that the bridge they have just crossed is the original one. Many stone bridges are successors to a sequence of timber or rope and plank bridges that were carried away by a river in spate. Stone bridges were durable, but they were also extremely expensive, so that communal resources or bequests, endowments and taxes were stretched for the provision of the earlier examples. Bridges need to be looked at with care, and many a medieval bridge, like the one at Killinghall (see Fig. 7 and the photograph on page 74), lies camouflaged by later transformations.

Clapper bridges

These are the most primitive-looking of bridges and consist of a massive horizontal stone slab or slabs supported on boulders or slab-built piers. A fine description of such a bridge was provided in Camden's *Britannia* of 1695: 'Where this Shire touches upon the County of Lancaster, the prospect among the hills is so wild, solitary, so unsightly, and all things so still, that the borderers have call'd some brooks that run here, *Hell becks*, that is to say, *Hell* or *Stygean rivulets* [actually meaning 'hill']; especially that at the head of the river *Ure*, which, with a bridge over it of one entire stone, falls so deep, that it strikes a horror into one to look down to it'. Really, it is the *design* that is old and individual clapper bridges are probably the work of recent centuries. Examples like the Tarr Steps on Exmoor must periodically need extensive repairs after flood damage.

Medieval bridges

These were generally quite narrow, with stone examples only being built at the busier crossings. Medieval bridges were important places. Some had **bridge chapels**, like the fine example at St Ives in Cambridgeshire. Here the medieval bridge gained two upper storeys (later removed) in 1736 and was used as a house. Monmouth boasts the only remaining fortified bridge gatehouse, built in 1272. Characteristic features of medieval bridges, though not shared by *all* bridges, were pointed arches, pointed **cutwaters** that protected the piers by dividing the oncoming waters, and **ribbed arches**. The projecting stone ribs ran around the under-surfaces of the arches, parallel to the road above and at right angles to the river beneath. The ribbed arches may survive after the bridge has been engulfed by later additions.

St Ives bridge still has a bridge chapel.

Monmouth bridge, an unusual surviving example of a fortified medieval bridge.

Moulton bridge, a medieval packhorse bridge built from the local flint.

The packhorse bridge at Ashness in the Lake District, probably the most photographed little bridge in Britain.

Pack-horse bridges

All medieval bridges must have been used by pack-horses, but the rather archaic designs for these little bridges persisted into the nineteenth century. In the uplands, where roads were poor, the reliance on pack-horses was high and the rivers were prone to sudden and violent flooding; bridges that looped over the rivers and becks in a single arch avoided the dangers of having a pier standing in the torrent, where it was exposed to pounding by the water or the trunks of fallen trees. Their **parapets** are low to allow the passage of the panniers on the passing ponies.

Later bridges

As industrialisation spread, traffic grew and the availability of official revenues for bridge-building increased, new generations of stone bridges were provided. These were usually wider than the earlier bridges, and robust, with dressed or

ashlar stonework in regular courses. Their rounded arches gave them a somewhat Classical appearance. Some of the military bridges built in the Highlands combined these features with those of the old pack-horses bridges. In many places an old, sometimes medieval bridge was adapted to the new demands by widening it on one side only.

14. MAKING SENSE OF IT ALL

Routeways are not the most amenable of subjects, but with some dogged efforts a picture of the history of a local system of roads and lanes will gradually take shape. The following points will be helpful:

- The **appearance** of a road will very much be influenced by its current function and condition. Two Roman roads that began in similar fashion as metalled aggers standing above flanking ditches may now look very different. One could be a faint holloway or a ridge running across pasture, while the other could be a thundering trunk road.
- **Prehistoric roads** are seldom easy to identify. In the lowlands they have been either ploughed out of existence or else enmeshed in the networks of living lanes. On high ground one may see incised patterns of braided routes, particularly where a convex slope is traversed. Long-distance trackways are often punctuated by prehistoric monuments and finds of trade goods. Be careful of any historic 'Ways' introduced by local authorities with their eyes on the tourist trade. How do you know that the routes they have set out are real, and not just themed tourist trails cobbled together from various roads and lanes? The most convincing ancient routes are those associated with cross-country salt trading. Very often these still have links to 'Salt-' place-names, though the old meaning of a name may be long forgotten and the name itself distorted, for example to 'Psaltergate' ('gate' comes from a Viking word for a road).
- Enthusiasts delight in discovering 'lost' **Roman roads**. However, for such a designation to be credible it must be plain that the route connected places that the Romans needed to link up, such as towns, camps, forts, ports, etc. Former hedgelines can be deceptive. Medieval ploughmen would toss stones into the nearest hedge bottom and over the centuries a ridge of cobbles and rocks would build up there and become overgrown. When the hedge is removed, one is left with an agger-like ridge, perhaps even with a flanking ditch, and anyone looking for Roman roads is likely to be

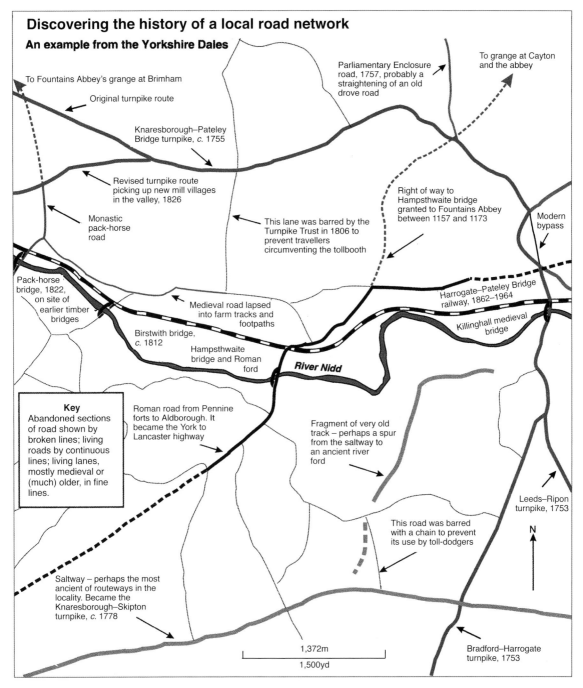

Discovering the history of a local road network

An example from the Yorkshire Dales

To Fountains Abbey's grange at Brimham

Original turnpike route

Knaresborough–Pateley Bridge turnpike, c. 1755

Parliamentary Enclosure road, 1757, probably a straightening of an old drove road

To grange at Cayton and the abbey

Revised turnpike route picking up new mill villages in the valley, 1826

Monastic pack-horse road

This lane was barred by the Turnpike Trust in 1806 to prevent travellers circumventing the tollbooth

Right of way to Hampsthwaite bridge granted to Fountains Abbey between 1157 and 1173

Modern bypass

Pack-horse bridge, 1822, on site of earlier timber bridges

Medieval road lapsed into farm tracks and footpaths

Harrogate–Pateley Bridge railway, 1862–1964

Killinghall medieval bridge

Birstwith bridge, c. 1812

Hampsthwaite bridge and Roman ford

River Nidd

Key
Abandoned sections of road shown by broken lines; living roads by continuous lines; living lanes, mostly medieval or (much) older, in fine lines.

Roman road from Pennine forts to Aldborough. It became the York to Lancaster highway

Fragment of very old track – perhaps a spur from the saltway to an ancient river ford

Leeds–Ripon turnpike, 1753

This road was barred with a chain to prevent its use by toll-dodgers

N

Saltway – perhaps the most ancient of routeways in the locality. Became the Knaresborough–Skipton turnpike, c. 1778

1,372m
1,500yd

Bradford–Harrogate turnpike, 1753

Fig. 7. Discovering the history of a local road network: an example from the Yorkshire Dales.

confused. The Saxons often referred to the Roman roads as 'streets', and the labels have sometimes stuck, while occasionally, field names with the element 'stony' may relate to a road (because of the rubble). Real abandoned Roman roads may be seen as faint ridges, but they often appear as anonymous holloways, perhaps with traces of flanking hedge banks. 'Living' Roman roads tend to have a hyphenated appearance, with their straight sections linked by curving roads that mark places where the original course became impassable and a new line was pioneered around the ruts and bogs.

- Lowland Britain is criss-crossed by the traces of former **medieval roads**. Most frequently they are seen most clearly as **holloways** traversing areas of permanent pasture. Occasionally there may not be much of a holloway and the roadside hedgerows may have gone, but the hedgerow trees may endure and still trace out the routeway. These roads can come from a wide spectrum of origins: market roads; village-to-village links; tracks to the common or its peat diggings or **turbaries**; lanes that were part of a little network of tracks radiating into the surrounding fields; routes to a great field used for fairs; ways used by pilgrims; and many other uses. There were also the corpse roads of the upland valley communities, used, *inter alia*, in medieval and sometimes later times to get corpses from farmsteads to the designated churchyard before chapels of ease were provided. The chapels in turn attracted their own lanes and tracks. If a reasonable length of the old track can be identified, it should be possible to deduce its origin and destination. Bits may survive as lanes or green roads and a name may also survive. If the track is named after a nearby village that was its original destination, a double discovery is made if that village has become 'lost'. The name might refer to a market centre used by the villagers, while a name like 'Badger Way' reveals its use by the itinerant traders in farm produce.

- The long-distance **drove roads**, once they left the high ground, tended to sink into the pattern of day-to-day lowland trackways, though on the high ground the old routes may still be visible. Centuries of use by cattle shod with iron have grooved the landscape and outcrops of stone may be smoothed and furrowed by the passage of countless hooves, just as the passes in the Old West were grooved by the iron-rimmed wheels of the pioneers' covered wagons. In Scotland, particularly, one can still see unusually green patches of upland pasture marking the **stances** where herds were penned to graze overnight, enriching the poor, leached soils.

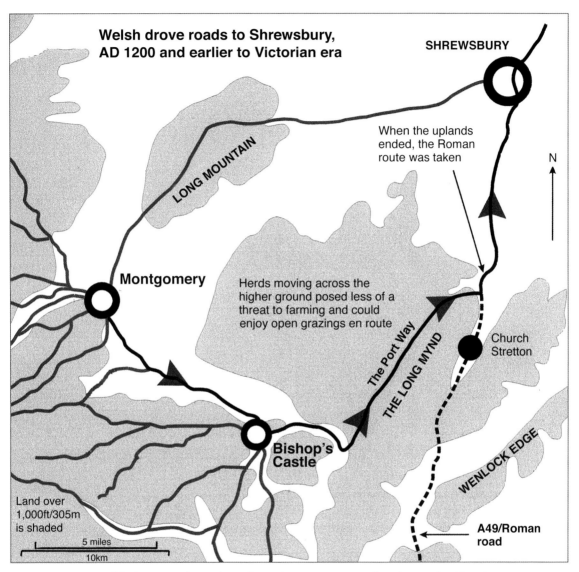

Fig. 8. Welsh drove roads to Shrewsbury, from AD 1200 and earlier to the Victorian era. Cattle trails from the Welsh hills converged on Montgomery and Bishop's Castle. Then the major drove roads favoured the ancient Port Way, the high route over The Long Mynd, rather than the Roman road.

('Stance' was also used for cattle markets, though **tryst**, meaning an appointed meeting, was used for the greater Scottish markets.) Drovers tended to avoid lowland communities and their vulnerable farmlands. Inns with attached grazing were provided for them on the ridge and watershed routes, and 'The Drovers' is an inn name that reveals the former use of its road, as do several less obvious English pub names that make reference to Scottish things or people (Highland lad, bonnet, etc.) in commemoration of the Scottish drovers, often men who spoke only Gaelic. In 1800 about 100,000 Scottish cattle came down on the drove roads, but any developments affecting a road after about 1880 should post-date droving. Scores of lowland tracks – some going to commons, some to markets and some to agisted grazings (see Chapters Two and Eight) – were also used for droving. Many very old tracks, like the East Anglian **drifts**, can be seen to have had wide verges that provided grazing for the ambling herds on either side of the road itself.

- The **military roads** of the eighteenth century are well documented. So too are the **turnpikes**, though their appearance can now be less distinctive. In their heyday the pikes, the toll houses, the barred side lanes and the general air of improvement left travellers in no doubt that they were on a turnpike (with no excuses to avoid the toll). But, today the picture is less clear. Many toll houses have disappeared or been converted into dwellings, while many roads that were never turnpiked have since been upgraded. A short session in the local history section of the nearest reference library should identify the turnpikes in your locality. In terms of appearance, the turnpike could consist of completely new road, old roads incorporated in the new alignment or a mixture of patched, straightened and little-modified sections. The nature of the roadside hedgerow trees can be informative. As the turnpikes were coming in, the old practice of pollarding (see Chapter One) was going out. Thus sections of old highway embedded in a turnpike may be suggested by roadside pollards, while hedges without any trees or without pollarded trees are likely to reveal new or improved sections of highway. Where hedgerow pollards are seen, a stretch of old road within a turnpike is suspected. **Enclosure roads** are likely to be of a loosely similar age but can be recognised as they invariably end at the parish boundary, as described above. (The parishes in a Forest like the Forest of Knaresborough are different, for the whole Forest was enclosed at once.)

- Many **bridges** conform exactly to the stereotypes described above. Most confusion is likely to arise from medieval bridges that have experienced considerable widening and modification. In such cases what is happening *under* the arches is likely to be more important than what goes on above. Ribbed arches should identify the original medieval component, while smooth arches will show later additions. What one may not learn without fairly detailed archive work concerns the negotiation of the river before the stone bridge was built. A search may perhaps reveal the wills of medieval people who left money for the repair or rebuilding of a local bridge, or refer to the timber bridges that got swept away; there may even be mention of coffin bearers who were drowned as they tried to transport a body for burial.

- The ancient **river port** functions of a village may not be obvious. Commonly the merchants' houses-cum-warehouses that once faced the waterway will have been replaced or else turned around to show their backs rather than their faces to the river. The quays and wharfs will be silted up, and the broadened river or pond where the narrowboats were turned may also have gone. Shallow earthwork traces of the waterways running up to each property may still be found, but the plainest evidence may be discovered in street or property names that include the elements **hythe** or **staithe**, both of which refer to a landing place. Other names may be more difficult. Stalbridge, for example, signifies a bridge, presumably a timber one, that was built with piles. **Ford** names are easier, as they denote old river crossings. They also imply fordable shallows that might have been barriers to all but the most shallow of craft. 'Hipping-' and 'Hippen-' names are associated with stepping stones. In the north of England, 'wath' names reveal fords and sometimes the commodity carried across might be specified, as with Lead Wath near Pateley Bridge in North Yorkshire. Also in the north 'force' names denote waterfalls that could never have been navigated (though look out for hints of old **sheep-washing places** in the pools below the cascade. These were vital for submerging and cleaning sheep and their fleeces before chemical dips were available.)

- Old maps can be extremely helpful in re-creating old road patterns. A beginning can be made by checking whether the library has, or can obtain, a reproduction edition of John Ogilby's *Britannia*, an atlas of roads in England and Wales published in 1675. Some of the main highways depicted are today little more than bridleways. Next one can check out the appropriate county maps that were being produced by people like Norden or Speed at, or a little before, this time. The various county surveys at a scale of 1in to a mile that became numerous in the eighteenth century should also be looked at, while mid-nineteenth century Ordnance Survey 6in to a mile maps give precise local detail and preserve names and information from earlier periods. For the large-scale parish tithe and enclosure maps, a trip to the county record office is needed.

- As pieces of the historical jigsaw of local routeways fall into place it is best to plot them on an **annotated map** and watch the picture grow. There is almost certainly going to be a cluster of anonymous little lanes, mostly inherited from the medieval or earlier periods. However, the main routeways that have formed the skeleton around which your locality has grown are likely to be identified and catalogued. They provide a framework that will prove invaluable when the other components of the historical landscape are explored. It is something of a thrill to discover where a former lane was going, and new discoveries can be expected as the pieces fall into place, in the way that lanes and paths converging on what is now an empty field can reveal a lost village, hamlet or fair site.

FOUR

Villages

1. SOME IDEAS ABOUT VILLAGES

'Villages are genuine timeless symbols of stability in a stressful, ever-changing world' WRONG

'English villages were created by the Anglo-Saxons when they arrived from the continent, and they still have more or less the same shapes and layouts' WRONG

'Village layouts may preserve some very old features, but villages grew, shrank, prospered or failed according to local circumstances and the forces of history' RIGHT

'The Olde Worlde character of most villages is a modern concoction produced by tourist interests, gift shops and landlords. Look below that veneer and you come face to face with a history that will often be cruel, painful and unjust, yet deeply interesting' RIGHT

2. WHY VILLAGES?

The settlements of prehistoric households and some native communities of the Roman era can often be recognised by the presence of **hut circles**, circular arrangements of stones that represent the footings of dwellings with low circular walls and tall cone-shaped roofs of thatch. In other cases one may find platforms shelved into slopes that once supported houses. But prehistoric settlement tended to be footloose; sometimes village-sized settlements would form, but they did not tend to endure for more than a few generations.

In the countrysides that archaeology is able to re-create for the prehistoric era and for the four centuries after the Roman departure in AD 410, villages were usually far, far fewer and further between than today, even though Britain was very well populated at the end of the Bronze Age. This shows that a place could support lots of people without necessarily having many villages. Even in parts of Essex today, on the very doorstep of London, there are areas where villages are

Hut circle near Dun Beag broch on Skye.

The ruins of a Bronze Age dwelling in the village below Rough Tor on Bodmin Moor, perhaps a settlement of tin workers.

The grandeur of this massive (roofless) house at Din Lligwy suggests that the local Roman-age society was already highly stratified. The presumed chieftain's house was grouped with dwellings and workshops.

outnumbered by hamlets and farmsteads. These examples show that it is quite possible to farm the countryside and practise essential crafts *without* having villages. Villages arose because particular ways of working the land and organising communities required them. Thus far, most have had reasons to survive. But if things were to change in a fundamental way (say, by steep rises in fuel prices encountered by commuters) then there are no natural laws to prevent the villages being deserted, as thousands were in the past. They have to serve a *role* and meet a *need*. With these factors in mind, the following things are important:

- In early times 'special villages', like industrial villages or fishing villages, were very unusual. There were a few settlements of prehistoric tin workers or Roman-age potters, but such places were rare.
- The overwhelming majority of villages were agricultural settlements, places where the people who worked the surrounding land congregated and slept after toiling outdoors all day and where they discussed how to organise their work in the days to come.
- Whether or not such people gathered together in villages depended very much on the way that the land was tenanted and how the work was organised.

Feudal lords played an important part in shaping medieval villages. The immediate descendants of Sir Thomas Ingilby and his wife, the local heiress, were responsible for creating the village of Ripley in North Yorkshire.

Imagine a countryside populated by substantial freeholders, yeomen and free tenants. They would probably prefer to live on their landholdings in isolated farmsteads, or perhaps in little farmstead clusters or hamlets. In the Middle Ages yeomen often lived outside the feudal villages on their own separate holdings.

In contrast, feudalism and open field farming (see Chapter Two) greatly favoured the creation and survival of big villages. Tenants were locked into a highly complicated system of farming and much depended on mutual cooperation. They had to pool their oxen or horses to form plough teams. Their holdings were fragmented in scattered strips, with the village at the heart of this local farming empire. Also, they frequently had to combine in teams to perform boonworks on their lord's demesne. So there was every advantage in having the feudal labour force concentrated in village dormitories, disciplined by the manor court and organised by the reeve, and with every opportunity for teamwork.

There were also intermediate patterns, especially in places where the domination of open field farming was less complete. In these places one tends to see a few big villages, interspersed with smaller villages as well as numerous hamlets and farmsteads.

When the 'glue' of feudalism began to weaken, villages might begin to fragment. Some other village-binding agent would be needed to hold them together, like village industries, commuting, and so on. Between Parliamentary Enclosure and the nineteenth-century mechanisation of farming on one side, and the development of commuting and village retirement cottages on the other, many villages took a few steps towards disintegration.

3. VILLAGE NAMES AND ORIGINS

Throughout most of the twentieth century it was thought that the study of **village place-names** could unlock the mystery of village origins. Some quite elaborate interpretations were produced, but it became increasingly clear that the place-name evidence was not supported by the growing number of excavations of early villages.

It had traditionally been believed that villages were created by the waves of Anglo-Saxon settlers who were thought to have rolled across England in the period directly following the withdrawal of the Romans. Thus a great surge of new village formation was believed to have occurred in the fifth and sixth centuries AD. Later, a second swarm of English villages (**secondary settlements**) was believed to have been created by settlers who expanded from the original villages in order to colonise their nearby woods.

However, archaeology has not really confirmed that there ever was such an overwhelming invasion, on a scale that drove the native British into the western fastnesses or exterminated them. Instead, British and Saxon communities may often have coexisted and the domination of the land by English culture may have been more to do with ruling dynasties than mass migrations. In fact there is little to suggest that the earlier Saxon settlers were interested in village life. Many generations of their English descendants lived and died before the real village revolution occurred, around the eighth and ninth centuries AD. This did take place against a background of invasion and instability but it seems to have been part of a larger revolution that laid the foundations for parish church creation, open field farming and estate reorganisation. Often the churches must have provided the nuclei around which people gathered, while the new method of working the surrounding farmland gave the reason for the changes.

It used to be thought that some village names plainly demonstrated a foundation by the first waves of Anglo-Saxon 'invaders'. An example is a name like 'Hastings'; the element 'ing', which derives from *ingas*, refers to the 'people or followers of . . .'. Thus, Hastings would be 'the place of the people of a patriarch called Haesta'. There are multitudes of such names – Walsingham, Markington, Reading, and so on. The notion that these 'ing' names revealed the influx of a warband and local occupation force, the followers of a patriarchal leader or warlord, was very persuasive. *However*, if the villages did not materialise until Anglo-Saxon immigration from the continent was long since over and Viking invasion was becoming a real threat, such ideas must be fatally flawed. Even so, village names all do or did mean something and the old language in which they are named (Early English, Middle English, Old Danish, etc.) can be revealing.

4. A TABLE OF VILLAGE NAMES

Where villages are concerned, place-names should be treated with great suspicion. A village must frequently have taken the name of a long-existing nearby feature. A place called 'Ashford' has obviously taken its name from a river ford shaded by ash trees – but things are never quite so simple with place-names and there is a good chance the odd Ashford name might not come from the Old English *aesc*, meaning ash tree, but from *ecles*, which relates to oak wood pasture. And to illustrate the trickiness of place-names further, some 'Eccles' names derive from vulgar Latin and denote ancient church sites!

Place-name elements were adopted in various combinations, sometimes in conjunction with the name of a person who might have been the local landowner (just as the medieval Spark family gave their name to Sparkbrook near Worcester) and sometimes with adjectives. Some names mean just what they seem to mean, with 'Holywell' indicating a holy spring, while others are quite deceptive. It is tempting to translate 'Heslington' as being the farm of the people of a Dark Age patriarch with a name like Hessle or Hesla. It is more likely to be the farm where the hazel trees (*haeslen*) grew.

Place-name translations are really *guesses*. The better the translator's grasp of half a dozen ancient languages and the ways they have evolved, the better his/her guesses are likely to be. There are no definitive answers, just informed guesses, with scores of words having a number of possible origins, some seeming more probable than others. However, taken across a locality spanning a few parishes or several townships, the place-names will produce a broad picture of the different peoples who have occupied the area and the contributions they have made to its history. Welsh place-names are still numerous along the eastern margins of the principality, where the displacement of Welsh culture by English settlers is often quite recent. In the Yorkshire Dales the very numerous Old Norse names and the thinner spread of Old Danish names show that Vikings from Norway and their recent descendants who migrated to the region via the Northern Isles, the Western Isles, Ireland, Cumbria and Lancashire were more numerous than the Danish Vikings, who moved up the rivers from the east.

Place-names provide some of our best evidence for the mysterious Picts, whose culture evolved in northern Scotland during the Roman occupation of England and Wales. Names containing **Pit**, which seems to describe a share of land, such as Pitmedden or Pitlochry, appear to belong only to the lost and unknown Pictish language. The names trace out the extent of the Pictish homeland in North East Scotland.

Among the most interesting names are those that seem to show the coming-together of people from different cultural backgrounds. Launceston in Cornwall is one of these 'hybrid' names, combining the old English 'ton' or 'farm' word with a Cornish word for an enclosure (*lann*). Between the two words may be another Cornish word for an elder grove (*scawet*). Similarly Salkeld in Cumbria combines an Old English word for sallow or willow (*salh*) with the Old Norse word for a spring, *kelda*.

By the time of Geoffrey Chaucer (1345–1400), Old English had evolved into Middle English and many of the words embedded in place-names had become redundant and then forgotten. Confronted with apparent gibberish, people will adapt the syllables into forms that are more easily said or, more likely, bend the word so that it coincides with something that does have meaning. Thus Odiham in Hampshire is nothing to do with oddities or ham, but was recorded at the start of the twelfth century as *Wudiham*, derived from *wudiga* and *hām* and meaning 'wooded homestead', while the 'way' or (stream) course with the 'strang' (strong) current ceased to be Strangway and became Strangeways in Lancashire.

Many names appear to have developed on the large estates that were part of the Roman and Dark Age landscapes. Such estates could contain several vestigial villages, all of them taking their name from the estate. Means were needed to differentiate between these settlements. This might be done by labelling them north, south, east or west, according to their relative positions, or by grading them by size into Greater/Magna and Little/Parvum. It could also be done by attaching the patron saint of the village church to the name, as with

Table 4.1. *Table of village names*

Language	Comments	Examples
Old Welsh/ Cornish/Gaelic	In the English-settled areas these names survived for many topo-graphical features (hills, rivers, etc.) long after English became the language spoken, but they rarely link to settlements. In Wales and Scotland many of the villages were founded by/for English speakers, sometimes indigenous people who adopted English as part of a 'feudal package', but in Wales often an intrusive community of English or Flemish settlers was planted on a feudal estate.	*Aber* – estuary *Afon* – river *Beag* – little *Coed* – wood *Dun* – fort *Eglwys* – church *Lann* – enclosure *Llan* – church *Muir* – moor or sea *Pant* – valley *Porth* – harbour/estuary *Pwll* – pool *Rath* – fort *Tre* – farmstead *Ynys* – island, wet meadow
Latin	The Romans left surprisingly few names considering the length of their occupation. Some Latin words were established via other languages.	*Castra* (chester) – army base *Cum* – with *Magnus* – great *Mare* – sea *Parvus* – small *Port* – harbour/market
Old English	The various dialects of the Anglo-Saxons produced a profusion of place-names in England, and when developed as Lowland Scots, thousands of names in Scotland, too.	*Cirice/church* – church *Denn* – wood pasture *Denu/den* – valley *Ēg (ey)* – island *Feld/field* – expanse of open land *Ham* – homestead *Hamm* – meadow *Hām-tūn/hamton* – home farm *Ingas/ing* – people of . . . *-ington* – the place where X's people live *Lēah/ley* – a grove or clearing *Stān/stane* – stone *Stede* – a place *Stoc/stoke* – holy place *Stock* – tree stumps *Straét/street* – Roman road *Ton* – place, farmstead *Wald* – wood, wooded hills *Walh/wal* – Welsh/strangers

Language	Comments	Examples
		Wic/wick – outlying farm, cheese farm, sometimes a Roman road-side village *Wic-ham*/wickham – settlement near a Romano-British village
Old Danish/ Old Norse	The Danes colonised the eastern and north-eastern parts of England around the time that English villages were being created. Some of their names are similar to those of their Norse (Norwegian) Viking cousins and some were shared with Old English, the continental homelands of Saxons and Danes overlapping. The Norsemen ruled York for a while but many of the settlers arrived from the west, via Viking settlements in the North Isles, the Hebrides and Ireland.	*By* – farm or settlement *Carr* – swamp forest *Erg* – upland summer farm *Ey* – island *Gill* – upland stream/ravine *Holt* – thicket/copse *Kirkja/kirk* – church *Marr* – fen *Ness* – headland *Skáli/scale* – hovel, summer hut *Thorpe* – subordinate hamlet or farmstead *Thwaite* – meadow, clearing or enclosure *Vik* – inlet or creek

Weasenham St Peter, Norfolk. In some cases the current landowner's name could be adopted, with Stratfield Mortimer in Berkshire taking its name from the family who owned it at the time of Domesday Book. Steeple Gidding near Huntingdon had a steeple; so, too, did Great Gidding, but the 'Great' prefix removed any confusion.

5. RESEARCHING YOUR VILLAGE NAME

If you want to do things the hard and independent way, you will need to scour the archives for the earliest possible recorded form of your village name. In this way the distortions wrought by time and linguistic evolution are kept to a minimum. For most of England the Domesday Book provides an accessible source of names as recorded in 1086, and most reference libraries will provide you with a facsimile or translation. But remember:

- Domesday Book lists *estates* and their contents, not *villages*. You may well find the village name there, attached to a piece of territory, perhaps a manor or a section of one, but this does not mean the village existed then. Domesday was compiled to reveal the king's taxable assets, not to help local historians!

- Equally, if the village name is *not* there, it does not prove that no settlement of that name existed. So far as taxation documents were concerned, the people could have been living up trees, it would not have mattered.

- If Domesday Book cannot help, as it cannot for the Celtic lands and the far north of England, then one may scour the local history books for any early mention of the name.

Taking the easier approach involves going directly to the place-name dictionaries in the reference library. A good library will keep several and it is instructive to look up the same words in different dictionaries and see how many conflicting translations are offered.

Picture your village in its setting and see which of the (possibly) varying translations seems best to accord with the local topography and countryside character. For example, you might live in a village called 'Radford', and different authorities might translate its name as 'Road ford' and 'Red ford'. There should be an old ford close by, and if the river banks or the boulders on the riverbed are of red sandstone, then the latter is probably the right translation. To be right, a name translation *must* accord with the setting. Always opt for the name that has the 'best fit' with the features of your locality (rather than the most romantic or flattering one).

After doing your best with the village name, it should be interesting to look at its broader setting. More likely than not there will be lots of very old names that reveal the environment as it was long ago. *Salh* or willow names will reveal the wet places, which the trees may have shared with *alor* or alder, with alder swamp being 'carr' in some places settled by Vikings and '*gwern*' in Wales. You may find a 'Swinden' or hollow where the village swine foraged beneath the trees. You may find the Broxbourne, where the badgers once crossed the chalk stream, or perhaps find references to displaced wildlife – the Arncliffe where the eagles soared, or the spring at Cranwell that the cranes once visited. Place-names remind us how much wildlife we have driven out of our homelands.

If your village was named some time before the Norman Conquest, then a study of the local names in its surroundings that belong to Anglo-Saxon and Viking times should give you an idea of the setting – woods, pools, swamps, meadows, copses and so on – around the time of its foundation.

6. THE LIVELY VILLAGE

It is true that countless villages contain features that have endured since medieval times. However, the early stages in village life seem to have been quite lively and the places that we see today look far different from how they appeared in their early years. The preoccupation with the myth that villages are stable and timeless places is a great barrier to a proper understanding of villages. Real villages are far, far more interesting than the chintzy places found in glossy books.

By the time of the Domesday Book many, perhaps most, villages in England (though not in the Celtic lands) had taken on a 'structured' appearance. High Streets, market greens or squares, house frontages lining the High Street or through road with long plots or 'tofts' running back were becoming established parts of the village landscape. And so they remain.

However, the first generations of English villages seemed more like loose bunches of farmsteads, with the dwellings set in and among little fields and enclosures. They had a 'paddocky' sort of appearance. These settlements of the eighth and ninth centuries AD were by no means the first villages to exist in Britain. But they – or those that survived – were the ancestors of today's villages. Prehistoric villages came and went without leaving a legacy.

Villages were certainly established in Roman Britain. Some were quite large, some small, some thoughtfully set out and others jumbled; some were industrial and others agricultural. There were some quite important ones that were set beside routeways, but only a very small proportion of the villages that survive into modern times have lineages going back before the time of the great Saxon kings of Wessex (rulers who established small fortified towns or *burhs* within the gradually gelling village networks).

Village England can only have been created at the expense of an earlier farming landscape. Did feudal tenants desert their hamlets and farmsteads voluntarily to populate the new villages or were they herded in with the flat of the sword? As yet, we know very little about the birth and early days of village England. It is very likely that the typical village acquired its landscape very gradually. The gaining of a market charter would encourage the creation of a place for trading, and as it prospered a court house and a market house for storing the market gear might be added. Meanwhile, as the farming economy developed, specialist workshops for wheelwrights, cartwrights and smiths might appear, and the warehouses and showy houses of merchants might enhance the High Street.

As the village grew, certain of its features would play vital roles in the

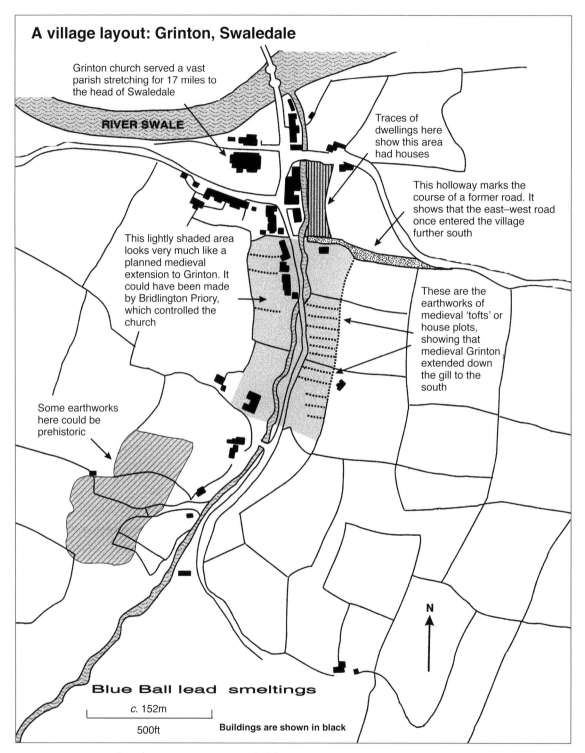

A village layout: Grinton, Swaledale

Grinton church served a vast parish stretching for 17 miles to the head of Swaledale

RIVER SWALE

Traces of dwellings here show this area had houses

This holloway marks the course of a former road. It shows that the east–west road once entered the village further south

This lightly shaded area looks very much like a planned medieval extension to Grinton. It could have been made by Bridlington Priory, which controlled the church

These are the earthworks of medieval 'tofts' or house plots, showing that medieval Grinton extended down the gill to the south

Some earthworks here could be prehistoric

Blue Ball lead smeltings

c. 152m

500ft

N

Buildings are shown in black

Fig. 9. A village layout: Grinton in Swaledale.

preservation of aspects of its layout. The through-road tended to provide the village spine, although villages could develop new alignments, while the church represented a stupendous investment and was hardly ever relocated.

7. PLANNED VILLAGES

When we think of new towns such as Cumbernauld or Peterlee, straight lines and right-angled corners seem very much the norm. For better or worse, planning is very much a part of modern life. However, when we think of the past, for no specially good reason, we think of roads that wiggle and wind and houses all jumbled together in a higgledy-piggledy way. There are certainly villages that did develop piecemeal along a snaking track leading up to the church. But there are a great many old villages that had no spontaneous aspects to their layouts. They were as planned as planned could be. That this was so need not be thought remarkable, for the Romans had planned their settlements and King Alfred (AD 871–99) and his kin had founded numerous planned towns. What is remarkable is that the clear traces of planning can often be picked out in village layouts that are nearly a thousand years old.

Edmonton, Cornwall, a planned nineteenth-century quarry village of twenty-four cottages and a chapel, all built around a courtyard and in the view of the manager's offices.

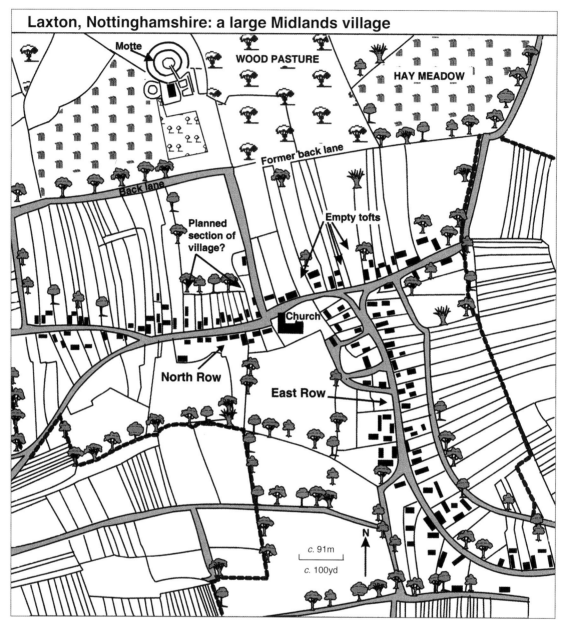

Fig. 10. Laxton, Nottinghamshire: a large Midlands village. Laxton, as it was mapped in 1635, was a complicated village. It had a Y-shaped layout, though one limb was much less developed than the other two. To the west of the church and on the north side of North Row a tidy little section of housing hints at a planned medieval addition to the village, and further west along this row the tofts of plots attached to the dwellings seem like strips taken from the communal ploughlands as the village grew. To the east of the church a few empty tofts show local shrinkage. North Row and East Row have back lanes on one side, though one of the lanes has been partly abandoned. In 1635 hedges with old pollards outlined some furlongs, but by this time many strips had been amalgamated to form more compact blocks of ploughland. Laxton motte was the medieval administrative centre for Sherwood Forest and the castle motte is just to the north of the village.

Planning involves building to a preconceived plan. It usually follows simple, geometrical patterns, because these are thought to be the most efficient or the easiest to build. The opposite of planning is spontaneous, piecemeal development. Planning tends to produce straight roads and right-angled intersections, and generally produces whole sections of development, like a row of houses, all at once. Spontaneous development produces gradual, seemingly haphazard growth and is seen in curving routes, uneven shapes, straggling houses and a mixture of dwellings of different styles and sizes.

Planning is associated with the masters of the countryside. They had the means to finance the larger developments, and the power to coerce their tenants to live in them; furthermore, they owned the land designated for development and had the financial incentive to wrest more rents and profits from their estates and manors.

Many villages were precisely planned from the outset, as the creations of feudal lords seeking to rationalise agriculture on their estates or to develop commercial activities, such as markets or crafts. There were also many other villages that may have begun life as rather disorganised agglomerations and yet gained planned additions. The lord might want to provide improved quarters for a merchant community near the market or pursue some other re-organisation.

Planning has a long history and it has never left us. Hundreds of medieval villages were set out to preconceived plans. Scottish landlords, for example, shifted thousands of tenants into villages every bit as planned as Manhattan during the Improvements of the Georgian era. Often free to work in landscapes unencumbered with obstacles to their designs, they were able to impose geometrical layouts as they pleased. New Pitsligo was neatly set out on a hillside in North East Scotland between the quarry that produced the stone for its houses and the peat beds that yielded the fuel for their fires. Today we can see scores of residential developments around little rectangular courts which resemble medieval ecclesiastical and charity housing in plan if not in charm.

The **model villages** that Georgian landowners set up to glorify the approaches to a mansion or park or to house communities evicted in creating the park were all carefully planned, often on an architect's drawing-board. Some might be set out in straight, 'rational' lines but others were carefully planned romantic parodies of 'traditional' or unplanned villages! Beneath their extravagant pie-crusts of thatch or alpine arrays of tiled dormers, the houses might draw on the vernacular styles of Switzerland, the Rhineland, Alsace or

Wimpole, near Cambridge, began life as a planned roadside village that housed tenants evicted by the creation of the park for Wimpole Hall. The vaguely Tudor dwellings date from the 1840s.

Norfolk. These villages were anything but ordinary: eye-snatching rather than eye-catching. They often conjured up a romanticised image of a rustic cottage community that had grown organically from a fairytale landscape and that basked in the patronage of a cultivated and munificent patron.

The last great flourish of the unplanned came with the development of the 'Plotlands' along the southern coast of England during the first four decades of the twentieth century. Settlers, many escaping from the increasingly feverish world of London, set up makeshift homes in old carriages, shacks and bungalows in settlements like Jaywick Sands, Canvey-on-Sea, Shoreham Beach and Peacehaven. Arbiters of taste and members of the rising breed of professional planners detested everything about the Plotlands. But at least the ramshackle places offered freedom and exuded a certain jolly, whimsical quality – features sadly absent from the planners' creations.

8. SO WHAT DOES PLANNING LOOK LIKE IN AN OLD VILLAGE?

Strange as it may seem, the understanding of village landscapes is very much about **shapes**. Because of this, it is often much easier to read a village story by studying its outline on a map than it is by actually walking through the place. Every line and angle has a story: pick up the important threads and one is well on the way to teasing out a village history.

First, one should realise that there are some sorts of shapes that cannot form by accident. The simplest type of planned medieval village layout had a through-road forming the village spine. Dwellings were arranged with their long axes aligned along the roadside, usually on both sides of the road. A long, narrow plot or toft ran back from each house frontage, providing land for gardening, hogs and fowls. In most cases the plots terminated at a back lane. Think about it and you will realise that such a layout could not form by accident. It has to have been planned. Of course, some features may change over time. In the little Yorkshire town of Skipton small streets behind the market place fit neatly into the spaces of the tofts of the earlier market-side houses, and an island group of shops has encroached on the market area.

The basic building blocks in such medieval plans are the rows of roadside dwellings together with the parallel tofts running back from them. These are termed **toft rows** and they can be arranged in various ways. In Yorkshire medieval planned villages of a Y-shaped layout of toft rows is common, with a forking road providing the basis of the Y and with a market place sometimes located at the junction.

Larger planned medieval settlements, usually small towns rather than villages, were set out on a rectangular grid or chequerboard pattern. Driving through such a settlement, like Castleton in Derbyshire or Boroughbridge in Yorkshire, involves a succession of right-angled turns as one picks a way through the rectilinear grid of streets.

Variations on these simple plans were used by the post-medieval builders of replacement villages for settlements levelled during park making and by the Scottish landowners enforcing the Improvements on their estates. One variation that they adopted was that of the straight through-road straddled in the heart of the settlement by a rectangular green. Anglo-Irish landlords of the same era used similar models when they introduced planned villages on estates that had quite different traditions of settlement. Occasionally, they incorporated a note of sentimentality (or propaganda?) by incorporating an English village green into the layout.

9. THE OCCASIONS OF VILLAGE PLANNING

Evidence of planned layouts can be seen in some Roman and Saxon villages, but the first occasion for village planning on a massive scale came in the aftermath of the terrible Harrying of the North. In 1069–71 William the Conqueror launched his armies on a vicious campaign of retribution for the uprisings in the north of England. The devastation was immense. When the Normans began the rehabilitation of their estates north of the Humber they created flocks of precisely planned villages. They seem to have employed standard measuring rods in many cases and created settlements like those described above. Even today, with the aid of a map one can see that the great majority of villages in the Vale of York preserve traces of this medieval planning. In some places an older church seems to have provided a nucleus for a post-Harrying village.

The lord's gaining of a market charter could spell both opportunity and trouble for the village concerned. With a good measure of luck, the market might quicken the pace of commerce. However, somewhere had to be found to house it – which could spell doom for a good many dwellings. The likeliest choice of spot for a market green would be at a convergence of routeways in a village, either in the angle of a bifurcating road, or at a crossroads. The lords concerned seem to have had no qualms about clearing houses from the chosen spot during the insertion of a planned market place after a charter had been obtained. Presumably the households involved would set up homes again on the margins of the village.

Another feature of medieval village life was the insertion of planned blocks of properties in an existing unplanned village landscape. Such interventions were always easier if the village was **closed** or under the ownership of a single lord (many villages were divided between different manors, and thus more difficult to reshape). A lord might want to create more attractive accommodation for traders, while the church might intervene to create housing for a body of priests attached to a chantry. Such interventions might involve straightening a section of a winding through-road and the setting-out of house plots using a precise geometrical plan. Seen on a map, the straight angular lines of the planned additions will contrast with the curves and uneven sizes of the neighbouring properties.

The use of simple geometrical motifs, like the straight road spine, the row of identical houses, the rectangular green and the grid of lanes, featured in the post-medieval village creations throughout Britain and Ireland. Numerous villages were created by improving landlords in the North East of Scotland, as I have mentioned; some of these were just a straight, double line of roadside

The market house at Wymondham in Norfolk. Such buildings often served many roles over the passing years, but most began as venues for the market court, where the paraphernalia for making stalls could be stowed. They are signs of medieval affluence.

dwellings, like Lumsden, and some were more elaborate creations, like Tomintoul, said to be Britain's loftiest village, with a rectangular green at its core. These Georgian and early Victorian village founders would often furnish their new developments with a kirk and an inn. In some cases the extravagant dimensions of the public buildings demonstrate the often-unfounded optimism of the provider. Villages are still gaining planned additions today, though for modern estates curving road layouts and open, unhedged frontages are favoured (though not necessarily by the residents). Most of these estates began with the speculative sale of plots of land by farmers to builders/developers. Thus one can generally recognise the old, squarish field boundaries that define the estates.

10. THE VILLAGE OF CLUSTERS

A great many villages are agglomerations of clusters of buildings that were formerly distinct. Scholars refer to them as **polyfocal villages**, or villages with several foci, but 'village of clusters' will serve just as well.

Imagine a corner of the landscape where a church has become the magnet for a little cluster of dwellings huddled around it. A little way down the track there is a row of dwellings occupied by tenants of a local manor. A different manor has its own hamlet dormitory where its own feudal tenants live, while yet another cluster of dwellings beside the manor house is home to a small community of retainers. Over the years some of these clusters expand until they meet and then merge. Before very long there will probably be a single village with a single name, but embedded in its fabric will be the little clusters that were once free-standing. Unpicking the story of a village of clusters is seldom easy. The names and roles of the different components can be very hard to recover from across the centuries.

When seen on the map, the village of clusters can have a 'lumpy', rather uneven appearance, with the different clusters being strung out along the High

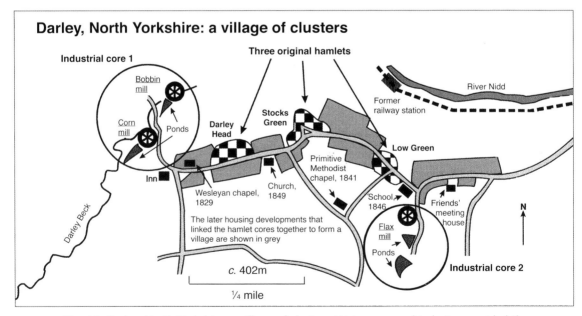

Fig. 11. Darley, North Yorkshire: a village of clusters. Water-powered industry provided the energy that allowed the village of Darley to develop from three separate roadside hamlets. The appearance of public buildings and services or 'central places' buttressed and confirmed the village identity of the new settlement.

Street like beads of uneven shapes and sizes on a string. Sometimes the 'necklace' has more than one strand, slung out in different directions.

It is much easier to understand how such villages have formed by looking at examples from times more recent than the Middle Ages. In the case of Darley in Nidderdale, the valley lane passed through several separate hamlets, each with its own little green. Water-powered industry in the valley created mills and these generated employment, so the mills became new nuclei for growth. With the rise in population, facilities like chapels and schools could be supported and the arrival of the railway and recent overspill housing cemented all the clusters together in a single, now-continuous settlement (see Fig. 11, page 114).

The village of clusters needs a source of energy if the separate clusters are to expand and gell. This might simply come from an increase in the local agricultural population, or it might be due to the quickening of trade brought by a successful market, while in the case of Darley and many other late additions to the village fold, it was industry that provided the energy.

11. SHRUNKEN VILLAGES

Once created, the village might achieve local stardom on the strength of its successful market, though this would be unusual and most village markets just ticked over or sputtered. Typically the village would grow very gradually in size. However, some villages failed utterly (see Chapter Seven) while numerous others contracted rather than expanded. These belong to the class of shrunken villages.

Shrunken villages have lost dwellings, but the degree of shrinkage varies greatly. In some cases just a short row of dwellings has gone, while in others up to 90 per cent or even more of the homes have been lost. Shrinkage can lead to a 'gappy' appearance, with sections of farmland, orchards or gardens filling the gaps where houses used to stand. It might also lead to the contraction of the whole village, with 'limbs' of settlement being lost from the roadsides at the margins of the settlement.

When shrinkage becomes very pronounced, so many buildings are abandoned that the whole layout of the settlement is distorted. It can be hard to decide which of several lanes was the original High Street, while the settlement is reduced to a few scattered and incoherent groups of farmsteads and cottages.

The causes of shrinkage are varied. Misfortunes might involve an outbreak of plague, causing a market to be suspended and its trade lost to a neighbouring rival. Tenants may have been evicted by a lord who was inclined towards sheep keeping rather than traditional agriculture. An upstart settlement nearby may capture the old village's commerce, or a waterway that was crucial to its trade could have silted up. More recently the Parliamentary Enclosure of the parish could have encouraged village farmers to move to new farmsteads on their new holdings. These and many other causes made shrunken villages quite common.

In the case of the Swaledale village of Grinton (see Fig. 9, page 106), the church, which served the whole of the upper dale, came under the control of Bridlington Priory. The priory may have created an extension to the village along the lane leading to local lead reserves. But, for whatever reason, the neatly planned enlargement of the village failed, leaving only the earthworks of the former house plots behind.

12. EXPLORING SHRUNKEN VILLAGES

Various medieval records from Domesday Book onwards give indications of village sizes, but those who want to work through the old records should remember that they were not always compiled with accuracy and villagers may have been ingenious at evading inclusion in tax assessments.

- The locations of former dwellings can often be revealed by earthworks. These may be the traces of the houses themselves, but more frequently the ditches, walls or hedge banks marking out the boundaries of tofts or closes containing houses leave clear marks. Where a manor house has gone, the earthworks of its stables, outhouses and garden divisions may be seen.
- Look for such diagnostic earthworks beyond the extremities of the remaining village and in any broad gaps between the properties lining its lanes. Similarly look for any holloways that could have been village lanes or side alleys.
- Look, too, for any traces of ridge and furrow. Ploughland would often run up to the margins of the settled area, so the presence of ridge and furrow might indicate the former village bounds.
- Where the implosion of the village has been quite severe, the hedges bounding its house plots could survive yet be stranded at some distance from the remaining village. Parallel lines of old, often rather tatty and gappy hedgerows could be the remains of old tofts.
- Patches of nettles sometimes flourish in the enriched ground of a former dwelling, where food debris, eggshells and so on have been trampled into the dark earthen floor. Coating the pounded earth of a floor with cow blood would also cause enrichment.

- Remember, however, that these clues do not always prove the existence of a *shrunken* village. Villages could wither and withdraw at one end, while growing and advancing in another direction. Thus, all the signs of decay would be produced in one place, even though the village itself could actually be expanding.

13. SHIFTED VILLAGES

The points mentioned above take us to the strange cases of villages that have actually moved across the local map. One can think of lots of reasons why this should *not* happen: the amount of investment tied up in village buildings; the problem that might be posed by moving across property boundaries and all the rearrangements that a relocation of a community would cause. Nevertheless, cases of villages that have moved are not uncommon and there are sure to be lots of as yet unrecognised examples – perhaps hundreds of them.

There are two ways in which a village could move. The first is by drifting, whereby the village develops new buildings at one extremity, while dwellings are abandoned at another extremity. In this way the settlement would advance gradually, slug-like, across its own fields. The second way is through being abandoned in favour of a new village that was purpose-built elsewhere in the parish/township. In this case the village leapfrogs over its fields rather than crawling across them.

Archaeologists are now discovering that it was commonplace for communities to migrate over quite short distances during the prehistoric era. The reasons why they did so are less clear, though a build-up of contaminants and disease after a few decades of occupation at a site might be the reason.

The villagers of the Middle Ages often tolerated foul conditions, with rats scuttling in the thatch and along runs in the wattle and daub walls, with cesspits intruding on the roadways and with sewage contaminating their wells. The villagers were prey to a spectrum of parasites and were threatened by awful diseases, but these things do not seem to have urged them to leave. Occasionally they did take advantage of an opportunity to move. After Cublington in Buckinghamshire was devastated by the Black Death, the returning survivors colonised a more lofty site that overlooked the poorly drained ground of their former homes.

Routes and commerce could foster the urge to move. The status of medieval routes was not fixed but rose or fell as trade blossomed in one place and stagnated in another. A community side-tracked down a lane that was abandoned by

The church at Comberton in Cambridgeshire, with its tower of clunch or chalk, was left stranded when the village migrated to a more promising setting.

tradesmen and dealers might opt for a move to a more lively thoroughfare nearby. This seems to have been the case at Comberton in Cambridgeshire.

A feudal lord might reorganise his estate, perhaps gathering his demesne together in compact fields and relocating the village close to the watchful eye of the manor house. Alternatively, he might move his tenants away from land designated for a deer park and into a new settlement.

The costs of such a move could be less than one would imagine. Most village dwellings were at least in part 'home-made'. Their structures were provided by rather poor-quality posts, braces, beams and rafters that were mostly jointed together, with the joints secured by removable pegs. Thus a dwelling could be dismantled and its main timbers carried away, just as the victims of the eighteenth-century Clearances in the Scottish Highlands departed carrying the curving **cruck blades** that supported their dwellings. Feudal tenants would normally have the right to take timber for wattle from the woods and to gather heather, reeds or straw for thatch, so building a new village was not so daunting a task. There would be one problem, however: the church.

The church embodied much of the wealth of the community, both of the tithe-paying villagers and the lord, who would probably have provided much of the fabric. It could well be the village's only stone building and could not readily be moved. (Ripley in North Yorkshire was an exception. The original church, quite recently rebuilt, was demolished about the late fourteenth century and its materials transported for several hundred metres and re-erected. That this happened is demonstrated by the rood screen, which had to be shortened before it could be incorporated in the new building.) Normally the church was reluctantly left behind, as at Comberton and at Castle Camps, also in Cambridgeshire.

14. SPOTTING THE SHIFTED VILLAGE

Shifted villages can be much harder to pick out than, say, shrunken ones. The following clues could be helpful.

Isolated churches, or their surviving towers, stand out like a jagged tooth in an otherwise empty mouth. They can be seen from far away – but what story are they trying to tell?

- The church could be a relic of a deserted village that never went anywhere and simply decayed where it stood.
- The church could have been forsaken by the community that once clustered around it, but now trekked back for Sunday worship and other services. In other words, the village shifted away from the church.
- The church could *always* have stood alone in a region where the whole settlement tradition was based on hamlets and farmsteads.

The characteristic earthworks of abandoned village streets and lanes, house platforms and house plots can be expected near the church, whether its village is lost or migrated. Furthermore, some investigations of the old parish layout and names should be helpful. If the parish, the church locale and the separated village all share the *same* name, then it is likely that the village drifted away. But if the old church, or the field it stands in or the nearby farmstead have *different* names, this could indicate a discrete lost village site. However, to complicate matters again, in the north of England particularly a parish can comprise several townships, each with its own differently named settlement but all sharing the one church. In many places a church could be kept alive after the

Weobley, near Hereford. The perspective here helps to emphasise the medieval dominance of the church over all the other village buildings.

death or departure of its village by continuing to be used by another, neighbouring, community.

A village might shift and *then* acquire a church. The memory of its old location might be perpetuated in field names referring to the village or its original church, in the way that the furlong called 'Chapel Flatt' flanked the ancient church site at Ripley.

Heavy scatters of medieval pottery of the coarse types used in village homesteads, spread over a village-sized area, might be found after the ploughing and harrowing of a field. In Norfolk the scattered pot fragments have sometimes seemed to trace the drift of a community from one place, often beside an ancient church, to a new perch beside a green some distance away. The availability there of common pasture would have been the bait.

15. HAMLETS

Hamlets are sometimes thought of as the poor relations of villages, failures that could not achieve village status. In fact, hamlets seem to be the 'natural' forms of rural settlement in many regions, like Cornwall, Cumbria and the Yorkshire Dales. They also have a longer and more numerous history than villages, for, along with scattered farmsteads, they were the norm for prehistoric settlement.

People often expect that hamlets and villages can be defined precisely according to their size and population, but this does not really work. A hamlet with more than 20–30 homesteads would be hard to imagine, yet one could imagine a large hamlet with a dozen farmsteads and a small village with a similar number of dwellings. Much depends upon how they are set out or structured.

The old **fermtouns** of eastern Scotland that existed before the Georgian Improvements could have had village-size populations, as did many traditional Irish settlements. But they were rambling, shambling places, sometimes served only by muddy paths and lacking the sort of structure and organisation that we associate with villages.

Both villages and hamlets can have greens and churches, but villages tend to have more structured layouts and more public buildings, and they present a fairly continuous display of house frontages to the traveller on the through-road.

A great deal of research has been done on villages, but hamlets are still rather poorly understood. In upland areas, where the population was quite thinly spread, the resources of hill farming would not have sustained villages, but households may have liked to live together in little farmstead clusters, perhaps for mutual protection. They could have shared some tasks and any joint obligations to their lord could have been organised more easily.

The ancient hamlet tradition may have been partly rooted in extended families of brothers, cousins, nephews and grandparents, with each household within an extended family occupying a farmstead in a hamlet.

Hamlets were no more misfortune-proof than villages and the sites of many of the failures are known to archaeologists. Like villages, hamlets could also shrink. In Wales many declined and eventually became single farmsteads, but the frequent presence of *Hendref* or *Trev* in the farmstead name reveals that previously it was a cluster of farmsteads.

In England and on the Improved estates in Scotland landowners could see an advantage in removing a clutch of impoverished tenants from a hamlet, fermtoun or **clachan** and combining their tenancies under just one man, who could be expected to produce a decent rent.

For all this, it seems quite remarkable that hamlets of around four or six dwellings should seem quite often to have sustained their existence, never getting much bigger or smaller, for century upon century. In some ways, the sort of hamlet-dotted countryside that one may see in places like the fringes of Dartmoor provides a porthole on the way that England may have looked before the reigns of the great Wessex kings, when open field farming was still a fad and the drive to corral tenants in great agricultural dormitory villages had yet to dawn.

16. MEETING THE GREENS AND ENDS

Most English readers will be living within a few miles of a hamlet or small village that is called Something Green or Something End. These **greens** and **ends** are a most intriguing facet of the rural scene. They are not, however, scattered randomly across the countryside. Very often they are associated with larger villages, where two, three or more of these minor settlements may be seen around the outskirts of the fully fledged village.

The greens are so-called because they have, or used to have, little greens around which their dwellings were grouped. In contrast, the ends might or might not have greens. Their names suggest that they were considered to be at the end of something, but what? It may be used in the sense of 'outlying', though 'corner' seems more likely. Thus in Bedfordshire, Stevington village's satellite 'Park End' lay towards the old deer park.

The greens and ends could, perhaps, represent a movement of medieval

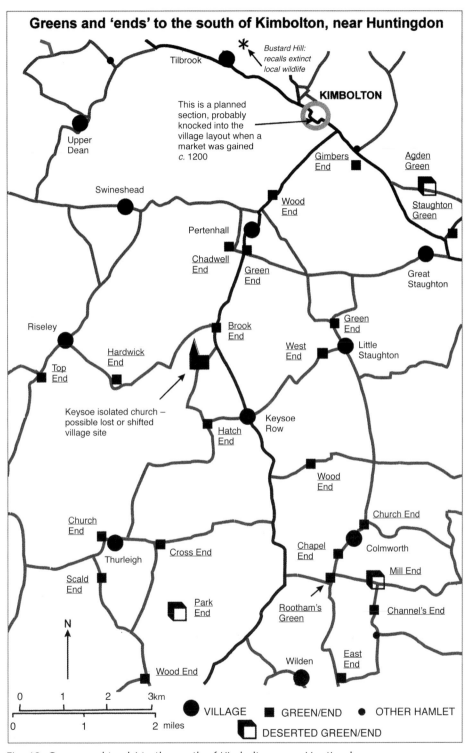

Fig. 12. Greens and 'ends' to the south of Kimbolton, near Huntingdon.

villagers to settle beside nearby common pastures (greens) but equally they might be the relics of an old pattern of hamlets and mini-villages that dates back beyond the birth of Village England.

Readers who scan a 1:50,000-scale map of their locality may be surprised at just how many places have 'Green' or 'End' as the second part of their name, particularly in regions like East Anglia and the Midlands and in areas with widespread woodland. They still pose a great challenge to our understanding of the countryside.

17. THE OLD VILLAGE GREEN

The old **village green** has been celebrated and romanticised in countless songs, verses and pictures, to the point where it has become something of a rural cliché. We have come to associate the green with rustic dalliance, maypoles and morris dancers, and homely values. Many greens, probably most of them, were not associated with any of these things and the churchyard was more of a social venue. Despite all the romantic literature, there are few convincing explanations of what village greens were actually there for. If we take a good look at a few then we cannot avoid the conclusion that they show so many differences and contrasts that they could not possibly all have been there for the same purposes. Some helpful pointers are as follows:

- The one thing that greens did have in common, apart from grass, was the fact that they were all packages of **common land**. They were there for the use of the community even though the squire might covet the green and sometimes manage to incorporate it into his garden.
- Pasture of any kind was in desperately short supply in most medieval communities. Therefore it is impossible to imagine that a community would enjoy communal rights to a piece of grazing and yet not use it for their livestock.
- Many of the very large greens, like the one at Barrington in Cambridge-shire, are highly likely to have existed as common pasture before the birth of the village that they came to serve. A glance at the plans of some real villages suggests that some villages formed as commoners set up house on the margins of the common, which soon became the village green.
- A common that was not really large enough to serve as a cow or sheep pasture would still be useful for grazing smaller livestock. Geese were frequently kept during the Middle Ages and they delight in feeding on

grass (although they make quite a mess of it). A green would also provide the village herd with a spot of grazing as the 'neat' or cowherd prepared to move them along, while a pond in the green would supply water for driven cattle and, perhaps, provide a home for ducks.

- One cannot credit the traditional notion that the green was a defensive corral for livestock, with cottages ranged round it like the circled covered wagons of the Wild West homesteaders. Highland clansmen were warriors but English villagers were not. They saw more sense in running away from armed raiders and they would drive their livestock away into the woods rather than hanging around to defend them and perhaps get hurt or killed in the process.

- When a village with a green obtained a market, the green would be the obvious venue for it. In other cases a market square would probably be knocked into the village layout, often at the expense of several dwellings. However, the charters that granted weekly markets would normally also grant an **annual fair**, often on the day of the patron saint of the village church. Fairs were much more exciting than the rather dowdy markets, attracting merchants from further afield and numerous visitors. A modest green would be inadequate and some adjacent field would probably be employed. The great fairs of the national calendar also tended to be held in open spaces, sometimes quite distant from a town.

- Some little common spaces that came to be regarded as greens may originally have been set aside for special communal uses, perhaps to accommodate stocks, a whipping post, a pinfold or a lock-up.

- Communal dancing features in the popular mythology of the village green. People did dance together, but the dancing was linked to ill-remembered semi-pagan concepts about fertility and the rebirth of the year. While there was dancing on some greens, the wealth of place-name evidence, as well as at least one early landscape painting, shows that it took place in fields, as field-names like Dancers' Mead demonstrate, while the morris ('Moorish') men certainly danced in the fields from which the harvest had just been taken. The green was a more likely venue for the maypole – some people regard maypoles as part of village mythology, but they did indeed stand on some greens. The provision of a venue for dancing to celebrate the arrival of summer could not justify permanently setting aside a block of land for the festivities, so dancing must have been an ancillary use for some greens.

- Many villagers did engage in games, often of a fairly brutal nature (the village lout has a long ancestry). Greens might sometimes have been used, but some games ranged far and wide across parishes and between churches,

The lock-up at Castle Cary in Somerset: road widening has probably gobbled up its little green.

while others were associated with special playing areas outside the village. These can sometimes be recognised by the name 'playstow', **'plaistow'** or 'plaster', meaning 'a place for play', which frequently endures in place-names. Less common are the 'Laker' names, from an Old Norse word for play that is still current in Yorkshire.

- The village green that we see today is likely to have been reduced since medieval times. Numerous greens were completely obliterated when Parliamentary Enclosure took its toll of common land. Although the green was a common resource, it was not immune to **encroachments** by members of the village community. Large greens might be settled by squatters, while households living around the green might pinch pockets of land from its edges. Cottage front gardens did not exist in the old world of villages and wherever they are seen in a village, encroachment on a green is strongly suspected. Piecemeal encroachment could gradually remove a green, while there are many places where a somewhat projecting cottage row can be recognised as an intrusion on an old green.

- Most greens are old and it is generally hard to discover what a piece of land was used for *before* it became a green. The one at Piecebridge in County Durham was a Roman encampment, while one (complete with maypole) at Aldborough near Boroughbridge was part of the Roman town of *Isurium*.

18. THE FISHING VILLAGES

Fishing villages tend to be so encumbered with the tat of the tourist industry that it is difficult to discover their real stories, but there are meanings behind every feature and facet of such places. Here are some of the less obvious aspects:

- A fishing village may seem to be steeped in antiquity, but in the past there were great restrictions on the importance that such places could achieve. In medieval times religious convention required that only fish protein be served on Friday, and sometimes other days as well. Sea fish could be wind dried and cured or pickled in barrels, but given the inadequate roads and the lack of refrigeration, fresh fish could only be traded in the immediate vicinity of the fishing port. Before very long fish trundled along in a handcart or carried in the fishwife's baskets would go bad.

- At first fishing tended to be a seasonal pursuit for tenant farmers who happened to live close to the coast. They might line fish for cod or mackerel or net herring during slack periods in the agricultural year.

- Over time twin settlements evolved in many places, with the agricultural settlement being perched on or near the cliff top with a fishing settlement or **sea town** being down below. The fishing settlement might be in two parts, one right by the fish quay or the shore where the boats were beached, and the other, the residential component, on a shelf near the base of the cliffs or in a gully running up from the shore.

- In some places the terrain was quite uncompromising and the settlement could only be built on a level cliff top overlooking the precipitous drop to the harbour, as at Whinnyfold near Peterhead.

- Sometimes a settlement or habitation of some sort might pre-date the fishing community. For example, Pittenweem in Fife developed right around the cave that had been frequented by St Fillan.

- As fishing became an occupation in its own right, fishing communities became very insular. Marriage outside the fishing fraternity was often frowned upon, while the constant risk of danger, death and bereavement

Pittenweem in Fife seems to have a greater antiquity than most fishing villages. Its name begins with what is believed to be a Pictish term for a piece of land, while the '-weem' element, which often relates to an underground passage, probably describes the cave here of St Fillan, an early saint.

Pittenweem's neighbouring village, St Monans, also has a link with an early saint and a venerable church.

might explain the adoption of fundamentalist Protestant codes. Insularity created its own problems in the smaller communities, including in-breeding: I can recall one little fishing village in northern Scotland where everyone shared the same surname.

- Modern times brought efficient refrigeration for fish both on land and in the holds of the boats, but the railway determined which few privileged fishing villages would flourish and expand; those bypassed by the rail network were left to struggle on uncompetitively, and were sentenced to survive through tourism.

Inland villages had the freedom to develop in a variety of different ways, but the development of fishing villages was usually strongly controlled by the stark demands of the local topography. Here are some things to look for:

- Settlements would normally adjust their forms to take advantage of whatever shelves the cliff terrain offered. Frequently the existence of a natural harbour that could be entered under difficult conditions of wind and tide was the main determinant for the presence of a fishing village, with building sites for houses being a secondary consideration.
- Some of the larger fishing centres developed artificial harbours and success could bring about such transformations. During the Middle Ages Scarborough advanced seawards, colonising former anchorages as it went, so that old harbour lines were engulfed by the town.
- Coastal settlements are regularly exposed to gales and storms advancing unimpeded across the sea and individual houses were often carefully sited to minimise the impact of bad weather. In particular, such cottages were often built with their gable ends directed towards the sea – this is particularly evident along the North Sea coast of Scotland.

Given the severe topographical restrictions imposed by a site on a rocky coast, the deliberate planning of fishing villages might seem to be out of the question. In fact, some highly planned ones were built, particularly in Scotland, where landlords spearheading the agricultural Improvements sometimes saw fishing as an alternative form of employment for the rural population. St Combs, near Fraserburgh, was set out to a neat plan, while the existing fishing villages of Cullen and Portknockie, just along the Moray Firth coast, gained large planned extensions. The planned fishing village climaxed in the new settlements built by the **British Fisheries Society** during the early decades of the nineteenth century in an attempt to stimulate the local economies in the Scottish Highlands and Islands. Ullapool, Tobermory, Lochbay and Pulteneytown were the results.

The typical modern fishing village has experienced many changes during the last century. Much character may have been lost by the decline of sea fishing, but many lives have been saved. In many cases the fish quays have gone and the only boats in the harbour may be tourist craft and boats for hire for fishing trips. The fishermen's cottages, where the family lived above the ground-floor room where gear was stowed and nets were mended, have now become retirement homes and guest houses. But with a little thought and effort the history of the fishing village landscape may yet be pieced together. One can think of worse things to do than explore a fishing village.

19. DISCOVERING YOUR VILLAGE

Armed with this book and a good measure of persistence, you should be able to discover a good deal about your chosen village. There is no fixed order for the enquiries, but you could proceed in the following way:

Names

Visit a good reference library that contains a selection of place-name dictionaries and compare the interpretations offered for your village's name. Remember to favour any that seem to reflect the local geography. It is also worthwhile to use the evidence of place-names, including old field names, in an attempt to reconstruct the setting of the young village. Margaret Gelling's *Place Names in the Landscape* (Dent, 1993), and John Field's *Field Names* (David & Charles, 1972), should be very helpful.

Shapes and images

The history of your village may well be reflected in the details of its shape. To recognise these shapes, a study of images of the village may well prove more helpful than a stroll down the High Street. The main kinds of image available are *air photographs* and *maps*.

Air photographs of particular localities can be obtained from certain agencies at prices that are not particularly high, but before investing it is best to see what is available through public services. The reference library may hold a local air photograph collection and others should be obtainable from the county archaeological/heritage unit.

The photographs will have been taken at various times, mostly from 1947 onwards, while the Luftwaffe wartime archive is held by the Pentagon. The date when each picture was taken should be recorded on it, and most will be in monochrome. The pictures vary in both quality and content. *Vertical* photographs are map-like views taken directly downwards from a normally high-flying aircraft. They are good for recording layouts in a manner that can easily be transferred to a map. 'Oblique' photographs are taken out of a side-window in the cockpit with a hand-held camera using a smaller film size; these do not resolve as much detail as the large, floor-mounted cameras. Obliques are in a 'landscape' format rather than the large square form of the verticals. Obliques are taken at low level and are good for resolving topographical detail (verticals seem rather 'flat'), and they can give quite dramatic renditions of earthworks. However, they are less easy to link to a map as they have strong perspective distortions.

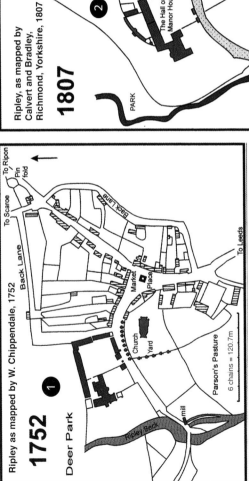

Ripley, as mapped by
Calvert and Bradley,
Richmond, Yorkshire, 1807

1807

A scale of yards

0   40

A scale of chains

0   1   2   4   6   8

▦ Glebe or Church Lands

■ Property of Sir John Ingilby Bart

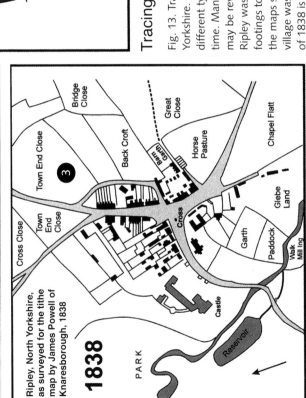

Ripley as mapped by W. Chippendale, 1752

1752

Deer Park

6 chains = 120.7m

Ripley, North Yorkshire,
as surveyed for the tithe
map by James Powell of
Knaresborough, 1838

1838

PARK

Tracing a village history through successive maps

Fig. 13. Tracing a village history through successive maps: Ripley, North Yorkshire. A sequence of maps of different dates, and possibly of different types, can reveal the stages in the evolution of a village through time. Many significant changes will be discovered, but not everything may be revealed. For example, between the surveys of 1807 and 1838 Ripley was transformed from a village of timber-framed houses on stone footings to one of whimsical stone cottages in fanciful styles. However, the maps show that the basic Y-shaped planned layout set out when the village was created in about 1400 survived the changes. The tithe map of 1838 is additionally useful because it names the fields of the parish.

If two air photographs were taken looking in exactly the same direction and from exactly the same position but at different times/seasons/weather conditions, one might be devoid of archaeological information while the other is bursting with it. Low light, closely grazed grass or growing crops can all seem to magnify archaeological details, just as diffused or high illumination, heavy snow cover, harvested crops or heavy cloud are most unhelpful. The fact that an air photograph seems 'empty' of useful information does not mean that the information is not there on the ground. Sites of former towns or Roman roads can vanish before the camera if the soil or crop or weather conditions are unhelpful.

Air photographs are useful for resolving significant features that are not obvious to the earthbound eye. The holloway of a lost village lane, the boundaries of abandoned medieval house plots, a planned row of dwellings that was sloughed off as the village migrated: these are the sorts of things that air photographs may reveal. To enjoy the benefits of working at home, you should ask if an inexpensive yet very acceptable laser copy can be obtained of the desired prints. Copyright conditions will vary from case to case.

Maps. Your village will have been mapped on numerous occasions, at different times and to different scales. This is wonderful because you are able to trace its growth/decline in considerable detail during the last 150–250 years or so. However, it is likely that it is the centuries before this that really interest you, and then the coverage is unpredictable, with luck playing a large part. Your reference library should have a run of Ordnance Survey maps at the useful 6in to a mile scale and the very large 25in to a mile scale, and these should take you back into Victorian times. Beyond this, an appointment at your County Record Office, the British Library or the Scottish Record Office may be needed.

You can never be sure what these searches will turn up. In England and Wales there is a fair chance that a detailed tithe map of the 1830s–40s, with the village surrounded by lots of interesting field names, will have been preserved. Otherwise there could be a large-scale pre-Enclosure or Enclosure map of the 1750–1850 period. The assorted maps at an inch to a mile produced by the various independent cartographers of the eighteenth century may be worth a glance, though their scale is rather small. The real treasure, if it can be found, will be a large-scale, beautifully coloured estate map from the Elizabethan or Jacobean era. If there is one, it will show you an astounding image of your village centuries ago.

Ideally maps of the village should be set out in time sequence so that the course of ongoing developments can be seen. Every map should be scrutinised and interrogated if all its details are to be assimilated. Record offices are not always the jolliest of places and it is best to work at home, if possible. Sometimes the curator will only allow pencil tracings to be made, and these are always third-rate. If the documents are robust, a photocopy may be obtained, while in other cases photographs may be printed or commissioned.

Talking to villagers

Oral history – recording the recollections of others – has long been considered a most inferior activity by the snobs of the historical world. In fact, the preservation of memories for future generations seems a quite admirable activity. There is no doubt that people are at their best as sources of information when they are describing events that they witnessed *personally*. Once one enters the world of hearsay and hand-me-down stories it is surprising how rapidly and extravagantly myths and errors appear. Elderly villagers can be amazing sources of information about events that shaped a village decades ago. They may tell you about a row of squatter cottages that was demolished, how a now ploughed-out track was once plied by steam lorries, or how workers uncovered a lost paved road when the sewers were being dug. Dialogue can flow in an uninterrupted way if a small tape-recorder is employed, and if you allow people to 'ramble' they may well come up with answers to good questions that you had not thought of asking.

Out in the village and getting out and about

Use your eye and a map to quiz the village as you have never quizzed it before. Each kink in the line of house frontages could tell a story; a little row of front gardens could tell of a green devoured, and each gap between houses might contain the traces of abandonment. Keep the models outlined above in your mind and scan the village landscape for evidence of shrinkage or shifting as well as the angular lines that spell planned development. The answers will not fall easily into your lap and, like a good detective, you must make all that you can of evidence from *every possible source*. This is why the maps, earthworks, air photographs and place-names all have to be taken into account and considered together. Persist, and you will be surprised what you can discover. Solve one little problem and several answers may drop into place. When the village survey is complete, make sure that others can benefit from your curiosity and hard work – place a copy in the local library.

FIVE

Sacred Landscapes

1. SOME IDEAS ABOUT SACRED LANDSCAPES

'There are books about changing styles of medieval architecture – that is probably all there is to know about understanding churches' WRONG

'We know maybe half a dozen prehistoric temples in Britain. The people were savages and their ideas about religion were pretty primitive' WRONG

'Because we live in a very materialistic society, we are poorly placed to comprehend ancient and medieval communities that were motivated by spirituality' RIGHT

'Ancient people created hundreds upon hundreds of temples, tombs and sacred landscapes. After a century or more of serious enquiry, we still do not understand them' RIGHT

'Because the study of churches was left to architectural historians, our understanding of the role of churches in the community and of the placing of churches within the landscape have been neglected' RIGHT

2. PREHISTORIC SACRED LANDSCAPES

We can understand things like field walls, millstones or fortresses because they all serve practical purposes, but religious monuments cannot be interpreted in such simple, functional terms. Nevertheless, archaeologists have acquired the habit of branding every discovery they cannot make sense of a 'ritual site' or a ritual artefact'. Perhaps we should not be too critical of this. If we had no understanding of Christianity we might make many blunders in interpreting a simple church. The orientation of the church and of the bodies in the churchyard might seem to relate to the sunrise and indicate sun worship. The altar might be associated with human sacrifice, as might the bodies under and around the church, while a steeple might be thought to point to a significant celestial event or to direct spirits skywards. It is only because of our detailed understanding of Christianity that we can avoid such mistakes and make sense of every facet of a church layout.

Notions that some religions are more 'primitive' than others are difficult to sustain. If parallels with societies that have low technological levels of development are relevant to our own ancient communities of Britain, then ancient people did not make a narrow distinction between religion and other aspects of life. Everything flowed together, so that all the animals, plants, rocks and watercourses in their settings had spirits, and spirituality permeated every aspect of day-to-day life. Everything was a part of a whole, and as such it merited respect. From the perspective of a modern world afflicted by frightful crises of humankind's making, this does not seem a bad basis for belief.

In terms of the setting, perhaps the most significant difference between Christianity and earlier beliefs concerned the fact that pagan beliefs (whatever their weaknesses) regarded humans as being *alongside* other creatures as parts of the setting, while Christianity awarded humans *dominion* over the landscape and all that it contained. It shifted the emphasis from coexistence to exploitation and consumption.

Just as one would struggle to understand a Christian church without recourse to Christian believers or biblical texts, so we still struggle to understand ancient sacred monuments. In some cases unpleasant suggestions of human sacrifice are found, but whether the victims were volunteers, criminals, deviants of another kind, hostages, captives or terrified members of the local community, we simply cannot tell. Such sacrifices might have been associated with the dedication of a monument, and most monuments seem to have been concerned with the organisation of worship in a 'proper' way or with the disposal of the dead of a community according to prescribed doctrines.

Our possible disgust when faced with some of the realities of ancient life must partly reflect the sanitised nature of modern existence. We may never see a decomposing body, never stand by a funeral pyre or have to cope with levels of infant mortality that make the loss of children a commonplace occurrence.

3. ENCOUNTERING SACRED LANDSCAPES

Many people still believe that the only prehistoric religious monuments were the famous ones seen in glossy books: Stonehenge, Avebury, Maes Howe, Newgrange, Callanish and the Ring of Brodgar. In reality, hundreds upon hundreds of ritual sites were created in the New Stone Age and the Bronze Age. In struggling to understand monumental constructions that seem to offer no advantage to agriculture or commerce, we tend to look for labels from our own religious experience, such as church, temple, cathedral, mausoleum, tomb,

The Ring of Brodgar on Orkney is one of the most impressive and celebrated of British stone circles.

churchyard and so on. But if the people concerned considered that a tomb could also be a temple and that the dead ancestors contained in it were currently actively at work as spirits standing sentinel over the homeland, then our own vocabulary is wholly inadequate. The main types of monument produced are discussed here, but we should remember that the people of the Middle Stone Age mainly led peripatetic existences as hunter/gatherers and thus they may not have created any *permanent* structures for worship. Their hunting bands may have sustained a shaman and have worshipped animal/ hunting gods.

When farming brought a more settled life, after around 4000 BC, a great investment of energy in massive communal monuments and tombs soon followed. Among the earliest were the **causewayed enclosures**, massive ceremonial and meeting foci, with the chosen hilltop being encircled by one or more rings of banks and interrupted ditches. **Cursuses** (or, more correctly, cursūs) seem to have been impressive ceremonial avenues, and burial mounds were often built close to them or at their ends.

The sacred landscapes of this time were communal creations and each community may have had its own local complex of monuments. Tombs feature prominently among the assemblages, but there were far too few great tombs to have accommodated all the people that lived in those times. Therefore it is thought that they were reserved for members of a ruling dynasty or priestly caste.

Where a boulder litter could be exploited, communities tended to build **chambered tombs** with an entrance passage and burial chambers; they were built using dry-stone walling techniques and some had an impressive façade of boulders or slabs. Such tombs had the advantage that they could be sealed with a boulder and reopened to admit new burials. In the chalk downlands and elsewhere, earthen **long barrows** were erected over the human remains. In both cases it seems that bodies decayed in special timber **mortuary houses** before the skeletons were gathered up and placed in the tombs. Whether we should really think of the gathered bones as being 'buried' in a chambered tomb or long barrow is uncertain. Rather than the ancestors being 'laid to rest', it seems that bones might be removed from chambered tombs and used in rituals. It could well have been that a tomb, well-stocked with the bones of high-status ancestors, was seen as an engine that pumped fertility into the ground or as the barracks of a ghostly garrison that would repel intruders or aggressors.

As the Age of Stone gave way, via a brief Copper Age, to that of Bronze, beliefs seem to have undergone a fundamental change. The profile of the

The entrance passage to the West Kennet chambered tomb near Avebury. It is flanked by chambers in which bones were stored.

Remains of a chambered tomb with an entrance passage, one of the many prehistoric antiquities on Jersey.

community tended to subside, while that of the individual rose. Burial mounds became smaller but much more numerous as **round barrows** of different designs proliferated. On the whole these were the graves of solitary men and women from the aristocracy who were buried with goods for the afterlife, though the magnetic sanctity associated with the barrows often attracted secondary burials in their sides.

Beneath the **bowl- or bell-shaped barrows** the burial ritual varied, though in the earlier burials the body was placed in a stone box or **cist** in a tightly crouched position and was furnished with goods such as copper or flint daggers, small gold items and a clay beaker which is thought to have contained a ritual drink, probably alcohol, for the journey to the next world. As ideas diversified, food vessels were provided and cremation was sometimes adopted, while later on cremated bones would be placed in urns and buried in **urnfields**.

As the Bronze Age came to a close, the fanatical interest in monument-making dwindled away and the natural elements seem to have captured the attention of society. In the Iron Age votive offerings, often in the form of valuable swords, were cast into rivers, lakes and swamps. The nature of human burials is uncertain, except for the territory in the east of Yorkshire, where warriors, their mounts and their carts/chariots were buried with costly trappings under **square barrows**. Some victims of ritual executions were thrown into peat bogs, where their bodies have sometimes been preserved. Iron Age belief seems to have had a dark and a watery character.

The spectacular importance of belief in most phases of ancient life is demonstrated by the assembling of immense amounts of scarce and valuable labour in the making of monuments. Each represented a huge investment. At Avebury a ditch that was originally 30ft (9m) deep surrounded a sacred area of some 28.55 acres (11.5 ha), all hacked from the chalk using picks made from antlers. About 200,000 tonnes of rubble were shifted, presumably in baskets, to form the bank on the outer lip of the ditch. Stonehenge was redesigned more than once, and leaving aside the Welsh bluestone components, the sarsen stone monument alone is thought to have embodied more than 30 million man-hours of toil; the shaping of the sarsens prior to their erection would have occupied fifty masons equipped with stone mauls for three years.

4. LOOKING AT THE MONUMENTS

Any attempt to seek an understanding of ancient ritual monuments through analogies with aspects of modern life usually ends in confusion and

Part of the remarkable henge and standing stone arrangements at Avebury in Wiltshire.

disappointment. If we had a prehistoric person at our shoulder then they would doubtless furnish a comprehensive explanation of the stone circle or chambered cairn that seemed entirely consistent and sensible, for to understand what the religion was all about would be to understand its expressions or manifestations. In the absence of such an interpreter it may be useful to follow some lateral lines of enquiry and think what monuments *might* have been for.

Henges were creations of the New Stone Age. Generally they do not seem spectacular today, though in their day they were far more numerous and more significant than famous stone circles like Stonehenge. The typical henge had a layout like a circle formed of two bananas, the two curving banks being separated by opposed entrances/exits. It is tempting to see the henge as a great open-air cathedral, with the congregation seated on the curving banks, separated from the sanctified inner space by the deep ditches inside the banks. This analogy would be excellent were it not for the simple fact that henges often appear in threes or in loose groupings. One does not need several churches close together; we disperse them, usually one to a parish. Were the various henges in

The Welsh tomb of Bryn Celli Ddu, a remarkable passage grave inside a henge. The tomb entrance is shown.

the groups used for different rituals, or in different seasons, or by different tribal factions? We do not know, but this example shows the weakness of simple analogies.

Stone circles attract stacks of attention, but little sensible reasoning. For decades now much has been made of their supposed role as astronomical observatories. A few fairly credible alignments on heavenly events have been put forward. However, my house has a lightning conductor but this does not mean it exists as a device for focusing electrical discharges. Were the circle-makers solely interested in establishing astronomical alignments they must surely have employed materials with more inherent precision than a massive lumpy block of granite or sarsen stone.

Stone circles were variants of henges, and Avebury henge contains several great stone settings. Both the circles and the henges were doubtless places for

Swinside stone circle in Cumbria is also known as the 'Sunken Kirk' because the Devil caused the stones used in building a church in daytime to sink into the ground at night. Prehistoric monuments often became associated with the Devil in the minds of people who knew no other explanations.

important ceremonies, but the mere fact of their prominence in the landscape suggests other uses. They would have been excellent venues for commerce and for exchanging the resources and products of different regions. They would also have been good places of assembly for debate and diplomacy. With their religious associations they might have conferred sanctuary on visiting delegations.

While just the few gigantic and well-publicised examples tend to find their ways into the popular media, both henges and circles can be found in a multitude of lesser forms. Also, in characteristic prehistoric fashion, the divisions become blurred, so that we find fairly modest stones providing a circular kerb around a barrow in monuments that seem more tomb than circle. Tomb-builders, meanwhile, were attracted to all other important monuments, which must have seemed to exude sanctity. Stonehenge sits amid a great constellation of Bronze Age barrows.

Although single, immensely compelling religions seem to have existed in both the New Stone Age and the Bronze Age, parochialism, the fragmentation of society and difficulties with travel must have encouraged the growth of local and regional variations. Thus we see reinterpretations of the great monumental icons being developed in scores of different directions. In northern Scotland, for

An example of a recumbent stone circle at Loanhead of Daviot in North East Scotland, where this particular variation on the circle theme became popular.

The haunting and complex ritual monument at Callanish on Lewis.

example, **recumbent stone circles** appeared, with a great horizontal stone, altar-like flanked by uprights, being incorporated as part of the stone ring. On Dartmoor particularly, rows of fairly small stones can be seen stretching across the landscape in mysterious alignments, while the great monument at Callanish on Lewis combines a tomb, a stone circle and several stone rows. All sorts of regional variations of chambered tombs developed, some with forecourts in front of their façades, where rituals concerning the dead must have been performed.

The great chambered tombs (some penetrated by passageways and thus known as **passage graves**) and the long barrows had obvious associations with the ancestors, but they could also, like some recently excavated pits of the New

Stone Age on the Dorset downs, have been seen as means of communing more effectively with Mother Earth.

Countless prehistoric monuments have been destroyed and the process is continuing, particularly where ploughing gradually eats away notionally protected barrows or where moorland is being reclaimed and coniferised. The destruction has gone on for centuries, and in medieval times it was often motivated by superstition. The vogue among the Georgian and Victorian landowners and intelligentsia for digging barrows left countless monuments ravaged and their contents pillaged and unrecorded. Now the metal detector operators who ransack and rob archaeological sites in the dead of night, are a far greater threat.

Because we tend to be preoccupied with Stonehenge, Avebury, Silbury Hill and other famous monuments we may overlook the multitude of small monuments all around us. People tend to be unaware of things like the gatepost-sized **menhir** or monolith; the nondescript little mound that is a **clearance cairn** of stones gathered from new farmland in, say, the Bronze Age;

The old antiquarians sometimes did terrible damage to ancient monuments. This Cornish tomb, Zennor Quoit, suffered a nineteenth-century attempt to open it with gunpowder.

This monolith stands close to a stone row at Merrivale on Dartmoor. The purpose of such standing stones is still uncertain.

the faint trough that was once an imposing boundary work; or the circle of boulders that once walled an ancient house. Any upland or downland locality may be packed with such things and while one may have no competence to excavate, it is as well to be aware of the prehistoric possibilities.

Prehistoric religions were not 'primitive' and not necessarily barbaric. They provided people with the beliefs and motivations that helped them to make sense of an often-threatening world in which natural forces, ranging from the blackness of night to torrential rain and thundering waterfalls, might seem overpowering. They helped people to believe that by creating the 'right' monuments and performing the 'right' rituals they might exert some control over their lives and maintain some links with their dead ancestors. They also provided people with a sense of kinship with the topography, woods, watercourses and creatures with which they shared their environment – and in this sense at least, the ancients were more progressive than modern people.

5. THE FIRST CHRISTIAN MONUMENTS

Imperial Rome controlled England and Wales for almost four centuries, but the various pagan deities of the Empire had little lasting effect. The legacies of Roman religion consist largely of a few altars, relics and images at abandoned fort and villa sites. The Empire was, however, responsible for the introduction of Christianity. This persisted in the remoteness of the Celtic west and appears to have endured in the backwaters of northern England through much of the era of pagan Anglo-Saxon domination.

In Ireland and Wales the arrival of Christianity was marked by the 'conversion' of the ancient standing stones that must have been associated with the old beliefs. This was done by chipping the symbol of the cross or the start of Christ's name on the stone concerned, which now became a 'pillar' of Christian belief.

In northern Scotland, meanwhile, a remarkably rich, elaborate and unusual repertoire of symbols – animals, combs, mirrors and intricate abstract forms – were being engraved on stone pillars and slabs and even on jewellery. These **Pictish symbols** came to be joined by the cross on stones that were carved as Christianity penetrated Scotland. Eventually the pagan symbols were excluded and the cross stood alone on the last generation of stones.

In England the displacement of Christianity by pagan beliefs during the last days of the Roman Empire and the early centuries of the Dark Ages seems to have been incomplete. Priests still visited congregations in their churches in

An inscribed pillar at Llanfihangel-y-Traethau.

1 Parkland landscape at Studley Royal, showing similarities to the medieval deer park landscape of groves and lawns stippled with trees (see Chapter Eight).

2 The chalk scarp face remodelled by the ramparts of Bratton Castle Iron Age hillfort in Wiltshire. Note the terracettes or sheep tracks on the slope in the middle distance (see Chapter Six).

3 The green at Finchingfield in Essex (see Chapter Four).

4 Port Errol, one of a large flock of planned villages in North-East Scotland created during the Improvements. These villages housed tenants removed from often destitute hamlets or 'fermtouns' and perhaps offered the hope of local manufacturing work (see Chapter Four).

5 Detached church towers are a feature of the West Midlands. If they simply reflect foundations that will not support an undivided building, why is the problem peculiar to that area? This detached belfry is at Richards Castle near Ludlow (see Chapter Five).

6 Castlerigg in Cumbria, an imposing stone circle in a spectacular setting (see Chapter Five).

7 Castle Crag in the Lake District was fortified in the Iron Age, becoming one of scores of minor hillforts offering a measure of shelter to local communities (see Chapter Six).

8 Ingleborough hillfort occupied a summit of the Pennines, a place so cold and exposed that the puzzling Iron Age dwellings there could never have been occupied in winter (see Chapter Six).

9 The stone keep at Conisbrough, near Doncaster, had a massive splayed stone base to defend its corners against undermining by sappers (see Chapter Six).

10 Ruined crofters' houses on the shore at the head of Gruinard Bay. Their inhabitants may well have been evicted to this bleak spot from an inland Highlands estate (see Chapter Seven).

11 Fallow deer were reintroduced to Britain by the Normans and became the most coveted quarry for hunting (see Chapter Eight).

12 Coastal mudflats on the Moray Firth at the Lossiemouth estuary (see Chapter Nine).

13 A surviving fragment of Fenland landscape at Wicken Fen, Cambridgeshire, where reed is cut for thatch (see Chapter Nine).

14 The West Kennet avenue is a ceremonial way associated with the great religious focus of the Neolithic era, Avebury (see Chapter Five).

southern Yorkshire and perhaps in parts of the Yorkshire Dales. The evidence for this comes from clusters of 'Eccles' place-names, which are thought to come from *eclesia*, a word derived from the vulgar Latin word for a church.

In the Celtic lands Christian communities with poor links to the declining capital of the Empire and the heartlands of Christianity had developed their religion along monastic lines. In Ireland and in areas of Britain influenced by Irish Christianity, religion was pursued by communities of aristocrats-turned-monks and it had an ascetic and somewhat introspective character. This differed from the religion organised hierarchically and by diocese that Rome had favoured. After the landing of a mission to pagan England from Rome in 597, the two competing strands of Christianity came into conflict in the north of England. In 663 the great assembly known as the Synod of Whitby gave the north to the Roman cause that had dominated the conversion of the rest of England.

Many place-names are derived from the ancient religious associations. The name elements listed in Table 5.1 are among the most numerous and are usually to be found combined with other words.

A Pictish stone at Aberlemno near Forfar, showing some of the strange Pictish symbols and warriors.

Table 5.1. *Place-names derived from religious associations*

Name	Language	Meaning
Betws	Welsh	Chapel
Capel	Welsh and Old French	Chapel
Cill/Kil	Gaelic	Church, graveyard, monk's cell
Cirice	Old English	Church
Clasau	Welsh	Minster church
Cros/cross	Various	Cross
Cruc	Old Welsh	Barrow, burial mound
Gwyn	Welsh	White or sacred
Eccles, eglwys	Latin *eclesia*, Gaelic, Welsh	Church
(H)ermitage	Middle English	Hermitage
Hearg	Old English	Pagan temple
Kirkja (kirk)	Old Norse	Church
Llan	Welsh	Enclosure, often for a church
Lundr	Old Norse	Wood, sometimes sacred grove
Stow	Old English	Place, sometimes a holy place
Teampull	Gaelic	Church
Temple	Middle English	Holding of the Knights Templar
Yshyty	Welsh	Hospital

Remains of the cells occupied by early Christian monks at Annait on Skye.

6. MEET THE MINSTERS

The conversion of the pagan English kingdoms was probably motivated as much by considerations of political expediency as by religious conviction. The kings saw advantages in enjoying the recognition of the great continental church and in having its authority and support to buttress their power. Conversion started at the top and spread gradually downwards. The missionaries concentrated their efforts on converting the heads of kingdoms and their most influential advisers, and once converted, such kings could command the allegiance of their families and the aristocracy. Only gradually were facilities for Christian worship extended to ordinary people, though in this respect the churches of the first generation, the **minsters**, played a crucial role.

Minsters were 'mother' churches (the word comes from the Latin *monasterium*) and they represented different ideas about the organisation of worship from those we associate with churches of the Middle Ages or the modern era. Each minster was staffed by a priest, a number of monks and several lay helpers, and the emphasis was upon each monk setting out from the minster to preach and minister to the communities dwelling in a fairly substantial surrounding territory.

Some of the fragmentary early relics of Christian worship, such as stone fragments of **preaching crosses**, may be associated with this practice, while

There is nothing in its outward appearance to show that the church at Horningsea, Cambridgeshire, was an early minster.

numerous later churches grew up at places where minster priests had habitually held services in the open.

At first there does not seem to have been a great concern to furnish every community with a minster. A very high proportion of the minsters were associated with estates controlled by a king. The Saxon kings were responsible for founding scores of minsters and they must have seen great advantages deriving from their associations with the church. Not the least of these advantages was the fact that priests were virtually the only literate people in the English kingdoms. Their ability to record the taxes, dues and obligations of a king's subjects, to frame laws in an unambiguous manner, and record proceedings and edicts would have made them very welcome on the king's estates.

Only slowly, in a process that extended into the Middle Ages, were the minsters overtaken by churches of a different type. Gradually, as Christianity broadened and intensified its hold, other estate owners chose to establish churches. At first these **proprietorial churches** were little foundations that served just the dominant family and perhaps a few of their leading retainers, but in time they were opened to the whole estate community, and in this way

parish churches were established. It was then that the country became divided into parishes (generally, old estates) that were grouped together within compact regions to form dioceses.

While the gradual and halting conversion of the English lowlands was in progress, missionaries from the Celtic west continued to make landfalls on the western margins of the British mainland. These 'saints' were simply monks – sainthood went with the territory in that time and place. Most of them are now so shadowy as to be almost invisible, but St Gwennarth, St Mawes, St Mewan and scores more all left their names in the dedications of churches that quite often they actually had founded.

Discovering which churches within a locality or region were the original minsters can be a surprisingly difficult task. There are a few obviously easy cases represented by those churches, like Ripon Minster, Wimborne Minster, and so on, that still retain the word 'minster' in their names, but these are a tiny minority of the actual minsters. An old church may have been fairly comprehensively rebuilt on one or several occasions since the distant time when the old minsters were lost in the burgeoning ranks of parish churches. Thus the physical appearance of the building may be of no help, although the older a pre-Conquest church is, the more likely it is to have been a minster.

Minster churches were often to be found on royal estates, and the location of these, at least as they existed in Domesday Book of 1086, rather later than the heyday of the minster, can be easily discovered by consulting a reproduction of the great survey.

Minsters may also be identified by the rather time-consuming and difficult exploration of medieval links between churches and places. Long after the parish churches had come to dominate the scene, minsters still maintained some of their ancient attachments to outlying places. A former minster might still send a clergyman across miles of hard terrain to hold a service each week at a particular place or chapel, or might still be entitled to tithes from a relatively distant locality or be due certain rents from it or perhaps control the appointment of its priest. These links, difficult to unearth and buried in old church documents, can help to rediscover members of the minster flock. There must be dozens of minsters still to be identified.

Roman *Isurium* (Aldborough near the River Ure in Yorkshire) was the administrative capital of a sub-territory of the Brigantes. After the Romans left, the town became largely derelict, yet it maintained some sort of leadership over its old territory. In the era of the Saxon kings this territory surfaced as a royal estate, known as Burghshire, while Aldborough itself exerted some sort of ecclesiastical leadership, even though it was eventually superseded by a new, planned, medieval town nearby, Boroughbridge. Though Burghshire fragmented and Aldborough lost its old dominance, the first of the medieval parish churches that formed in the dale away to the south-west were all strung along the small Roman road that had carried troops to *Isurium* and minster priests to their distant congregations. The church at Aldborough maintained connections with places to the south-west through much of the medieval period, even though the contacts ran against the grain of economic and political development.

7. NUDGING THE PAGANS ASIDE

Conversion was a very political affair. In the confrontation between the old and the new, Christians in Britain might have adopted a strategy of full-blooded aggression towards pagans, such as Charlemagne had employed on the continent. Instead, one discovers a more subtle, more tactical approach to the battle for hearts and minds. It involved the commandeering of the ancient holy places rather than their destruction and replacement.

Because of the nature of the pagan beliefs, the pagan holy places were linked to certain features of the natural landscape, which were often associated with particular gods and goddesses. Christian missionaries were specifically instructed to take over such sites of pagan worship. In this way, not only would the old deities be displaced and robbed of their perches in the landscape, but also the Christian foundations would 'inherit' some of the sanctity that the common people believed was attached to such places.

Springs were judged to be particularly important and were the places where the forces of the underworld made contact with the surface world. The original church at Ripley in North Yorkshire was perched on a nigh-impossible site on a shelf on a river bluff – and was bracketed by a pair of springs. Many medieval churches were associated with **holy wells**, like the one at Stevington in Bedfordshire, whose waters were thought to cure eye diseases.

Even when churches were not built to 'Christianise' the site of a pagan well or spring, measures were taken to divert their magic from pagan to Christian patrons. Wells dedicated to the grotesque Celtic child-eating goddess Annis emerged in a much-sanitised guise as dedicated to St Anne, while St Helen was conveniently on hand to commandeer all of pagan Elen's springs.

In 1893, when more old superstitions could be remembered, sixty-seven holy wells were counted in Yorkshire alone and many more must have been

The Welsh church at Holywell was associated with one of the most celebrated of holy wells.

overlooked, while Scotland and Wales probably have more than 2,000 examples between them.

St Michael hilltop churches are more puzzling. Almost 700 of these dedications are found in England and Wales, an unusually high proportion of them being located on hilltops. In many cases it seems likely that the militant archangel was seen as a suitable saint to oust the pagans from their hilltop strongholds. Perhaps, too, he was seen as a fitting successor to Hermes and Mercury, who had special associations with the dead. St Michael probably preceded St George as England's patron saint and his early popularity in militaristic societies made him a likely choice in any reallocation of gains from the pagans. Even so, the association between this saint and hilltop settings is so marked that one feels that there must be something more involved as well.

The well house covering the Dupath holy well in Cornwall.

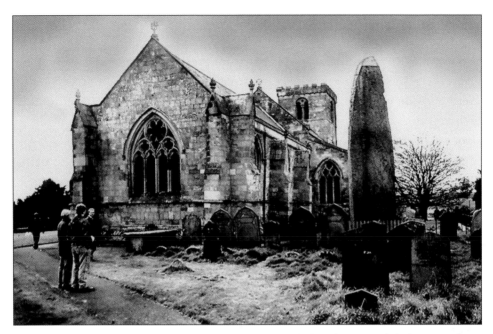

The church at Rudston, near Scarborough, was built right beside a monolith that must have been considered sacred since Bronze Age times or earlier.

In some cases the association with a prominent prehistoric monument was so blatant as to leave no doubts about the Christian intent to evict the pagans from their settings. At Knowlton in Dorset the church was built *inside* the great circular earthworks of one of a trio of henges; at La Hogue Bie, on Jersey, the chapel of Jerusalem and that of Notre Dame de la Clarte stand perched on top of a huge chambered cairn above its monumental entrance and passageway to the underworld. The church at Rudston near Scarborough stands on a knoll overlooking a plain where the courses of cursuses must once have been obvious, and right by the church stands Britain's tallest monolith. Juxtapositions such as these tell their stories very clearly.

8. THE WORK OF THE CHURCH

The medieval church had a very obvious duty concerning the souls of its congregation, but its responsibilities certainly did not end there. Modern devotees of paganism imagine that a well-organised and well-supported pagan religion pursued a parallel existence alongside the medieval church. That was not so. However, ordinary people led lives permeated by superstitions, some of them useful and some of them now seen plainly to be silly. But from whatever religion preceded it, the Christian church inherited a form of responsibility for ensuring the fecundity of the land and the benign character of the weather. (However, when failing on one or both counts it does not seem to have suffered greatly, the deficiencies normally being attributed to human frailties and sins so great that they had provoked the Divine beyond endurance.) Remote and unfathomable in some ways, the medieval church was still deeply involved in communal affairs.

The church's tolerance of blatant pagan imagery in the very fabric of its buildings is quite surprising. It is hard to see how bishops on visitations could have been blind to things like the explicit earth-mother and goat images carved on a slab set in the church tower at Whittlesford in Cambridgeshire, an image known as a **sheila-na-gig**. It is not known if the sheila-na-gigs represent lingering pagan ideas or a separate medieval fertility cult.

Much more numerous in England are the **green men**, identical to, or companions of, the various woodwose, jack-in-the-green and man-o'-the-woods characters – man/tree beings that anticipate Tolkein's ents. The green man is commonly represented as a hirsute male head with paired vines issuing from its mouth. It is clearly a fertility symbol and a very popular one, though the nature of the cult concerned is uncertain. Green men can be found all over a church, sometimes in places where they are bound to be seen, and sometimes, puzzlingly, up in the dark recesses of the roof timbers and largely invisible. They seem to be of a jollier nature than the grotesque sheila-na-gigs but are not well understood. However, their presence seems to show a church that was ready to hedge its bets and take aboard any fragments from paganism if they could help with the burdensome responsibilities for the fertility of the parish.

Surrounding the church was the **churchyard**, though in the case of Ripley, mentioned above, the original church site was so cramped that the yard had to be placed on level ground above it, actually overlooking the church roof. Churchyards deserve our attention for all sorts of reasons.

Where, we may ask, did the churchyard come from? During Saxon times plots of land of a generally rectangular shape were awarded to new churches for burials. There seem to have been other cases where a rather circular or oval plot of land had an earlier existence as a freestanding cemetery. Certainly, churchyards of such rounded shapes are regarded as indications of a very early, often Celtic, church foundation.

We have come to regard the village green as the venue for social activity and fun. In reality, and sometimes in flagrant defiance of authority, such activities tended to flourish in the churchyard rather than on the open green. While ordinary people were generally in awe of, if rather mystified by, the church, this did not spoil their wholehearted indulgence in fun and games in the churchyard that could go beyond dalliance and playfulness. Impromptu dancing might begin, with the dancers barging through the knots of gossips and distracting the people who were trying to strike deals among the pits and earth mounds of waiting graves.

Some deceased VIPS might have **tomb slabs** to mark their graves in the yard, but most of them were buried inside the church, under the floors, giving the building, at best, a rather musty smell. Generally the churchyard was unencumbered with stones and monuments. The most worthy members of the tenant community tended to be buried on the sunny south side of the church, though exactly where is uncertain in the absence of accurate plans. The least of the village community, and those weighed down with burdens of shame, were buried on the dank and shady north side. In the seventeenth century the introduction of tombstones began to disrupt the ball games, and for a couple of centuries a very mawkish set of motifs based on the death's head were favoured. As attempts to gain medical knowledge began to impinge on the churchyard in the shape of bodysnatchers, more wealthy people might seek to protect the bodies of their deceased families under heavy iron cages or **mortsafes**. These tend to be particularly numerous in the vicinities of old Scottish universities with medical schools.

Far more went into the graveyard than ever came out on people's boots or shoes. Therefore, over time the level would tend to rise and rise. I find this most obvious where an old churchyard has forced a later road to divert around it and one can see a height difference of several feet between the level of the road and that of the yard above.

The Church seems to have regarded the common people as loutish sinners constantly posing a threat to the stability of society and the evidence of manor court records suggests that there were grounds for this view. The Latin gospels would have been understood little if at all by most ordinary people, but the Church seems to have been very well aware of the impact of liturgy and spectacular ritual on the 'simple' minds of country people. For them, going to church was a breathtaking experience. The priest and his servants were resplendent in fine robes and the myriad pinpoints of candlelight revealed a highly decorated and brightly painted church, eerily moving with the guttering of the lights. Among the wall illustrations, most prominence was likely to be given to an immense mural of the Doom that awaited the multitude of sinners. Lost souls scorched by fires, bodies turning on spits, sinners munched by devils and prodded towards the fires with impish tridents – these graphic images must have impacted heavily on a community that knew no horror movies or hospital soaps. The service in Latin may have been confusing, but one left church in no doubt of what was in store for *you* if you did not heed its rules.

It is easy to let the loutish and sometimes brutal aspects of peasant life blind one to the strong and caring sides of medieval rural life. People who died in the rugged outposts of upland parishes knew that their kin and neighbours would carry their body, often in a simple wicker coffin, for mile upon mile across rock and beck for burial in consecrated ground (see Chapter Three). Meanwhile, in the world of mortals, the Church was each community's insurance policy against the droughts, floods, famines and pestilences that were frequent accompaniments to medieval life. 'God speed the plough' was a heartfelt slogan, and the act of blessing the implement displayed no coyness or theatricality in medieval times. Of course the Church had a stake in all this. In a good farming year its tithe of the produce would be greater than in a bad, and though it claimed a **mortuary** of their second-best beast from those who died, a healthy and expanding community produced more dues and fees than one that was impoverished and declining. Furthermore, the priest himself was also a small farmer. In his spare hours, unless he was of noble birth or affluent, he worked on the plots of his allotted **glebe** and this must have given him not only a stake in the harvest, but also an understanding of the culture and concerns of his village flock.

9. THE CHURCH BUILDING

Our appreciation of the village church within the landscape and the community has been overshadowed by the preoccupation with church architecture. Railway stations can be very interesting and sometimes attractive buildings in their own right, but this does not leave us in any doubt that they are what they are: railway stations. Too often it seems to be thought that all one needs to know about a church can be found in the appropriate volume of Pevsner's *Buildings of England*, and that the relative importance of a building can be gauged by the length of its entry there. The medieval builders of churches may have sought to create beauty and so glorify God, but this did not prevent them from knocking down millions of cubic metres of historic masonry that modern aficionados would have drooled over. Admiration was fine, but churches were there to perform their jobs within the community. Once people ceased to believe in this, they stopped building them.

The Saxon church at Earls Barton in Northamptonshire, with strapwork decoration on the tower.

The Norman church at South Lopham, in Norfolk.

Saxon churches embody rather simple techniques, with narrow doors and windows and rounded arches (small windows sometimes have triangular heads), which seem to express an uncertainty about the loads the walls could bear. The corners or **quoins** of buildings are often built of **long and short work** of alternating upright stones and horizontal slabs. Occasionally a **strapwork** of raised stonework is employed, apparently in imitation of timber buildings. Most Saxon churches have a certain rustic charm, a feature not generally passed on to the next generation.

Norman churches perpetuated this Romanesque style in a more monumental and often overbearing manner. They tend to be very heavy, with walls composed of inner and outer skins of masonry packed with rubble bonded in mortar. Arches and some piers are decorated with chevron, dogtooth and other motifs, usually fairly crude devices that were hacked into the stones with axes. Throughout England and parts of Wales this was the architecture of conquest and subjugation. Political inspiration may explain why new and replacement Norman churches were so numerous.

The **Early English** style that roughly spanned the thirteenth century was the first Gothic style and its experiments with vaulting offered exciting possibilities. Windows remained relatively small, taking the form of narrow, pointed **lancets**, which could be grouped in twos and threes. The Early English style superseded the Norman style in countless parish churches and it was also displayed in many young monasteries. There one may often see a **Transitional** style, with Norman decoration around the new pointed Gothic windows. At its best it has a graceful austerity.

The **Decorated** style of around 1290–1350 was a development of the Early English style, with the more confident and sophisticated vaulting techniques allowing walls to become thinner and windows larger. The generally restrained decoration of the previous era became more extravagant, with foliate forms appearing in the spectacular **window tracery**. This style, displayed in enlargements and rebuilding work at many cathedrals, was widely introduced in modernisation works at countless parish churches. It must have been greatly admired and highly popular, with all who could afford it seeking to rebuild their parish church in the new style. This followed a time of great population growth and many new churches were built in this style to catch up with the expanding populations.

The **Perpendicular** was the last of the Gothic styles and in various forms it has endured to the present day. By concentrating the architectural thrusts of walls onto buttresses, the builders of churches were able to maximise the

Lavenham in Suffolk has one of the finest Perpendicular churches.

window spaces and produce soaring buildings with bright, airy interiors. Towers were developed to emphasise the upward lines, while tracery abandoned the swirl for vertical lines that emphasised height. The arrival of the style (experiments had begun around 1335) was accompanied by the eruption of the Black Death and the plummeting of numerous populations. At the end of the Middle Ages, however, the prosperity of various regional woollen industries funded some spectacular expressions of the Perpendicular.

Although these successive styles are quite distinctive, it is difficult to discover churches that are *wholly* in one style. As communal buildings they evolved with the communities they served, which might grow, shrink, enjoy some disposable wealth or become impoverished. The churches we encounter display the products of several phases and fashions of building. When they are demolished and the archaeologists move in, then evidence of even more building phases are likely to be discovered.

Numerous churches must have gone through one, two or even three timber phases and then a couple of stone phases before the Anglo-Saxon era was even over. Then, in the course of the Middle Ages, all clear traces of Saxon work might well have been removed as the building was remodelled. An expanding medieval community meant an expanding population, so that the little nave-and-chancel buildings had to be enlarged. Some Saxon churches had begun by serving just the landowner and his immediate family, so that the base of the tower might have acted as a nave, and the masonry above as a dynastic stronghold or refuge.

Fashion, too, was important, and the Romanesque liking for rounded apses tended to be overtaken as the nave was greatly lengthened to accommodate a growing population. Then the building might expand sideways as the nave walls were breached and side aisles added. Meanwhile, the opening of the nave walls at a higher level produced a clerestory, with the new windows allowing extra light to flood in.

There would, of course, also be communities that shrank and the maintenance of an over-large building would place a heavy burden on the lord and his reduced tenantry. Evidence of contraction can be found in shortened naves, lowered nave roofs (leaving a telltale inverted V-shaped crease at a higher level on the wall of the tower), and masonry and new windows filling the gaps in the walls after side aisles were shed.

Equally the evolving church embodied the fashions in worship and the degrading emblems of intolerance and bigotry. The brightly coloured medieval glass that once graced the windows was smashed by state-sanctioned vandals, as evidenced by its colourless replacements. The whitewash covering the colourful Doom painting, the headless cross in the churchyard and the niche robbed of its statuette tell similar stories. The walls of Ripley church are pocked with pits at chest height, which are thought to be the legacy of the executions of Royalists by Cromwell's firing squads.

Church architecture can be very beautiful. For me, however, the church is much more interesting as a building that, in its stones and scars, records the history of a community. In the light of its existence as a unique repository of communal history, arty talk about the 'superior' or 'provincial' or 'dis-appointing' quality of its various architectural facets seems much less important.

10. COUNTRYSIDES OF CROSSES

The cross was as much a part of the Dark Age and medieval scenes as signposts are of our own. The cross was the symbol of Christ's passion and death and crosses announced proximity to places of importance, often inviting God to treat them in a favourable manner. Having said this, they came in many different forms and were expected to perform a variety of roles. And so when one encounters a cross in the open countryside it may not necessarily be easy to understand just what it is doing there. The following roles are suggested.

Christianised standing stones

These were originally erected to serve some ritual functions – often as ancient grave-markers – and over the years local reverence became attached to them. For this reason, after the arrival of Christianity it was felt essential that the stone be 'converted' to Christianity by the addition of a cross symbol. On the Pictish symbol stones (see page 149), the later cross joined the pagan symbols, as though their commissioners were hedging their bets, although the last generations of stones displayed the cross alone. Christianity had plainly triumphed. In the west of Britain this urge to convert pagan stones was most active in the fourth century.

Memorial stones

These date from around the sixth century and mainly belong to the period preceding the conversion of England. Thus they are found mainly in the Celtic west. The stones may be of modest size and some carry just the Christian symbol, a cross in a circle. Others bear the 'Chi-rho', with the Greek letters X and P superimposed to represent the first two letters of Christ's name, or sometimes have the Greek alpha and omega to the left and right of the X to signify that Christ is the beginning and the end. There may also be an inscription to commemorate the dead noble or priest, usually along the lines of 'Here lies x, son of y'. This will generally be in simple Latin, but may also be in a Celtic language or in the old **Ogham alphabet**, where the 'letters' are strokes of different kinds through a line.

Preaching crosses

In the west the erection of crudely executed **cross pillars** was followed by the development of the most elaborate and ornately decorated **high crosses** and grave slabs adorned with crosses in the ninth and tenth centuries. In England, as

The lollipop-like Cornish cross in the churchyard at Altarnun may have originated as a preaching cross that pre-dated the church.

long as the minster system prevailed, services were frequently conducted in the open, beside a stone cross. Many crosses still stand in churchyards and one may assume that an eroding Dark Age cross is the one that sanctified the preaching site *before* the church was built. This is often true, but preaching crosses are hard to distinguish from other crosses, like those erected in established churchyards near existing churches. Both the preaching crosses and the churchyard crosses of the Saxon era can display astonishing skill in replicating in stone the intricate interlace patterns seen in contemporary illuminated manuscripts. The English,

A Cornish cross at Crows-an-wra, near Land's End.

Welsh and Scottish examples almost rival the amazing craftsmanship and beauty of the high crosses that were fashioned at Irish monastic sites at around the same time. The majority of **churchyard crosses** belong to the medieval centuries, and crosses continued to be erected to sanctify churchyards in the centuries that followed. Unlike market crosses, the churchyard cross would often culminate in a small tabernacle displaying carved religious images, though for this reason very few survived the assaults of the Reformation and Civil War. Some preaching crosses, made redundant by the building of a church, were incorporated into the fabric of its walls.

Cornish crosses

One may scarcely visit Cornwall without seeing a good few stumpy Celtic crosses with circular heads like lollipops. They seem to belong to the centuries that bracket AD 1000 and to have been 'general purpose' crosses, guarding churchyards, establishing the limits of church land or even marking routeways. The intractable nature of the local granite or 'moorstone' may explain why their decoration was far coarser than that of contemporary high crosses in Ireland or most Saxon preaching crosses.

'Functional' crosses

Crosses were employed to serve a variety of roles not directly connected to worship. They were like great exclamation marks fashioned from stone and they told passers-by that something of importance was at hand. Village markets were usually signalled and sanctified by a **market cross**. Many of these crosses still stand on market greens centuries after the demise of the market concerned, while others were vandalised as 'popish symbols'. They vary considerably in size, but the typical cross consisted of an upright shaft on a stepped stone plinth. The tops of these monuments have not usually survived, but they normally consisted of a lantern-shaped head rather than an actual cross. Any cross seen on a village green or beside the High Street is most likely to be a market cross. **Wayside crosses** were sometimes erected, though their uses seem somewhat arbitrary. They might sanctify spots where horrible events had occurred, or perhaps mark out the intervals where parties bearing a coffin could rest safely. Similarly tall pillars or crosses were useful to chart the line of a route across high, blizzard-prone ground. **Boundary crosses** marked divisions of many kinds, such as the limits of estates or warrens. Where a cross now seems stranded out in the country it might well have been a boundary marker; ecclesiastical authorities were keener than most to define the bounds of their estates, as well as to mark the boundaries of sanctuary offered to fugitives by a church.

Unusual crosses

There are just three **Eleanor crosses** surviving from the collection of very beautiful monuments that were erected after the death of Queen Eleanor in 1290 at the eleven places where her body rested en route from Harby, Northamptonshire, to Westminster. **Penitential crosses** were unusual and just a few medieval examples survived. They had a rather cylindrical form and were ringed by curved niches for the knees of the praying, inward-facing penitents.

11. THE CHURCH AND THE REGION

Even though particular fashions in church architecture exerted total domination at the times when they were current, no two churches in Britain are quite the same. This is partly because each church has its own history of building and rebuilding, demolition and modification, and partly because each region of Britain developed its own collective notion of what a church should look like. At first glance one might think this was simply because each region had its own

Breamore in Hampshire has a noted Saxon church, but a glance at the windows alone, where most medieval styles are represented, shows that it has experienced a succession of alterations.

set of building resources – sandstone, granite, limestone, straw, and so on – but this is only a part of the story, for some of the regional fancies were not related to the materials to hand. Seemingly inexplicable differences in taste helped to diversify the scene.

Perhaps the biggest restriction on any church-building plans concerned the weakness of the transport system. Stone is a difficult, bulky commodity and the builders would go almost to any lengths to avoid long or uphill journeys by cart or wagon. Rivers and lesser waterways could be exploited, but the emphasis was on discovering the nearest source of acceptable stone. This generally meant that the finished church became 'as one' with its setting, its walls and towers matching the surrounding cliffs, outcrops and cuttings. However, transport only became a serious problem in the period before the Norman Conquest when the first generations of **timber churches** were replaced by stone ones. Only one of these log-walled buildings survives, at Greensted-juxta-Ongar, though there are several, later, timber towers. Gradually the builders gained confidence and

The last-surviving Saxon timber church is at Greensted-juxta-Ongar. Vertical posts from the original building can be seen forming the wall.

fluency in the use of stone, but many churches remained the only stone buildings in their parishes for centuries.

Sometimes, an old church's fabric contains clues to earlier life in the locality. Courses or random scatters of narrow, russet Roman bricks or squared Roman stones tell of the pillaging of the ruins of forts, towns or villas by the builders. Corbridge in Northumberland devoured such remains more greedily than most, containing not only a wealth of recycled Roman stone but also an entire gateway at the junction of the chancel and the tower.

Particular problems arose if a locality was totally lacking in acceptable stones (such as limestone, hard sandstone or granite) or when a second-rate walling stone was insufficient for the making of heavy, load-bearing components, such as the lintels used above windows and doors or the quoins at the corners of buildings. In such cases 'two-tone' churches appeared, with walls made of flint from the fields or of poor-grade material from a local quarry contrasting with the commercial-grade stone brought in from much further afield for door jambs, window surrounds, quoins and lintels.

The downlands and chalk country of Norfolk were particularly dis-advantaged. The better-grade chalk or 'clunch' was soft and excellent for interior carving but it was easily attacked by rain and frost, so only occasionally was it employed for the whole building, as at Comberton in Cambridgeshire. Otherwise flint from the fields had to be used along with imported sandstone details. Flint was a low-status material, but it did offer decorative possibilities when each flint was **knapped** to present a flat surface and such flints were grouped in panels to produce a chessboard effect – Suffolk has many examples. Great problems were encountered in building towers because of the absence of good stone to build their corners, and so cylindrical towers were adopted in many places, like Beachamwell in Norfolk.

It is always particularly interesting to relate a church to the nearby quarry that gave it life. Medieval masons disliked shifting stone over difficult ground. Look for a spot at the edge of high ground with suitable rock strata outcrops. Blocks of stone might be split off from the exposed face using lines of wedges and then pre-shaped in a working and assembly area nearby to avoid moving any stone unnecessarily. Once ready, they were moved on sledges to the building

The round tower at Beachamwell in Norfolk, a shrunken settlement that supported several medieval churches.

site. Using such tactics, a block of stone might reach the building site without ever having moved uphill.

For the most expensive and prestigious buildings a top-quality building stone was required and some of the best churches built in the south of England after the Norman Conquest utilised the products of the Norman quarries at Caen, shipped in across the Channel. Normally the preferred stone was a top-grade limestone of a pale silver or golden hue that would 'case-harden'. Such stones were easy to work or saw but, after exposure in a building they would develop a very hard outer coating. Masons in Northamptonshire, the Cotswolds and Somerset were lucky in that a belt of limestone from the Jurassic era was ready to hand. Otherwise architectural luxury came at a high price.

Originally, most churches must have been thatched. This would also have underlined the regional character of their locality. Places of worship by fens or broads would have had dark roofs made of the local reeds, the village churches of the fat farming country would have used wheat straw from the surrounding fields in their roofs, while in Wales, Scotland and Ireland the shaggier oat straw would have been seen on some roofs, others being of heather or a **black thatch** of slabs of peat. Roofs thatched in reed or straw were relatively light, but they had to be steeply pitched to shed rainwater efficiently. Roofs covered in sandstone flags ('thack-stones'), like those of vernacular buildings in the Pennines, were heavy, so a minimal pitch was preferred. The change from a thatched roof to another type of roof can often be traced on the building. Above the place where the nave roof now joins the tower, the scar of a higher, steeper roof, usually one that was thatched, can sometimes be seen.

It is clear that churches were bound to differ, because their designers (usually an itinerant master mason instructed by a patron) were obliged to make the best use of local resources. However, there are other regional differences deriving from various causes such as prosperity. Some regions were relatively affluent and the legacy of lost settlements and abandoned churches in Norfolk reflects the fact that through most of the Middle Ages this was a disproportionately prosperous and well-populated county. Prosperity could come in surges, like the wealth deriving from the tin mines in Cornwall and the lead mines in the Pennines. Spectacular churches in East Anglia, Somerset and the Cotswolds often represent the investment of a family fortune raised in wool-trading – the church at Lavenham in Suffolk is the most celebrated. Parts of the Yorkshire Dales that had been deprived of churches through the medieval period gained several in the distinctive local 'Pennine Perpendicular' style as a little wealth trickled into the area from the woollen industry in the sixteenth century.

The late medieval church at Kirkby Malham in the Yorkshire Dales, one of the best examples of the Pennine Perpendicular style.

Even so, there were differences that derived neither from environmental resources nor from economic advantages, and these helped to determine the nature of regional identities without having any obvious origins. **Broach spires**, in which the tower developed into a steeple via complicated geometrical steps, were greatly favoured in the East Midlands, but did not spread until the days of the Victorians and their magpie-like approach to building. Essex has just one medieval spire, at Thaxted, while panoramas of some areas further to the south or west positively bristle with spires. East Anglian churches flaunt their magnificence in hammerbeam roofs, while Somerset churches do it with their towers. In the far south-west of England there was a liking for naves with double or triple gable roofs, and if the local stone did not lend itself to fine carving, this could be compensated for by spectacular woodwork in the rood screen. Altarnun in Cornwall has a double roof over some very high-quality woodwork.

Imitation could either concentrate or dilute a regional church style. Sometimes the masons might be instructed to base a new church on those of

Somerset churches built in the Perpendicular style are noted for their fine towers, like this one at North Petherton.

neighbouring parishes, though perhaps to build their towers or spires just a little taller and more impressively. In other cases models from other regions were introduced. Thus the Cluniac monks sent masons from Lewes to estates at Prittlewell in Essex with instructions to reproduce the sort of towers seen at Ashford, Lydd and Tenterden in Kent.

12. THE CHURCH MOVES ON

The Middle Ages effectively ended (in religious terms at least) with the break with Rome and Henry VIII's establishment of a national church under his authority. The medieval church may sometimes have been distant, greedy and even corrupt, but never again would one church exert a commanding leadership over entire, undivided communities. The dynamic era of magnificent church building that had lasted for five or more centuries ground to a halt and in the years leading up to the Georgian era more churches probably fell down than were put up. In the late Tudor period and beyond belief was often a cause for persecution and fear and a single church could never again embrace a whole village, confess its sins and apply spiritual bindings to its wounds. Various events contributed to the evolution of the landscape.

The **dissolution of the monasteries** in 1536–9 created a great vacuum in rural society. Since at least the arrival of the Black Death in 1348 most monasteries had been shadows of their former selves. Monks were satirised as symbols of overindulgence; monastic communities were greatly reduced; recruits were hard to find; and popular religious enthusiasm had become redirected towards the penniless orders of friars preaching hellfire and damnation and towards donations to guild and chantry chapels in churches.

None the less, the monks still played a leading role in rural affairs. They employed many rural workers; they leased immense estates to lay tenants; they frequently provided the priests for the parish churches, and in the case of the Augustinians they shared their churches with lay people. Monasteries, priories and nunneries permeated the affairs of rural Britain. This was particularly so in the north, where the Cistercians had their great agricultural empires. The failed Pilgrimage of Grace of 1536 was a popular uprising driven by fears of what might be in store if the monks were removed. Such fears were well founded. The monastic lands were frequently sold in large blocks to speculators and then fragmented, resold and often sold again. In place of the perhaps unpopular but familiar monks, people now had powerful strangers for neighbours. Some were profiteers with no interest in the communities (other than how much money

Churches always have a strong element of individuality. In the case of Swaffham Prior in Cambridgeshire, two churches share the same churchyard, the result of a long-forgotten feudal arrangement.

could be extracted from them) and some proved overzealous in pursuit of official dogmas and for generations their families brought terror and disruption to the Catholics or Quakers of their locality.

The English Civil War in the first half of the seventeenth century was immensely costly in life. Not only did it strike at the fanatics and bigots in the ranks of the Royalists, Parliamentarians, Covenanters and Puritans, but it took a heavy toll on all life. It also played a major role in the destruction of a spectacular heritage of sculpture, coloured glass, wood carvings and murals. The prejudice against idolatry gave vandals licence to smash a national artistic heritage that was many centuries in the making, with even the remains of kings at Winchester being wrecked.

As religious affairs began to settle, the new English national church embodied the fresh outlook. The whitened walls and plain glass windows told their own tales, and the towering pulpit announced that preaching had replaced the splendour and mysteries of the long-gone medieval church. But all the killing and persecution could not unite people under a single church. The Scots united with England and Wales under a single parliament after 1707, generally preferred a church without bishops, and different, nonconformist versions of the Protestant faith proliferated. In England the squire, still a dominating presence, might doze through the sermon, sometimes in the comforting glow of his own fireplace, though all around him the Quakers or Friends were meeting and youthful, less deferential religious notions were germinating and taking shape among the cottages of oppressed farm labourers and in the farmstead workshops and the little rows of houses beside the mills.

The established church had failed to capture the heart of the community. The lists of essential repairs lengthened, and by Victorian times, when an enthusiasm for making and fixing churches returned, countless village churches presented challenging subjects for renovation. What was attempted generally constituted imaginative rebuilding rather than the painstaking conservation that we know today. Fortunately the Victorian enthusiasm for all things medieval brought the Gothic styles thundering back into fashion. However, the Victorians were not too particular about the purity and authenticity of what they borrowed or how they interpreted particular motifs. This was also true with regard to the completely new churches that they built: a Northamptonshire broach spire, a West Country barrel-vaulted nave and a porch copied from a Norfolk church might all be united in one building.

At Wymondham, Norfolk, the two towers reflect rivalries in a church shared by the parish and the Abbey.

The rocketing growth of population in the expanding industrial towns provided an insatiable demand for new churches in the Victorian era. Nonconformists were also active, both in the provision of less spectacular places of worship for urban populations and in the creation of buildings to reflect and serve the different congregations produced by the fragmenting of the Protestant faith. In many a Welsh mining, quarrying or manufacturing village the main street was lined by chapels serving the various persuasions; a disagreement among the members of the governing body of a chapel could see a new branch of nonconformism launched. Scotland had fewer competitors, though none as uncompromising as the ones serving small fishing communities.

13. DISCOVERING YOUR CHURCH

Every church has a story, sometimes one that goes back over 1,000 years. For all that architectural sleuths and the aficionados of bell-ringing or bench-end carving may have scrutinised the building several times, it is quite likely that nobody has actually explored your church in terms of its setting and its role as the hub of a community through some of the most interesting periods of history. Here are some suggestions:

- Look at the immediate setting of the church. Does its site coincide with any significant geographical 'events'? Are there springs there that might have been thought sacred or does the church crown a commanding knoll? Such things may imply an earlier, pagan site, while some early churches were built where routes crossed rivers and then seem to have acquired a village 'tail' running back from the ford. A scan of place-names may help to reconstruct the ancient environment, as described in Chapter Four.

- What about the dedication? The majority of medieval churches favoured popular dedications like All Saints', St Mary's and so on. However, there are a number of English churches that have dedications to little-known Celtic missionaries, and these suggest very early foundations. In Cornwall and Wales, where such dedications are commonplace, various Celtic saints are so obscure that we only know about them through the dedications of the churches they founded.

- Most churchyards are of rectangular or trapezoidal shape. One that is circular or oval, especially if it occupies a commanding position, strongly hints at a very early foundation.

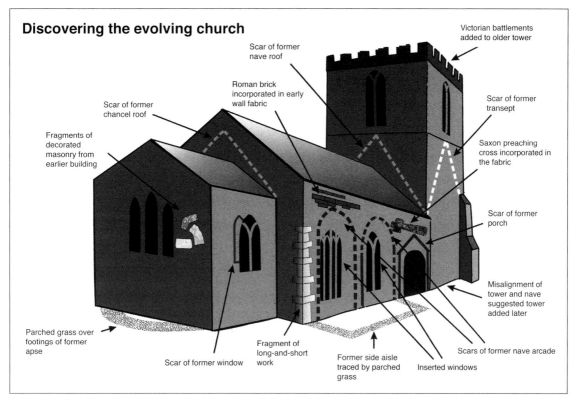

Discovering the evolving church

Victorian battlements added to older tower

Scar of former nave roof

Roman brick incorporated in early wall fabric

Scar of former chancel roof

Scar of former transept

Fragments of decorated masonry from earlier building

Saxon preaching cross incorporated in the fabric

Scar of former porch

Misalignment of tower and nave suggested tower added later

Parched grass over footings of former apse

Scar of former window

Fragment of long-and-short work

Former side aisle traced by parched grass

Inserted windows

Scars of former nave arcade

Fig. 14. Discovering the evolving church.

- Most old churches were established in young villages or else villages soon grew around them. There are, however, a large number of churches that stand somewhat isolated from settlements. In such cases it will be useful to refer to Chapter Four, Villages, and attempt to decide whether *your* isolated church served a village that was deserted, shifted or shrank, or whether it might always have stood alone on a site commandeered from pagans at an early stage in the Christian era.
- Look closely at the fabric of your church, remembering that original timber churches, and perhaps one or two stone successors, could have disappeared completely in the course of unrecorded rebuildings. Can you match up the stone used with the rock strata exposed in the immediate vicinity? If not, how far did the masons go to obtain suitable material? It is unlikely that the stones travelled far. A search of a zone within a couple of miles or so might reveal the irregular bumps of an old quarrying site or a high, hard rock outcrop that has been cut back by medieval quarry-workers. Fieldwork

like this will not reveal the source of the great roofing or spire-making timbers. These would have been prefabricated at some woodland workshop, and you may see the numerals, usually Latin ones, inscribed on them to guide their assembly. If records survive, they will be buried in contemporary accounts, and the beams may well have been transported much further than the stone. The church is probably the handiwork of peripatetic masons, many of whom were born in quarrying villages, and although a few church-building contracts and accounts survive, all that one is likely to find of the builders are the simple **mason marks** showing who was responsible for shaping which stones.

A plan of the parish should be well worth a look. In many cases the parish originated as the estate of the landowner who endowed the church. But parishes are not constant. In the uplands and dales medieval churches were few and they served huge parishes, where corpse roads from far afield focused on the church. In attempts to overcome the effective impossibility of worship in the remote hamlet and farmsteads and to make conditions easier for the burial parties, chapels of ease were established in such parishes, as we have seen. These chapels might become churches in their own right, and pockets of population growth could also result in new parishes being carved out from the old. Equally some communities might fail and the old church territory be absorbed into an amalgamated parish. Such parishes often have double-barrelled names that identify their components.

Look at the layout of the building and see if it offers any clues about the growth or shrinkage of the community. Only a thoroughgoing archaeological excavation can reveal the whole story. This would lift the turf from the surroundings of the present building and show, for example, if side aisles or an apse has been shed. Traces of a lowered roof line, a shortened tower or a porch that was dismantled rather than repaired can all tell of poverty and contraction.

A good look at the fabric of the actual walls can also be revealing. The old masons would often incorporate anything robust into a rising wall. A thirteenth-century wall might, for example, include a few narrow, russet Roman bricks or tiles, the shaft of a churchyard or preaching cross with carved decoration of the eighth or ninth century and some fragments of stonework decorated with Norman chevrons. Obviously such a wall can tell one a great deal about the earlier history of the church.

It may be worth while wondering about the inspiration of the design. Does the church reflect features seen in neighbouring churches, or does it seek to out-do them in any way? Local imitation certainly took place, but the newest cathedrals set the fashion for those who could afford to replicate in miniature their grand designs, such as like the octagon towers of a few churches in the region of Ely Cathedral.

Nonconformist chapels are also suitable subjects for investigation and their relative youth can make detailed research easier. Often middle-class members or sympathisers might donate the land on which a chapel was to be built, and details of the grant may survive in the chapel records. It may be possible to piece together a picture of the opposition they presented to the established church/local squire and also uncover the rivalry between competing nonconformist sects. The location of the meeting houses used by the Quakers, who often spearheaded the cause and paid a heavy price for doing so, may be identified, and also their little graveyards, so often islands of tranquillity. In any villages where nonconformism was a force, a surprisingly complex picture of shifting chapel sites and of sects that rose and fell and were eclipsed by others may, with diligence and patience, be re-created. Scores of sites of superseded or abandoned chapels have appeared in the last two centuries, and it is remarkable how quickly memories of a chapel can fade. Work on recent religious landscapes should be done before all memory is lost and old photographs fade away. The larger-scale maps of the Victorian era will normally indicate the different places of worship.

SIX

Strongholds

1. SOME IDEAS ABOUT STRONGHOLDS

'The Normans built the first defence works and the castles of the Middle Ages were damp, draughty places, while castle life was grim and gloomy' WRONG
'Castles were just bolt-holes for the nobles, and once gunpowder was invented, that was the end of castles' WRONG
'Medieval castles were part of a tradition of defence that went far back into prehistoric time. The main distinction between the prehistoric and the medieval citadels seems to be that the former were mainly *communal* defences and the latter the strongholds of *dynasties*' RIGHT
'The castles of the Middle Ages were about many things as well as defence. They were status symbols and places for gracious living that were surrounded by well-tailored landscapes. They had many points of contact with the stately homes of the post-medieval centuries' RIGHT

2. WHY STRONGHOLDS?

This question is not as simple as it seems, and the further back we go, the more uncertain the answers become. A magnificent construction that looks purpose-built for defence might actually have been created for other reasons. It might be a splendid and showy statement of the might or (self-) importance of the person who caused it to be built. Similarly a military work might have been created to convey a message rather than as the stage for a battle. The Mercian king Offa (757–96) is still renowned for commanding the construction of the great boundary work that faces outwards from the Mercian frontier towards Wales. But Offa's Dyke could never have been manned effectively by the troops at the king's disposal. It must therefore have been a great statement of the king's might and a dramatic warning against incursions from Wales.

To complicate matters further, monuments that do not seem to have had much military credibility appear, sometimes, to have been the scenes of battles.

Among the earliest yet most imposing of prehistoric monuments were the **causewayed enclosure**s. These were normally set on fairly modest hilltops, with the summits being ringed with one or more lines of banks and ditches. Rather than presenting a continuous barrier to any advancing force, the ditches were frequently interrupted by causeways (see Chapter Five). Therefore the monuments have been interpreted as ceremonial assembly places for the surrounding communities, with the encircling pits being dug, at least in part, to accept ritual offerings and the debris from feasts. However, several of these sites, like Crickley Hill in Gloucestershire, Hambledon Hill in Dorset and Stepleton, its near neighbour, have revealed evidence of epic battles involving archers, decapitations and great conflagrations.

We know that the castles of the Middle Ages had great symbolic importance in an age that was heavily permeated by symbolism. The castle was a symbol of

Situated on a rocky promontory, Dunottar Castle near Stonehaven was a powerful defensive castle on a site occupied since at least Pictish times. It was the seat of Scotland's Earls Marischal for 250 years and in the sixteenth and seventeenth centuries it evolved into a palatial residence.

status in a highly militaristic society. It was impossible to imagine an aristocrat of high standing who did not possess at least one castle, irrespective of its actual defensive merits. Battlements, too, had great symbolic significance and sometimes they appeared on coats of arms. When castles finally became redundant nobles continued to hanker after the displays of status associated with castle life and explored other means of showing status (through costly landscape parks, for example).

Some fortunate castles passed through several centuries without ever having undergone an attack or a siege. During this period, however, each would doubtless have hosted dozens of visiting parties, served continuously as the administrative centre of the surrounding estate and become far more opulently furnished within, while the recreational facilities outside the walls greatly increased. A castle might have spent just one-thousandth of its life under siege, while a really important noble might spend his time between two or three castles and several manor houses as he migrated around, consuming the surplus production of his scattered estates. When a castle was occupied, it normally operated in its capacity as a centre for local admin-istration, recreation and hospitality. For the tenants to be summoned to man the walls was unusual.

The later medieval baronial strongholds were more showy palaces flaunting the trappings of castles. When well and truly redundant, several largely sham castles became caught up in the Civil War. Some, like Castle Bolton in Wensleydale, performed surprisingly well in roles that they had scarcely been intended to perform.

We know all these things about medieval castles because the archives are packed with written and illustrative materials concerning medieval castle life. However, there is nothing in the archives to show how prehistoric strongholds served their communities and so we tend to opt for the most obvious explanations. Yet had we just the medieval *monuments* and not the *writings*, we might be quite blind even to the existence of fundamental phenomena like chivalry and courtly love.

We tend to project our own preoccupations onto the past. The English, particularly, have long been obsessed with invasion from the continent, both when such threats have existed and also when they have not. Much of what was written about prehistoric life has reflected this **invasionism**, creating foreign threats and bogeymen that are unlikely to have truly existed. It has blinded us to the fact that, rather than being periodically overrun, massacred and displaced by foreign invaders, British society seems to have very deep roots indeed.

3. THE FIRST MONUMENTS

By the Iron Age communities throughout most of Britain had begun to invest remarkable resources of energy into encircling hilltops with girdles of ramparts. We know, too, that societies were becoming unstable and circumstances more threatening. Even so, it is hard to deduce whether the earliest of the apparent strongholds were built for ritual, defence or both. Around the end of the Stone Age several massive hilltop enclosures were built and these might be regarded as fortified tribal capitals. Carn Brea in Cornwall, for example, was a large village that, around 3500 BC, gained defensive ramparts. It may have housed craftsmen making axes of the hard, local stone. Like several of the causewayed enclosure ritual centres, such as Hambledon Hill in Dorset, Carn Brea was redeveloped as a **hillfort** in the Iron Age, demonstrating the military potential of ancient centres that were traditionally thought to be concerned only with ritual and social gatherings.

The first stages in the creation of hillforts of the kind that would girdle so many hilltops with their ramparts and ditches may have come in the Bronze Age, around 1200 BC, when some hilltop sites that may have been associated with religious rituals were ringed with palisades of posts stout enough to repel attackers and to carry fighting platforms. Rams Hill on the Berkshire Downs seems to have been an example. An area of about 2.5 acres (1 ha) was enclosed by a deep ditch, with the rubble being cast inwards to build a rampart; a little later the palisade was added to enhance the barrier effect of this rampart.

During the centuries that followed the climate deteriorated. The population had been steadily growing and the farmlands of Britain were supporting as many people as would be living at the time of Domesday Book, over 2,000 years later. There may even have been more people than that. But as the summers became cool and cloudy and the climate wetter and windier throughout the year, the blow fell hardest on the frontiers of farming: the uplands and the damp clay vales. Autumn would be upon the households before their crops had ripened and disease ravaged the herds and flocks in the sodden fields. As the inevitable refugees from these frontiers of farming sought new niches in the countryside, the pressures of an overlarge population doubtless began to reverberate throughout society.

By the start of the Iron Age, around 650 BC, these pressures must have been intense and the archaeological evidence describes increasingly stratified societies dominated by warlords armed with fearsome slashing swords; these men may, in anticipation of the feudal world, have offered protection to communities in return for heavy payments of tribute. At the same time religion seems to have turned in a darker direction. As the rain swirled down and the watercourses burst their banks, people tried to appease the water gods, casting votive offerings of weapons or occasionally of sacrificial victims into the rivers, meres and bogs.

In the past scholars attributed the turbulent, warlike character of the Iron Age to successive invasions of Celtic people from continental Europe. However, Celtic languages now seem to have been established far earlier and the hillforts do not seem to correlate with these (presumed) invasions. The population was probably far more preoccupied by the threats posed by the people just beyond the wood or across the river than with any foreign threat. For them, foreign lands began at the dyke or hedge bank around their territories.

Prehistoric hillforts are very significant archaeological and landscape features in most of the regions of Britain. In some regions the summit of almost every hill seems to be notched and belted with ancient ramparts. They reflect a society that had become more class-ridden, more subservient to warlords and more militaristic. They also reflect the increasingly fearsome nature of weaponry. Slingers and their piles of slingstones were still perched on ramparts and fighting platforms, but the aristocracy now had swords made of iron rather than the brittle bronze blades of old. They trundled around battlefields on chariots, hurling javelins as they went, and could quickly dismount and split their opponents' skulls wide open with these swords. Yet the hillforts were not part of the paraphernalia of ritualised cavorting and posturing in the gory carnival of the Celtic battlefield. They were part of a much grimmer scenario, one of mass attacks on desperate communities. The farmer, his wife and their children were unlikely to live much longer if the fort's barred gate or rampart were breached.

4. MEETING THE HILLFORTS

The labour used to create our legacy of hillforts must have been absolutely stupendous. It has been calculated that England (south of the Lake District and the North York Moors) and Wales contain 1,350 hillforts. To the north of Hadrian's Wall around 1,100 hillforts are known and there are probably about 70 examples in northern England between these great zones. Ingleborough, the dominating fell of the Pennines, is crowned by a massive Iron Age fort. In Scotland the Mither Tap o'Bennachie, overlooking Strathdon, supports a wind-lashed hillfort that is 1,698ft (about 518m) above sea level, while also in the north-east Tap o'Noth has one that is even higher at 1,850 ft (about 564m).

Strange though it may seem, one does not have to have a hilltop to build a hillfort. There are some lowland examples, in Epping Forest, elsewhere in Essex, in Norfolk and in Suffolk. Some places have remarkable concentrations of hillforts – more than communal defence would seem to have required. They abound in the Welsh Marches, Wessex, Cornwall and Wales, particularly south Wales and Pembrokeshire. Strangely, in *Brigantia* – that part of England that the Romans found most unsettled and troublesome – spanning the Pennines, hillforts are present, but not very numerous.

It is not hard to think of other functions that hillforts might have served in ancient societies, perhaps as places for assembly, trading and ritual. However, they were very much concerned with defence. One needs only to look at one of these monuments from the perspective of an attacker to realise that they were expertly constructed with military matters very much in mind. The ramparts and the ditches that front them were disposed to get the maximum defensive advantage from the terrain and great care was taken to make entrances as secure as possible.

Hillforts were features of the Iron Age landscape in various parts of continental Europe, where some were packed with elongated buildings that seem most likely to have been barracks. Citadels rather like hillforts were built in a few places well after the end of the prehistoric era. Forts with massive ramparts and barrack-like buildings were built in Viking Age Denmark, and some believe that they were bases and training camps for the terrifying raids on England.

Some British hillforts are also known to have contained buildings and in some ways the later hillforts were approaching the notion of the town. Usually the buildings are interpreted as dwellings. The fort at Hod Hill in Dorset was packed with about 250 circular houses, and the hillfort that adapted the site of the ancient causewayed enclosure on Hambledon Hill had about 175 of them. At Tre'r Ceiri, on the Lleyn peninsula in North Wales, there were about 150 dwellings. Lofty Ingleborough had just a few, though it is impossible to imagine how anybody could have survived up there through a winter.

However, not all the buildings in hillforts were houses. There were some, supported on four corner posts, that have been interpreted as granaries. This has given rise to the idea of the hillfort as a symbolic local capital. Grain might be brought up to his fortress as tribute to the local king, who redistributed it as largesse to his subjects. However, the profusion of forts in the western uplands, where grain would struggle to grow, relegates this interpretation to a minor role.

Hillforts generally stood on high ground among the ancient commons, which would have been visited by people from the surrounding territories. Thus they may have served as neutral meeting places where the affairs of neighbouring communities could be debated and settled. Although their stupendous earthworks, towering palisades and carefully calculated defences made them formidable strongholds, some hillforts might also have been centres for ritual, perpetuating the role of the more ancient hilltop centres.

As the approach of the Roman invasion in AD 43 signified that the Iron Age was drawing to its close, a few vast, sprawling hillforts were evolving into tribal capitals and vestigial towns (**oppida**), with a few, like Croft Ambrey near Hereford, having an orderly pattern of streets flanked by presumed barracks and granaries.

5. EXPLORING YOUR HILLFORT

The crumbling medieval castle that one might see today is a very poor representation of the stronghold as it looked when up to date, viable and decked out for war. We do not hear the portcullis rattling down, see the scalding water pouring from the murder holes, the hinged wooden shutters closing the gaps in the battlements, the banners, or the wooden galleries or **brattices** built out from high walls to shower death on those attacking the wall base. The hillfort, abandoned for 2,000 or more years, looks even less like it did in its prime.

Over many centuries soil from the rampart will have trickled, washed and slumped back into the fronting ditch as Nature undoes the work of humans. Originally the rampart would have been much higher, the ditch much deeper and all the slopes much steeper. Attackers were obliged to advance from the depths of the ditch up a very steep and slippery rampart bank, while all the while being bombarded with sling-stones, spears and, perhaps, arrows. The essence of the hillfort as a military work concerned this imposition on attackers to storm uphill across difficult terrain. While the earthworks may have slumped, the palisades of upright posts or small tree trunks that were often used to crown ramparts have disappeared completely. With such timber palisades in place, the forts were much more formidable obstacles.

Hillforts varied greatly in their layouts, presumably depending on military fashions, the perceived challenges and the resources available. The most obvious distinction concerns the numbers of concentric ditch/rampart rings involved. The so-called **univallate** forts had just one ring; the **bivallate** forts had two and the **multivallate** forts had several. The entrance of a fort was likely to be its

A section of the ramparts at the multivallate hillfort of Badbury Rings in Dorset.

weakest point and so most likely to attract an assault. Some forts had just one entrance, some two and a few more than two. In some cases these entrances were flanked by outworks or **horn works** projecting out like horns, so that any attackers assaulting the timber gates would have to run the gauntlet of flanking fire. Often the entrance included a gatehouse with guard chambers, while towers, parapets and walkways were designed to concentrate defenders around and above the gate.

The ramparts that we see today can seem imposing, but these eroding banks give few clues to the original appearance of the fort until they are excavated. Frequently the tall palisade that overlooked the ditch was backed by a massive but neat construction of rubble quarried from the fronting ditch, all contained in a box-like structure of timbers. Such **box ramparts** could also be faced in dry-stone walling. Where such an elaborate construction was not employed, the earth and rubble dumped to form a rampart might be faced or **revetted** in stone. In hard rock country the stones hacked from the ditch might be used to form a rampart of towering dry-stone walling or of rubble faced in such walling.

In northern Scotland the timber-laced form of box rampart construction has given rise to a most mysterious class of fortresses: the **vitrified forts**. In these the timbers lacing the stone ramparts were ignited to create a conflagration so intense that the stones in the rampart were vitrified, or turned to glass. Why this should have been done remains mysterious, for the ramparts were worse rather than better for having undergone this process. Perhaps some now-unfathomable ritual was involved?

Ditches were originally far neater and more trap-like. Fashions changed, and some ditches were dug with V-shaped cross-sections, while others had flat floors and steeper sides.

Far less challenging to our understanding is the way in which each hillfort exploited the local topography. Hilltops have obvious defensive advantages, but so, too, do the margins of plateaux with precipitous edges. In such places, a relatively short stretch of rampart/ditch can 'detach' a fort. A similar logic is employed in the case of **cliff castles** or **promontory forts**, where defences are strung across the narrow neck of land linking a natural sea-girt promontory to the mainland. There is scarcely such a promontory in Pembrokeshire or Cornwall that was not exploited in this way.

Here are some leads to follow:

- Scanning around from the lofty perch of a hillfort, can you guess which community and territory your fort may have dominated/served?

- Look at the entrance(s). Is there any trace or hint of a trackway that would have been used as people came up to the fort to find refuge, bring tribute or debate affairs? In your imagination, can you project a pathway down to the lowlands where most people would have lived?

- Try to think like a military engineer. Judge how the slopes and hollows in the natural topography have been exploited by the designer of the fort. See how effective were the efforts to make *all* approaches to the stronghold difficult.

- Remembering that a fort is only as strong as its weakest point, try to deduce how *you* would have led an attack. Did the designers of the fort anticipate this challenge? Look to see if adequate attempts were made to strengthen the defences in places where the natural terrain was less steep.

- Bear in mind that hillforts tended to survive for several centuries, though there may have been intermittent phases of abandonment. Excavations show that they were often improved and redesigned. Thus a new loop of ramparts might be thrown out to enclose and protect an area beyond the original defences, that may perhaps have previously been used as a paddock for livestock.

- Are there any semicircular shelves, circular depressions or stone **hut circles** inside the fort that could mark the sites of Iron Age dwellings? In hard stone country hut circles with the wall footings still exposed can often be found.
- How would the fort-dwellers survive if a siege was prolonged? Water could have been carried in skins or held in cisterns, but in the chalk country particularly the need for deep wells would seem to have posed a serious challenge.
- What happened to the fort after the Roman invasion imposed peace on Iron Age society in England and Wales? In some cases Norman mottes were introduced into the ancient defences, the most famous example being that at Old Sarum in Wiltshire, but there are various less famous examples, such as Loddiswell Rings in Devon. Any elongated ridges or cigar-shaped mounds inside the ramparts might well be **pillow mounds** or artificial rabbit warrens (see Chapter Two), hillforts being favoured sites for warrens.
- If your fort is in Scotland, especially if it is north of the Central Valley, look among the rubble of the rampart and see if there are any dark, glass-like fused stones and boulders that indicate the mysterious vitrification rite.
- What about the name of the fort? Such names frequently reflect the old defensive function (see Table 6.1).

6. SMALLER PREHISTORIC DEFENCES

At the time of their construction the great hillforts were extraordinarily greedy of labour. Whether readily or under duress, members of communities provided only with antler picks and baskets shifted earth and rubble on a scale that might daunt even the operators of today's mechanical diggers. One estimate suggested that the (unfinished) fortifications at Ladle Hill in Hampshire offered sufficient work to employ 200 labourers for 115 days – yet this was a fairly small fort and plenty of others had many times its length of ramparts. As well as the hillforts, which had the capacity to shelter communities, other, quite different strongholds appeared in late prehistoric times, and they seem mainly to have been the defences and bolt-holes of families or very small neighbourhoods. They tended to appear in the Celtic uplands, where the centralised control evidenced by the hillforts may have been weaker. They comprise the following types.

Crannogs

These were dwellings standing on small, usually artificial, islands in lakes in Scotland and Ireland. In Scotland they are known to have appeared in the Bronze

Table 6.1. *Names reflecting a defensive function*

Name element	Language	Meaning	Example
Burh	Old English	Fort, manor house, town	Brough, Edinburgh, Scarborough
Caer	Old Welsh	Castle	Caerleon-on-Usk
Castel	Middle English	Castle	Castle Bromwich
Chester	Latin *castra* via Old English	A (Roman) military camp or fort	Chester, Godmanchester
Dic	Old English	Ditch, embankment	Devil's Dyke, Wansdyke
Din	Old Welsh	Fort	Dinas Dinlleu
Dūn	Old English	Hill	Dunmow
Ditto	Gaelic	Fort	Dundee, Dunoon
Pen	Old Welsh	Hilltop, headland, sometimes fortified	Pen Dinas, Pen y Gaer
Ràth	Gaelic	Ring fort, defended farmstead	Rathillet
Tomen, tump	Old Welsh/ Welsh Marches dialect	Mound, often a Noman motte mound	Also used for prehistoric tombs, e.g. Windmill Tump, West Tump and Nan Tow's Tump, all in Gloucester

Age. In Ireland, where almost 1,000 examples have been recorded, the greatest period of crannog building was in the early Christian period, though just a few were still occupied after the close of the Middle Ages. The crannogs therefore had a remarkably long history. The islands were created from brushwood, stones and piles and would support one or sometimes two or three dwellings, perhaps within an encircling palisade. They would seem to have been the homes of a family or an extended family and the crannog dwellers must have considered that the extra protection gained was worth the inconvenience of the building works and worth the aches and chills of life in the dank lake climate.

But this protection must have been limited. Most crannogs lay in range of missiles hurled from the lake shore and a few small boatloads of attackers could easily have overrun their defences. Today they appear as low, blister-shaped islands, often colonised by trees and shrubs. The larger Irish loughs and Scottish lochs may have accommodated dozens of examples, of which just a handful remain visible.

Brochs

Brochs were remarkable cylindrical towers, expertly built with a double layer of dry-stone walls. They appeared mainly in the north of mainland Scotland and on the Northern Isles at around the time that the Romans were conquering England, though the origins of the design are uncertain and the sources of the building expertise have not been traced. Within the hollow walls were built various chambers, though from outside the broch resembled an enormous windowless, sailless, tower mill, up to 50ft (15m) tall. A handful of warriors could have defended the narrow entrance and so brochs offered effective defence against raiders and skirmishers, though not against armies. They may have been the bolt-holes of local nobilities in turbulent times, or just possibly the defences of the ancestors of the Picts against raiding parties from Roman slaving ships. To see a broch in anything like its original condition, one must go to Mousa on Shetland, while the stumps of towers can be seen at Dun Carloway on Lewis, Gurness on Orkney and Dun Telve in Glenelg.

Souterrains

Known as **fogous** in Cornwall and as **weems** or **earth houses** in parts of Scotland, souterrains are no less mysterious than the brochs. They were underground passages, often lined with dry-stone walling and usually just a few yards in length, though occasionally more than 150ft (46m) long. They were generally associated with Iron Age and Roman age dwellings, but while some were fully underground and had stone slab roofs, many on the Scottish mainland took the form of a broad trench that was roofed-over with timber. They were assumed to have been defensive bolt-holes, but in the conditions of a violent raid it is hard to believe that they would have been anything other than death traps for any people seeking refuge there. There is always the possibility that they were used for rituals and the similarities to Neolithic passage graves are fairly obvious. A more prosaic and credible idea is that they were used for storing farm produce – cattle were the main source of wealth in the Celtic lands and such passages would have kept dairy products relatively cool.

Furnishings made from slabs of the local sandstone in the ruins of Gurness broch, Orkney.

In Ireland the souterrains lasted much longer, up to England's Norman era, and some believe that they were used as shelters from Viking raiders. Well-preserved fogous can be seen in Cornwall at places like Carn Euny, while throughout Britain and Ireland there are doubtless many slab-roofed examples that remain undiscovered.

Raths

These were the defended farmsteads of the higher orders of rural society in the early Christian era. They are among the most numerous of monuments, with almost 50,000 sites being identified or suspected, of which the great majority lie in Ireland. Traces of the farmstead itself have usually vanished but raths can often be recognised from the neat circle of enclosing ramparts, varying in diameter around a mean of about 100ft (30m). Scattered among them are some bivallate examples (having a double rampart ring), and these were presumably the abodes of the leading lights in early Christian society. As with the other examples mentioned, the defensive potential of the rath must have been very limited, though the ramparts could have harboured livestock during troubled times. In any flight over Ireland a scrutiny of the ground below is likely to reveal plenty of the ring doughnut-like rath patterns.

7. TOWARDS THE CASTLE

The occupation that followed the Roman invasion and conquest of England and Wales subjected these lands to a centrally organised and efficient military machine. For the first time politics, economics and the force of arms were integrated and imposed across the whole occupied territory. Hadrian's Wall, the British component of the Romans' quest to find secure frontiers for their empire, is the most celebrated legacy of these times, although the system of military roads was the most important and durable inheritance. The Romans used standardised camps and fortresses based on a playing card-shaped enclosure with rounded corners, and with entrances at the mid-points of the long and short sides. Smaller forts served by roads and coastal shipping were placed in a tactical way to provide bases for the policing and pacification of the more restless upland societies, while larger fortresses, like York, were positioned strategically to secure the rich commerce of the lowlands and support the frontier defences. As the stability and security of the British colony began to decline after around three centuries of occupation, a number of changes took place.

Barbarian incursions by Picts, Gaels or Scots from Ireland and Angles and Saxons from across the North Sea became more frequent, and attempts were made to bar access to threatened territories by casting up **dykes** or **linear earthworks**. These stretches of rampart-like banks fronted by deep ditches echo the old hillfort defences, though instead of encircling a defended area, they ran

Danes Dyke near Flamborough Head, one of many, usually puzzling, 'dykes' or linear earthworks. It seems to have detached and defended an estate sandwiched between the dyke and the sea cliffs.

in fairly straight lines, perhaps sometimes linking up areas of more difficult ground, like marshes and woods.

England contains many examples of these dykes but they are difficult to interpret. Certainly some of them belong to the Iron and Bronze Ages and were used to mark out important tribal boundaries. Many were constructed in the period when Roman power was waning and in the Dark Ages that followed, while a few examples are as recent as the Norman era. However, all the dykes tend to look rather similar, irrespective of their ages, and since they ran across country rather than through settlements which would deposit artefacts, they can be hard to date even when the cutting of roads or the laying of pipelines provide opportunities for archaeological excavation. Dykes that looked quite similar could serve different purposes, so that a **territory-marking dyke**, like Offa's Dyke or Dane's Dyke near Flamborough Head, will resemble **routeway-barring dykes**, like Devil's Dyke and Fleam Dyke, both in Cambridgeshire.

During the legendary times of King Arthur, when the power vacuum left by the Roman departure exposed England and Wales to barbarian attacks, British communities also attempted to refurbish and defend some of the decrepit prehistoric hillforts, like South Cadbury in Somerset. However, despite the Arthurian myths and the real terrors of life at these times, the Dark Ages did *not* produce exciting and revolutionary new castles. In the more rugged parts of Scotland members of the local ruling families occupied defended homesteads or **duns**. These consisted of a compact enclosure containing timber buildings that were built in lean-to fashion against a very massive, rubble-filled dry-stone wall. Duns had been around since about the start of the Iron Age but they were still being built and developed through the first millennium AD. The walls of these duns, resembling those of greatly scaled-down hillforts, can be found on many knolls, hillside shelves and crag-tops, especially around the western seaboard of Scotland. Otherwise, however, castles did not appear until the final stages of Saxon rule in England, when a few Norman favourites of Edward the Confessor built a small number of mottes on English soil.

After their victory at Hastings in 1066 the Normans dominated England, and later Wales, through an unpopular warrior aristocracy. The supporters of William, Duke of Normandy, were rewarded with estates forfeited by members of the former English ruling class. As they took control of these far-flung territories for the first time the Norman lords were vulnerable and often their first act was to create a makeshift stronghold that might later be improved. Most must have been built by the forced labour of their reluctant tenants. Various forms that did not require great constructional expertise or masonry were available.

Mottes, originating in France and the Rhineland, were huge, steep-sided mounds of earth excavated from a surrounding quarry ditch which some-times became a moat. These mounds were like flat-topped cones, with their circular summits being encircled by a palisade. The entrance was reached via a bridge over the moat and a spiralling track, and a timber gatehouse overlooked the entrance gate in the palisade. The range in size of the motte was immense, from the great borough-dominating examples at places like Cambridge or Thetford, with its 80ft-tall (24m) motte, to modest humps that might scarcely cow a handful of yokels. People do not tend to realise how small a motte could be.

Ringworks are seldom mentioned, though in some areas they were as important as mottes. Many were built soon after the Conquest, if not before, and most ringworks are rather like enlarged raths. Earth from the surrounding circular moat was cast inwards to form a steep bank resembling a ring doughnut. The bank would then be palisaded and the level internal space adapted for domestic life. Ringworks were exported to Scotland and Wales with the advance of feudalism, while some seem later to have had their interior spaces filled with earth to convert them to mottes.

The motte at Berkhamsted Castle, Hertfordshire.

Baileys were defensive enclosures with their own ramparts, ditches and palisades that could be attached to a motte or a ringwork. They offered the lord additional space within which to protect livestock and property, and secure sites for manorial buildings, stables and living space. On the other hand, they greatly increased the perimeter that the lord's retainers had to defend.

The remains of these early castles can often be discovered in the course of a ramble of discovery. In some locations, like the Welsh Marches, the military relics of feudalism may be encountered every half-mile or so. You should always remember that mottes can be quite small and unimposing. Some such modest mounds will sometimes have been used to support windmills. A few were converted from prehistoric barrows. Mottes were probably more effective as symbols of conquest rather than as means of physical domination and repression. Some were located to defensible positions, but others, like the one in the first village at Cublington in Buckinghamshire, stood on militarily poor lowland sites from where they glowered over the dwellings of the feudal community. Symbolic locations were exploited by some important examples, such as the one in Old Sarum hillfort, an ancient centre of control.

A very careful inspection of the remains can produce some interesting discoveries. For example, if the inner face of a bailey earthwork is seen not to be a smoothly arcing curve but rather to consist of several straight sections, one may deduce that it was cast up to surround straight-walled buildings that were already in position beside the moat.

If there are two or more medieval castle sites in your locality, consider whether they might be successive. For example, the archaeological evidence at Middleham in Wensleydale shows how the Norman intruders built a formidable ringwork on existing ridged ploughland at the crest of the valley slope. The site was well chosen, for the spring that filled the moat and provided a crucial supply of drinking water also revolved the wheel of a tiny mill. A bailey was added, but then growing prosperity and security urged a move to a much more commodious stone castle that was built on a shelf lower down the slope. This was a broad, squat **hall keep**, which offered more spacious accommodation than other stone towers.

Always consider the place-name evidence. Old field names gathered from farmers or old maps can be revealing. Names like Burrow Banks, Bury Mead, Castle Garth, Chester Lease and many more all have tales to tell.

8. THE CASTLE MOVES ON

Earthworks and palisades served their immediate purposes, but as baronial rivalries kept pace with the rising incomes of the status-conscious aristocrats, so they felt the need to obtain strongholds that were more secure, more permanent and more dynastic. However, the technology of offensive warfare was advancing quite rapidly and castles were obliged to evolve apace or risk perishing in successful assaults. The stages in this competition are embedded in the architecture of surviving castles and the following developments can be traced.

One means of strengthening a motte involved converting its palisade and (possible) timber tower into a thick-walled tower of stone: a **keep** or **donjon**. However, motte mounds were built of rubble, subsoil and slippery clay and it was often doubtful that a mound would, in fact, support a heavy stone structure without slumping into the moat with catastrophic results. Some keeps were built on motte mounds, but often they were erected as freestanding structures on firm foundations.

The load of masonry was more widely spread where a **shell keep** was adopted. This was a ring of thick stone walling that replaced the timber palisade running around the top of a motte mound or running around the ramparts of a ringwork. Buildings could be built in lean-to fashion against the inner face of this wall.

The towering stone keeps of the king and his greater barons were imposing symbols of feudal subjugation and dynastic power, but they were soon seen to have their weaknesses. If parties of sappers were able to undermine their angles then the corners of the towers would collapse and they could soon be stormed. Attempts were made to counter this by building the towers on massive splayed bases or plinths, as at Conisborough (meaning 'king's fort') in south Yorkshire. The necessity of keeping attackers away from the wall base remained, and was partly resolved by the use of **projecting towers**. These allowed defending archers or crossbowmen to sweep or enfilade the wall foot area between the towers, so that any sapping operations were driven underground.

The projecting towers or bastions could be employed in different ways. Some barons adopted a building plan derived from the bailey and its encircling defences and protected their homes with a **curtain wall** punctuated with **interval towers**. Alternatively, some pursued the keep concept and created a strengthened tower with turrets and enhanced gatehouse defences. Later the two concepts were merged, with a separate keep built on or inside the curtain wall. An early example of the latter was at Richmond in Swaledale, where the Norman keep was built above a gateway in the triangular bailey.

It also came to be appreciated that right-angled corners attracted sappers and towers were less vulnerable if built to rounded, polygonal or D-shaped plans.

Richmond Castle in Swaledale. Here, unusually, the great stone keep was built over the gateway to the triangular bailey.

Framlingham Castle in Suffolk, with early mural towers of a square type.

Thus a curtain wall with D-shaped towers is almost bound to be younger than one like Framlingham, in Suffolk, which has square towers.

Such developments were incorporated by the nobles who had the resources needed to keep abreast of the changes in castle design. The medieval castle achieved its highest development in the **concentric castles** built for Edward I (1272–1307) in his pacification of Wales. These had inner and outer wards, with the walls of the inner ward overlooking those of the outer. Such castles could position forces of bowmen armed with the formidable longbow on the raised battlements of the inner ward to fire outwards over the ranks of bowmen manning the outer, lower ward.

Concentric castles, perhaps most typically represented by the unfinished castle of Beaumaris on Anglesey, were the apogee of medieval military architecture. Thereafter, attention tended to focus on the gatehouse – and particularly upon the problem of creating a defensible bolt-hole for use if part of the mercenary garrison should change sides.

9. DEFENCE AND THE LESSER GENTRY

You are scarcely likely to stumble upon an undiscovered citadel of the king or one of his greater barons in the course of a country stroll (but one lives in hope!). However, the feudal castle had immense symbolic significance. Its battlements, moat and portcullis were emblems of status and power, and not surprisingly they were mimicked in the more modest creations of the lesser gentry. There might be times when vagabonds or organised robber bands roamed freely and there always seems to have been a loutish element in rural society. As a result it can be hard to deduce whether a little defence-work should be regarded as a status symbol, a refuge in times of cross-border raiding, or a place of safety to escape local ruffians. Of course some small strongholds might be all of these things. Examples that might be encountered are as follows.

Moats

The creation of homesteads surrounded, or partly surrounded, by moats was commonplace in England and Wales in the 150 years or so after about 1150, with 5,000 or more of them being made. The people who sought this kind of lifestyle ranged from the better-off free peasants or **franklins** to the aristocrats of sub-castle rank, who might own several manors, each with its own moated manor house. Meanwhile, the barons who did own castles would usually also have several manors, some with moated houses. Few of these moats had the sophistication of a formidable drawbridge that could be raised and none was broad enough to keep archers or artillery out of range. The moats might well have been valued at times of civil strife and anarchy, when scavengers and thieves roamed around. They might have held some rather unappetising fish, like tench or bream. They certainly echoed the moats of the great castles, and perhaps reflected a little of their glory. Inside the moat there was usually a modest timber-framed farmhouse, though occasionally there was a stone house with arrow slits and battlements. However, to fortify a house in such a way the occupant needed a special royal 'licence to **crenellate**'. This enabled the monarch to control the construction of potentially dangerous fortifications and to make some revenue from those that he did license. Unrecorded moats are among the most likely of discoveries, but do not expect always to see a perfectly rectangular example like the ones in the textbooks. Moats can be dry or heavily silted, have only three, two or even one side, while one arm of a moat may have been used as a tip by the neighbouring farmer. Occasionally a dump bank of some of the material excavated from the moat can be seen on its outer side, and rarely this shallow bank is more obvious than the heavily silted moat within.

Peles

In the south of England and the Midlands the building of small family defence-works came to an end with the moats. To the north, in Cumbria, Northumberland and other vulnerable territories, however, cross-border raiding and the realisation that kings had neither the resources nor the inclination to defend their border subjects resulted in a continuing tradition of fortification. Peles were defensive towers that appeared in the second half of the Middle Ages and persisted until the union of England and Scotland in 1707 signalled the end of border warfare. They ranged in scale from compact mini-castles to squat churchyard towers built to shelter a parson – yet seeming more like a death-trap than a refuge. Sometimes a protectively walled yard or **barmkin** was built beside the tower to hold livestock that was otherwise likely to be rustled in the course of a raid. Such yards were popular in the disturbed centuries bracketing the close of the Middle Ages.

Bastles

These defended houses proliferated in the decades following the close of the Middle Ages and were interspersed among the peles in the areas threatened by cross-border Scottish raiding. They were essentially fortified farmsteads with thickened walls, barred doors, ground floors that could accommodate cattle in

Nappa Hall in Wensleydale, an unusual pele with two towers.

times of danger and upper floors that were accessible only by means of a ladder removable from within, or sometimes via an external stone staircase. The bastles or bastle-houses were closely confined to the vicinity of the Scottish border and had a very restricted time-span, their day being well and truly over by 1707.

Tower houses

Tower houses revived memories of the long-defunct Norman keeps, though they had provision for more comfortable living and their wall bases were overlooked by projecting turrets. Immensely popular in Scotland, they were not confined to the lesser gentry; two Aberdeenshire tower houses, Craigievar, the early seventeenth-century stronghold of the Forbes family and Castle Fraser of around 1600, which proclaimed the power of the Frasers, were extremely imposing. The grander tower houses were home to the greater chieftains and lairds of clan

Craigievar Castle, near Aberdeen, is one of the most opulent of the seventeenth-century tower houses in North East Scotland. While the accommodation is spacious, no great effort was made to select a defensible site.

society, and since their owners were often men of great accomplishments and sophistication, they combined the means of civilised life with some defensive capabilities. Anyone doubting the symbolic importance of such places should see how the architecture, from the (possible) stone 'cannons' under the battlements downwards, proclaims the might of fortifications that may be more for display than for the harsh realities of defence.

10. DESIGNS FOR COURTLY LIFE

The greatest cause of the decline of castles in England and Wales was not gunpowder (some castles were specially adapted as platforms for the new cannon) but the centralised might of the Tudor monarchs, who put an end to baronial armies and their pretensions. In the meantime, however, castle life had advanced far beyond the rigours that Norman castle-makers may have endured. Interior chambers were colourful and draped with expensive hangings, troubadours had introduced romantic notions of courtly love, and the Arthurian legends had been rediscovered and interwoven with fashionable ideas about chivalry. The castle-dwelling communities were beginning to live the myths they had created, while outside the lofty windows the surrounding landscapes were being rearranged and embellished in a host of ways. Instead of just looking up at a castle, look out and around for any surviving aspects of the **designed landscape** that once surrounded it. Look especially at the approaches to the

Bodiam Castle in East Sussex occupied a designed landscape of sheets of reflecting water and surprise views.

castle. The approach roads were sometimes contrived so that the castle remained hidden and then suddenly burst into view. It might seem to be floating on the water of a carefully engineered artificial lake, and the final approach might be made via a low, water-flanked causeway. Such expanses of water may have vanished with the decay of leets and the silting up of little canals, but the levels of the ground may still hint at a former lake.

Water offered lots of recreational possibilities, including fishing and boating. Ponds provided in the adjacent deer park would have served in such ways. Some presumed 'moats' should probably be regarded more as water features than as defences.

Any castle of distinction would have had a garden, a carefully tended place with arbours and turf benches for dalliances, medicinal herbs and fragrant blossoms growing in neat, geometrical beds. Such gardens were normally placed on the south, sunny, side of a medieval castle, just outside the walls. Most disappeared long ago, but if the ground concerned has not been redeveloped you may be able to recognise the terraces and pathways of the former garden. Many such examples are probably still to be recognised. Somewhere beyond the neat garden there may also have been a **wilderness** with plants growing in more natural ways.

Deer parks (see Chapter Eight) were normally placed close to their parent castles, with the battlements providing perches for the ladies watching the hunt. Great use was made of vantage points and sometimes special towers or turrets were provided for observing the chase. The views from the top of a castle may reveal clues about the use of contrived features and vantage points.

Use your imagination. A damsel at a high window on the south side of an imaginary castle might smell the fragrance rising on the breeze and look out across the clipped shrubs, turf and little plant beds of the castle garden towards the lawns and groves of the deer park, where greyhounds chased the unfortunate fallow deer. Were she squeamish, she might turn her gaze to the wilderness, the fishponds or the horses of the baggage train, now grazing in a paddock nearby after the journey from another manor. The cruelty of the chase apart, there would probably be nothing in her view that was unharmonious. Had there been, it would have been removed.

Only quite recently we realised that landscaping was not invented by Lancelot 'Capability' Brown and his kind. A great deal remains to be discovered about the carefully contrived countrysides associated with medieval castles, abbeys and priories, and this is a promising topic for any enthusiast.

11. INSECURITY MARCHES ON

As the Middle Ages drew to a close 'real' castles disappeared. In England, united under successive Tudor monarchs of unchallenged authority, attention was directed away from internal rivalries and towards the threat of foreign invasion, which had been heightened by the Reformation and the break with Rome. Strongholds of many varying kinds continued to be built and their remains are often found. They include the following.

Sham castles

Although sophisticated fortifications were no longer built by members of the aristocracy, the castle was still a powerful symbol of dynastic authority. Consequently nobles built houses that had the outward trappings of castles, but were really comfortable homes lavishly equipped with suites of rooms for accommodating guests and their retinues. However, the relatively thin walls and large window openings of these 'palace castles' tell their own story.

Henry's artillery forts

In the years after 1539 Henry VIII, who was fearful of a Catholic invasion, caused a string of artillery forts and bulwarks to be built along the likely invasion coast of southern and south-eastern England. Frequently built of materials pillaged from ransacked monasteries, these forts were essentially platforms for cannon and housed garrisons for their defence in the event of infantry landings nearby.

Martello towers

These were drum-shaped buildings copied from a type that had impressed English commanders in the Mediterranean. Rather in the tradition of the Henrician forts, they were a response to the threat of invasion by Napoleon's forces. In all 103 towers were built, being constructed of brick; their walls were some 13ft (4m) thick on the seaward side and they had cannon mounted on their flat roofs and small garrisons inside. Some forty-five examples survive, of which only nine are in their original condition. The one at Dymchurch has been restored and is open to the public.

Relics of modern warfare

There are enough relics of recent conflicts around to interest and occupy a large swarm of enthusiasts. In the frenzy of modern warfare that took civilian

Martello Tower, Dymchurch. The Martello tower was a standardised artillery platform that housed a small garrison for defence against landing parties.

Town walls were symbols of status in the medieval world. As well as serving the needs of defence and regulating the comings and goings of traders, they also proclaimed the independence of the town or city from its feudal surroundings. Only one of York's barbicans survived nineteenth-century road-widening operations.

conurbations as its targets, records of the disposal of defences might be badly kept or lost. In many cases we have the relics of recent conflict, but the doctrines and strategies that spawned them have to be re-created. The airfields in eastern England that launched innumerable bomber raids are gradually surrendering to agriculture; pillboxes that guarded key points in the locality may still stand, though one may not yet have recovered the logic behind their patterns: in fact, they were all links in defensive chains. Relics of features like former searchlights, anti-aircraft and communications installations may mislead the landscape detective. We tend to look quite deeply into the past for our answers and may overlook more recent explanations.

SEVEN

Lost Villages

1. SOME IDEAS ABOUT LOST VILLAGES

'Lost villages are most unusual and there are very few sites that are known'
WRONG
'Most lost villages were deserted because their communities were wiped out by
the Black Death' WRONG
'Villages are fragile places that are very sensitive to changes in society and their
environment' RIGHT
'Many hundreds of villages have perished since the start of the Middle Ages'
RIGHT

2. MEETING VULNERABLE VILLAGES

In prehistoric times, in Roman times more often than not, and even in the
earlier centuries of the Anglo-Saxon era, villages were deserted as a matter of
course. The archaeological evidence for some prehistoric settlements and others
of the Dark Ages strongly implies that a community was resettling within a
locality after anything from a generation to a century or so of occupation at a
particular site. The reasons for this **desertion habit** are uncertain, but perhaps
the sites simply became foul after a few generations of human occupation?
Certainly the old settlements were unsanitary places where infection and
contamination could build up. However, medieval villages were scarcely more
hygienic, yet they persisted (see Chapter Four).

From about AD 800–900 villages seem to have been founded with the intent
that they *would* persist. Investment in costly churches of stone helped to tie a
community to one place, and it may have been harder to relocate when the
fields, taxation and property systems became entrenched; furthermore the manor
house and its court may also have had a stabilising effect. How, then, was it
possible for villages to be destroyed?

Godwick deserted village in Norfolk, a county that had a very large medieval rural population and proportionately large levels of desertion.

Under the feudal system of the Middle Ages the lord and his tenants/ bondsmen were linked by obligations on both sides, with the lords notionally defending their subordinates. In reality, the relationship was a one-sided one and lords could usually uproot feudal communities without redress. Even in the unlikely event that a king was sympathetic to his humblest subjects, there was no political logic in his siding with a community of bondsmen against an influential baron whose support he one day might need. Malnutrition, over-population, famine and epidemics could all reduce and weaken a village community, making it easier for a tyrannical landlord to remove a village.

Feudal society was a martial society of aristocrats either engaged in war or preparing for it. Conflict, whether national, regional or local, erupted quite frequently and at such times villages would habitually be pillaged and burned.

Normally they recovered, though some campaigns, like the genocidal Harrying of the North of 1069–71, impacted profoundly on the settlement pattern.

The Church offered salvation to members of the martial elite and was thus in a unique position of power, but it seldom used its influence to defend the weak. Its immunity from lay institutions might sometimes be questioned, as in the confrontation between Henry II and Thomas Becket, but the freedom of bishops, abbots or priors to run their estates as they pleased allowed countless evictions from Church lands. Christian principles seem seldom to have intruded between powerful Churchmen and their lay tenants.

The great majority of medieval villages existed as dormitories for the armies of servile land-workers, as described in Chapter Four. Where villages were sited on thin, hungry soils, the land could quickly become exhausted and the community might drift away to find better prospects. Changes in the climate could turn heavy land into a morass or undermine the livelihood of upland villages. Confronted by pressures from landlords, a deteriorating farming environment, rising rents and the lure of neighbouring towns and more prosperous villages nearby, a village might see its population bleed away over successive decades.

Therefore the village community can be seen to have walked a tightrope, never knowing when a challenge to its survival might arise. It could come from men of power and influence with new plans for the locality, from armies or skirmishers, or from transformations in the fickle environment – an environment either abused by farmers or changing under its own impetus. However, once the notion of the permanent village had taken root and permanence had become the norm, the seemingly aimless drift of settlement came to an end and there had to be a *reason* for any village desertion.

3. WHY WERE VILLAGES DESERTED?

War

Battles raged through villages on many occasions. The village of Branxton was caught up in the Battle of Flodden (1513) and Long Marston found itself squeezed between Royalist and Parliamentary cavalry at Marston Moor in 1644. Dozens of villages in the north of England were severely damaged by Scottish raiders following the English defeat at Bannockburn in 1314. However, one could not kill a village just by burning its buildings. The villagers always returned. One of very few possible war victims was the Yorkshire village of Leake near Northallerton, which was said to have been depopulated by 'The Black Douglas' and his Border raiders in 1318.

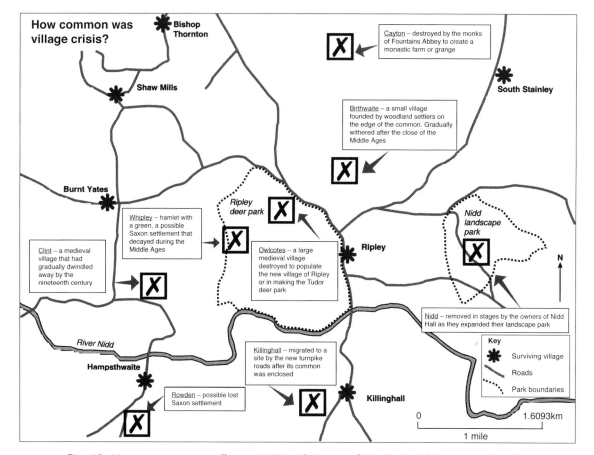

How common was village crisis?

Bishop Thornton

Cayton – destroyed by the monks of Fountains Abbey to create a monastic farm or grange

Shaw Mills

South Stanley

Birthwaite – a small village founded by woodland settlers on the edge of the common. Gradually withered after the close of the Middle Ages

Burnt Yates

Ripley deer park

Nidd landscape park

N

Whipley – hamlet with a green, a possible Saxon settlement that decayed during the Middle Ages

Ripley

Clint – a medieval village that had gradually dwindled away by the nineteenth century

Owlcotes – a large medieval village destroyed to populate the new village of Ripley or in making the Tudor deer park

Nidd – removed in stages by the owners of Nidd Hall as they expanded their landscape park

River Nidd

Hampsthwaite

Killinghall – migrated to a site by the new turnpike roads after its common was enclosed

Killinghall

Rowden – possible lost Saxon settlement

Key

Surviving village

Roads

Park boundaries

0   1.6093km

1 mile

Fig. 15. How common was village crisis? In this area of North Yorkshire, measuring less than 5 by 3.5 miles, there are many examples of village desertion, with a range of causes being apparent.

William the Conqueror's Harrying of the North was rather different, for the destruction of communities and crops in the north-eastern counties of England was not incidental to the campaign but rather its goal. It transformed the patterns of rural settlement.

Monks

Members of holy orders seem unlikely assassins, yet they were responsible for removing numerous villages. The White Monks (Cistercians) arrived in England at Waverley in Surrey in 1128. They were unusual in that they desired isolation from contamination by lay people and sought lives of austerity in desolate settings. Rievaulx, in the Rye valley on the edge of the North York Moors, was founded in 1132. In Yorkshire the Cistercians found the desolation they desired in the lands around their abbeys, and several more sprang up there, including Fountains, Byland and Meaux. This desolation was enhanced by the removal of over a dozen villages, such as Cayton and Herleshow that once stood on the doorstep of Fountains Abbey. The monks liked to impress the public, particularly potential donors, with **foundation myths** that glorified the hardships and tribulations that the community had faced in establishing an abbey or priory. In reality, the settings were not particularly challenging and the real hardships were faced by the victims of eviction.

Another generation of villages was destroyed when villages and hamlets were replaced by monastic farms or **granges**. Though the Cistercians had begun by seeking simplicity and austerity, they experienced remarkable worldly success and had 500 abbeys in Europe by 1200 and 750 abbeys by the fifteenth century. With such wealth and influence, they were able to operate their far-reaching estates as they pleased.

The environment

Environmental conditions are always in a state of evolution. If people pack the countryside to the maximum levels when conditions are unusually favourable,

This was the site of Herleshow, a village destroyed by Cistercian monks because it lay on the doorstep of Fountains Abbey.

then disasters will inevitably threaten whenever those conditions worsen. This happened in the years after about 1300. Up till then climate had steadily been improving, luring communities to settle in ever more marginal areas. Then it turned sharply in a cool, cyclonic direction. Summers were cloudy and wet so that crops would not ripen and hay would not dry, while cattle were afflicted with disease and there was foot rot among the flocks. Meanwhile, the coast was assailed by storms and flooding and settlements on the eastern and southern sides of Holderness were inundated.

These tribulations imposed on a bloated population produced weakness and stress, so that communities were less able to cope with the other challenges of the fourteenth century, such as Scottish raiding and the Black Death.

Of course, some environmental threats are beyond human control. For example, the eruption of Mount Hekla in Iceland about the end of the Middle

The village of Cublington in Buckinghamshire was devastated by the Black Death, but higher ground nearby was resettled and this church was built there.

The village of Wensley in Wensleydale was hit hard by the Black Death in 1563, leaving a hamlet with a church far too large for the surviving community.

Bronze Age period threw masses of ash and dust particles into the atmosphere. This resulted in a darkening of the skies and a cooling that is thought to have resulted in the wholesale abandonment of the British uplands (see Chapter Nine).

Plague

Terrible epidemics were commonplace among societies in the Middle Ages but the Pestilence or Black Death was unusually terrifying and devastating. The Black Death (its cause and nature are now disputed) arrived in England in 1348 and destroyed around 40 per cent of the British population. It returned many times before disappearing in the seventeenth century. It does seem permanently to have exterminated a few villages, but not many. Though communities could be almost annihilated, so long as the village lands were fair and fertile, then new populations were almost always attracted.

However, village communities weakened by the plague could be easy targets in the next round of adversity. Similarly a famine following harvest failure weakened populations so that they were less able to resist plague, cholera, typhoid and the various other illnesses that stalked the village.

Sheep

Seemingly dim and docile creatures, sheep were the greatest threat to village life, first in England and much later in Scotland. They destroyed far more villages than all the preceding threats put together.

Before the Black Death, and following a long phase of agreeable weather, the land was overpopulated. As a result there were more tenants than holdings, and labour was cheap. After it, both tenants and labourers were in short supply and for the first time in generations they were in a position to argue for better terms. On some manors lords threatened with the defection of their now-valuable tenants to neighbouring manors or to the expanding towns offered better terms. The remorseless demands for feudal services on the lord's demesne or for special gifts, like eggs or hens at certain seasons, were reduced or cancelled. A new class of tenants paying rent in cash appeared, while official attempts to peg back labour rates foundered.

Wharram Percy in the Yorkshire Wolds was a victim of Tudor sheep evictions. As the result of excavations spanning several decades it is our best-known deserted village.

Milton Abbas was created as a replacement for the Dorset country town of Milton that was demolished to make way for a park and lake for the Earl of Dorchester in the late eighteenth century.

However, many other landlords turned to the example set by the Cistercians, inspired by the fortunes they had made from sheep farming. In the Tudor era whole strings of villages were pulled down and the farmland converted to sheep ranges. In these places landlords derived their income from the flocks rather than from the rents and services rendered by feudal tenants. Solitary shepherds roamed fields that had once been crowded with village labour forces.

Landscape parks

The medieval aristocrats had lived in fortified manor houses and castles which often stood in villages. When the changes in the scale and cost of war and the concentration of power under the Tudor monarchs made the baronial castles redundant, the aristocrats looked for new ways to display their status. In this way the feudal castle was replaced by the stately mansion and its landscape park (see Chapters One and Eight). Unfortunately for the villages caught up in the new arrangements, the parks were cleared of any humdrum settlements of tenants, leaving the mansion and the old village church in isolation. Whether a new village was built to house the evicted villagers outside the park, or whether they were simply cast out on the road depended largely upon the lord concerned.

4. WHAT DO WE FIND AT LOST VILLAGE SITES?

Each site is a little different. The nature of the traces of the old village will depend on its appearance and layout before its departure; the way in which it went (for example, whether it perished at a single stroke or gradually dwindled away), and the uses made of the site after its death. Thousands of villages have been lost, and even though their dwellings have usually gone there is almost invariably some evidence remaining for the landscape detective to recognise.

Churches

One might imagine that, even if they tore down a village, lords would respect the sanctity of the parish church. In fact, churches were repositories of a rare and valuable commodity: dressed stone. Generally a church would be robbed of its stone, even having its foundations dug out, so that the old church site may be hard to find. There were many cases, however, where the church also served a neighbouring township where the community survived, and so it would tend to remain in use. Sometimes it would be shortened, narrowed or lowered to reflect the reduced needs of the smaller congregation (see Chapter Five).

Occasionally the robbed church stone would be reused in the local manor house or elsewhere around the manor. Occasionally it was used in building a new church at a different site in the parish, as at Ripley near Harrogate. The church might easily have been the only stone building in a village and any stone litter at a lost village site, particularly if some stones have been dressed, might well be the remains of a church.

If no decent building stone was available, as occurred in chalk downland country, then the body of the church would be built of flint nodules (derived from fossilised sea organisms) that often form seams in the chalk. Such nodules litter the fields in chalky localities so that there was no point in dismantling the abandoned church, except, perhaps, to remove the imported sandstone slabs and blocks used to make the lintels and quoins or corners. This is why crumbling flint churches are such characteristic landmarks in chalk and flint country, like much of Norfolk.

When villagers were evicted from a landscape park, the old village church frequently survived. The old congregation, now housed outside the park, might come in to worship on Holy Days. Often the church was effectively converted into a mausoleum for the proud family living in the mansion close by. Its interior became festooned with family memorials, so that the proverbial Martian might imagine the building was erected to worship the dynasty installed in the hall nearby, rather than the Almighty. Usually the earthworks of the lost settlement form undulations in the park outside.

Wherever you see a church standing in isolation, you ask whether it is a church that has always stood alone in a setting where farmsteads and hamlets are the norm; whether it marks the site of a lost village; or whether it could have been built to Christianise a pagan site, such as one with holy springs or wells, and so to take over the sanctity of the place. Examples can be found to demonstrate each possibility (see Chapters Four and Five).

Roads and lanes

As feet, hooves and cart wheels passed along a trackway it would gradually be worn down into the ground to form a **holloway** (or hollow way). These vary greatly in depth. This partly reflects the amount and nature of the traffic they carried, but also reflects the local topography, with holloways becoming more deeply incised where they ascend/descend a convex slope, like the brow of a hill.

Holloways are normally the most obvious of the earthworks at a lost village site, taking the appearance of troughs, sometimes quite shallow, with the widths of modest lanes rather than of modern main roads. They can often be followed heading across country to their old destinations: do not be surprised by the narrowness of most old lanes.

Where there are several holloways, the biggest one is likely to be the remains of the main through-road that so often formed the spine of the village, while the smaller ones may have been tracks to the fields, back lanes running along the margins of the house plots and gardens, or alleys between dwellings. Some villages took shape around greens, but most had their outlines determined by the spine of the through-road and the ribs of the tributary lanes.

A holloway alone does not signify a lost village site. Lots of roads have been abandoned and former lanes can be found in landscape parks, running across commons or beside old hedgerows in places well away from actual village sites. However, lost village or hamlet sites are suspected in places where several lanes and footpaths converge, for no apparent reason, at a place now devoid of settlement. Formerly they linked the community to their fields and the world beyond. At Great Childerley in Cambridgeshire (see below) five holloways can be seen to converge on the deserted village site.

House sites

These may not be obvious. Often the survival of evidence depends on how the houses were built. Dwellings of posts, wattle, mud, dung and cow-hair daub and thatch will soon tend to subside into a slumping mass of dirt, sticks and straw, though walls of stone rubble or footings of rubble tend to leave more traces. Whether the wall footings are overgrown by turf or still exposed, stone walls leave better traces, whether viewed from the ground or the air.

When most traces of walls have gone, the outline of a **house platform** may well remain. This is a level rectangular area representing the old floor space and tracing the dimensions of a building. I always think of medieval house platforms as being about the size and shape, although somewhat elongated, of one of those little old buses that plied the country lanes in the 1930s.

In better-preserved cases the house platform may have a slightly raised rim, representing the house walls, and a notch in the front wall (and sometimes also the back) marking the doorways. Normally the long walls were parallel to the roadside, with the door facing the road or any ribbon of green that flanked it. Frequently a **cross-passage** spanned the short distance between the front and back doors. In earlier medieval houses of the **longhouse** type, this marked the divide between the space where the family lived and that occupied by their cow or ewe. In the best-preserved sites both front and back doors are marked by opposed notches in the earthworks.

The main domestic building in or beside the medieval village was the **manor house**. These lordly dwellings were frequently moated (see Chapter Six), with the moats being more likely to survive as earthworks than the house itself, which would often be built of timber, wattle, daub and thatch. The moats sometimes protected just two or three sides of the house and the four-sided moats shown in textbooks were by no means the standard. Look for earthworks like deep holloways that bend sharply to form rectangular or trapezoidal shapes, sometimes in the form of L or C shapes. Sometimes a low **counterscarp bank** of soil upcast from digging the moat was left on the outer edge of the moat, and this may survive as a ridge, even in places where silting has filled the moat itself. The typical manor moat may have deterred small bands of robbers or kept the local louts at bay, but it was probably mainly a status symbol that mimicked the moats of the higher-status castles.

Other earthworks

- **Fishponds**. Manors frequently had fishponds that provided lawful protein on Fridays and held a reserve of food for the feeding of visiting parties (see also Chapter Two). The lord and his retinue or a large host of visitors might suddenly descend on a manor and the fishponds provided abundant fresh food. At such times the fish would have been netted, but there is also evidence that pond-fishing was also an adjunct to the aristocratic hunting in the deer park (see Chapter Eight). The ponds seem to have been stocked, at least in part, by fish hooked and netted in nearby rivers and lakes, and there were often chains of ponds of increasing size to accommodate fry and young fish destined for the main pond as they grew. Filled by local springs and streams, or fed by little aqueducts, the ponds were generally quite shallow. They seem to have been drained periodically so that a bumper harvest could be grown in the rich detritus of the fishpond floor. They can be recognised by the earthworks of the low retaining banks and can be square, elongated or trapezoidal in form. Some were placed on hillsides with strong retaining banks on the down-slope side. Where the pond was more ornamental in function, a walkway would follow the flattened crest of the bank.

- **Ridge and furrow**. Plough ridges were produced in arable land that was deliberately ploughed to form corrugations like corduroy (see Chapter Two). Ridge and furrow alone is not an indication of a lost village site. Rather it often begins at the place where the house plots of the village ended and the farmland began. Thus the regular corrugations are an indication of where the village was *not*. However, the fields of villages destroyed in Tudor times were usually turned over to pasture. Safe beneath the sward, the ridge and furrow will have survived, and wherever it is seen in old pastures or parkland, the question of 'where did the ploughmen live?' is raised.

- **Village greens**. These areas of common land often lay in the heart of the old settlements (see Chapter Four). They would not normally be built upon or ploughed, so at lost village sites they can appear as level areas without earthworks of buildings or ridge and furrow. However, before a village fell, its green might have been encroached upon by buildings if alternative sites had been lacking. Greens were either encircled by roads if they had compact forms, or formed narrow ribbons of common grazing alongside a through road; a few were far more expansive.

- **Boundaries**. Hedges, ditches, walls and banks separated the different village properties. Very often in medieval villages the houses were aligned along the roadside and long garden plots or **tofts** ran back from the dwellings to a back lane (see Chapter Four). The tofts were used for cultivation and for keeping animals like pigs, chickens or milk cows. Boundaries between them were formed by hedges, ditches or wattle fencing. Sometimes the houses stood in compact enclosures or closes rather than at the ends of tofts. Narrow troughs or faint banks may mark both these kinds of boundaries between households at lost village sites. Where hedges and ditches were used, the ditches are likely to leave the more durable traces, unless old pollarded trees originating in the village hedgerows still form recognisable alignments. Where walls were used lines of parched vegetation, like those sometimes seen marking the courses of old house walls, may sometimes be recognised during summer droughts.

5. FINDING LOST VILLAGES

Ruined dwellings may only be seen standing at the most recently deserted villages, like old mining and quarrying settlements – and even there they tend to be bulldozed to discourage vagrants and squatters. However, villages do not disappear completely and eyes can be trained to recognise the clues. Not all the deserted medieval villages have been discovered – I found three more at the start of this millennium. Here are some of the clues:

- **Map clues**. The farmland was divided between villages that were fairly evenly spaced: there was a limit to the distance that a plough could be dragged to an outlying plough strip. Thus it made more sense for the farm labour force to be distributed in villages dispersed across an area rather than concentrated in towns. In much of Somerset, for example, substantial villages tend to be around 3 miles apart, with smaller villages or large hamlets in the intervening spaces. Look at the pattern of villages in your area on the modern map and see if there are any suggestive gaps in the network. If there are, explore them in closer detail.
- **Old maps**. Maps drawn in the nineteenth century or earlier could pick up the final stages in the death of a settlement. Most useful are sixteenth- and seventeenth-century estate maps and mid nineteenth-century tithe maps, which should be available in the county record office. Almost equally useful maps may be held in your main reference library, such as the first edition of the Ordnance Survey 6in to a mile map from around 1850. Various commercial cartographers drew maps at scales of 1in to a mile in the second half of the eighteenth century, and these often record villages that subsequently died, especially the victims of Georgian park-making. Any old map is worth looking at closely, to see if settlements have vanished, drifted, shrunk or been reorganised in the intervening years. A map of 1586 was most helpful for it marked 'The place where the towne of Whateborough stoode'. This Leicestershire 'town' was actually a lost village, the word town being applied freely to villages in the past.

- **Tracks and paths**. The empty places in the countryside where routeways, including public footpaths, are seen to converge may well once have been settlements. A convergence of routes does not always prove the former existence of a village – a hamlet or an inn might have been the attraction.

- **Place-names**. The old village place-name sometimes survives tied to a farmstead or a field and thus acts as a grave-marker for the old settlement. Norton Hall marked the site of Pudding Norton deserted village in Norfolk. The use of 'town' rather than 'village' was normal, and any lane called 'Town Lane' may well have served a (lost?) village. Look out for double-barrelled place-names. Where two villages evolved from one estate, different prefixes, based on size, relative direction, church dedications and so on, were used to differentiate between them, like Great and Little Plumstead or Weasenham St Peter and Weasenham All Saints in Norfolk (see Chapter Four). Thus in the Yorkshire Wolds there is still a Wharram le Street, but Wharram Percy is Britain's best-known lost village site. Sometimes a *lost* village name will be preserved because it is bracketed with that of a *surviving* village in a combined parish, like Norfolk's Horstead-with-Stanninghall, where there is the village of Horstead but just a ruined church and 'Staininghall' Farm.

The ruins of the church at Pudding Norton in Norfolk. Walls of flint were not worth robbing for stone.

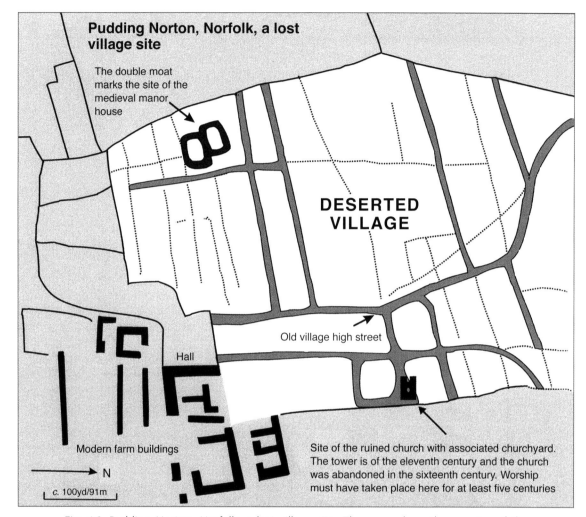

Fig. 16. Pudding Norton, Norfolk: a lost village site. The area where the remains of the village can be traced is shown in white; village streets and lanes are grey; broken lines show the boundaries between medieval house plots. In 1557 money was left for the repair of the church, but by 1602 it was said to be wholly ruined and to have been long since pulled down by unknown hands.

- **An isolated church**. As explained above, this could once have been surrounded by the dwellings of a community. However, this cannot be assumed and some regions with ancient settlement patterns mainly of farmsteads and hamlets are associated with free-standing churches. If the ruins preserve traces of a shrinking congregation – demolished side aisles, a lowered roof line (look for signs of gabled roof lines on the tower) or an abandoned chancel – then the lost village attribution is more likely.

- **Earthworks**. All the earthwork features, like holloways, house platforms, boundaries and fishponds, tend to be found in association at deserted village sites, though fishponds and warrens sometimes stood in isolation in a park. The degree to which they are obvious depends on whether stone was used as a building material and whether at some stage after the village was abandoned the site was levelled by ploughing. Earthwork patterns are much more easily interpreted in air photographs: check the coverage available at your main reference library, county record office or heritage unit, but remember that what is revealed depends very much on the altitude of the aeroplane, the weather and the state of crops at the time a photograph was taken.

- **Hedgerows**. Lengths of hedgerow, often gappy and unkempt, with maybe only a few pollarded trees remaining, might *just* have survived to mark the alignments of boundaries between long-lost village tenancies. Where the degradation of the old boundary hedges has gone a long way, it may not at first be apparent that the few trees in view actually form alignments.

- **Stones**. Many village dwellings were built of poor-quality timber, mud, wattle and thatch. During the Middle Ages efforts were made to raise above ground level the timbers on which houses rested to reduce rotting of the beams that were in contact with damp earth. Stone footings of locally quarried rubble were often used, while in stone-rich localities some dwellings were completely walled or encased in stone. Scatters of stone are always likely to be informative and if one can see exposed stones forming a corner or alignment, gentle probing with an iron-tipped stick may reveal the outlines of a house or barn lying hidden just beneath the turf.

- **Nettles**. Stinging nettles flourish in enriched ground, such as might be found over an earthen house floor that may have been coated with ox blood and had bones and other food remnants trodden into it over many years. Not all nettle patches indicate former dwellings, but when the patch is squarish in form and room-like in size then suspicions are aroused.

If you think that you may have discovered a lost village site, make sure that it is properly recorded and protected by reporting it to the archaeological or heritage unit of your local authority. If you are not sure, report it anyway and your interest should be welcomed.

6. SOME EXAMPLES

These examples help to show the way a picture (usually incomplete) can be pieced together from different strands of evidence.

Great and Little Childerley, Cambridgeshire

The two villages, Great Childerley, quite large, and Little Childerley, smaller, stood close together at a convergence of local routeways. In 1279 the hundred rolls recording tenants and their tenure show that both settlements seem to have been quite healthy, supporting eight free families and sixteen families of bondsmen and four free and nineteen bond families respectively. This situation continued for at least another century, for seventy-six villagers from the Childerleys paid the Poll Tax in 1377, and more may have managed to evade the collectors. However, problems of some kind, perhaps plague, occurred in the decades that followed, for the communities were granted relief from taxation in 1432 and 1489 – a sign of communities under stress and in decline, though the land around was still being worked in the traditional open fields at this time. Early in the sixteenth century some enclosures of the old village lands were reported and this seems to have signified the beginning of the end, for in the reign of Charles I (1625–49) the Childerleys were destroyed in the enlargement of Sir John Cutt's deer park. This example illustrates how misfortune was drawn towards those places that had already experienced hardship and had perhaps lost the ability to resist lustily.

Water Eaton, Oxfordshire

The locality was producing both grain and wool in the thirteenth century, but in 1359 the village and its land were taken over by Oseney Abbey, though village life continued. After the Dissolution of the monasteries, much monastic land passed to speculators and profiteers. At the close of the sixteenth century, the village seems to have been torn down by rioters objecting to the enclosure of village fields and commons; they blamed a certain Mr Fryer for the death of Water Eaton and the hedging-about of its open lands.

The Candovers, Hampshire

These seem to have been the small sorts of settlement that attracted trouble, with only eight taxpayers living at Chilton Candover in 1327. This village fell under the control of a man called Fisher, who destroyed the settlement in the 1560s, presumably enclosing the land for sheep, leaving only a church and a farm remaining. The church stood until it was demolished in 1876. In 1595 Brown Candover went the way of its neighbour, destroyed by one Mr Corham. Its church also stood for centuries more, being burned down in 1845.

Owlcotes and Birthwaite, Ripley, North Yorkshire

Owlcotes, meaning 'owl cottages', was recorded in the second half of the twelfth century. When I discovered it, lying just inside the wall of the Tudor deer park, I also found pottery that suggested the village had its heyday in the twelfth and thirteenth centuries and declined thereafter. It might have been depopulated, as so many villages were, when the park was created. However, I suspect that it had gone by then. It may well have been depopulated in the decades following the arrival of the Black Death. This was a time when the new lords of the Ingilby dynasty reorganised the patterns of settlement and worship on their estate, so that Owlcotes, a substantial village, may have had its population transferred to the new village of Ripley. The new village accommodated a new church and market and was under the gaze of the fortified manor house.

Birthwaite was a very different sort of place, a small frontier village on higher ground at the entrance to the partly wooded common. It stood in an area with numerous names associated with the clearance of woodland and must have been founded by a community of assarters. Though always small, it lasted longer than its neighbour down the hill, for in 1607 the manor court ordered the inhabitants of Birthwaite to correct the course of the stream that ran from their green. Thereafter the village seems to have dwindled away.

Lillingstone Dayrell, Buckinghamshire

At the end of the fifteenth century the estate belonged to the Earl of Oxford and was tenanted by one Thomas Darrell. In 1493 he enclosed 164 acres (66ha) of village land and some forty people were evicted. Only the manor house was left standing, yet by getting rid of the villagers Darrell caused the value of the land to double. This, however, was a time of mounting anger against enclosure and eviction. The authorities, concerned that the highways were swarming with desperate victims of eviction, fostering a climate of revolution, attempted to reverse the trend and bring the detested enclosers to book. Around 1519 Darrell promised to rebuild seven houses. But he and his son managed to evade the ruling and the case went through eighteen adjournments until it was dropped in 1545. Justice was greatly impeded by the fact that those serving in the courts came from the same social background as those brought before them to answer for evictions – indeed, often they were friends and hunting partners.

7. THE LOST SETTLEMENTS OF THE SCOTTISH HIGHLANDS

The beautiful landscapes of the Scottish Highlands are now soulful and desolate, but once they bustled with activity. Between about 1750 and 1900, when village destruction associated with landscape parks was petering out in England, the Scottish Highlands experienced a wave of sheep evictions that was more ferocious even than those that had ravaged Tudor England. These were the notorious **Clearances**. They were enacted on the brink of modern times and the wounds are still unhealed. Most countrysides in the Scottish Highlands still resemble battlefields, strewn with the crumbling corpses of homes.

The Clearances followed the Jacobite defeat at Culloden in 1746, after which both the traditional chieftains and the English interlopers who took over forfeit estates attempted to put the affairs of the Highlands on a modern economic footing. For untold generations the Highland clan chiefs had measured their status according to the numbers of armed retainers they could summon when the fiery cross was borne through the clan territories. Unlike the situation on English manors, here the clansfolk regarded their chieftain as an ancestral father figure as well as an overlord. Within their clan homelands the rule of the chief was almost absolute and loyalty to him was regarded as the paramount virtue.

But because status was measured in terms of the size of the clan army, chieftains were encouraged to overpopulate their territories accordingly. The defeat at Culloden pitched the Highlands into the world of commerce and profitability. Taking rents from the impoverished farmers of the clan was less rewarding than giving the estate over to commercial flocks and their solitary shepherds. Now, loyal Gaelic-speaking subjects were evicted from their homelands and driven to become crofters on the distant coasts, to take passage on emigrant ships or to find work in factories in the Lowland Scots or English-speaking lands to the south.

The features of the old Highlands countryside included the following:

- An absence of villages of the conventional type. People lived in hamlets or **group farms** where small communities worked the surrounding lands.
- In the Gaelic-speaking areas these hamlets were known as **clachans** and in the North East, where a form of Lowland Scots based on English was spoken, they were **fermtouns** ('farm towns').
- The hamlets were distinguished according to whether they possessed a church (**kirk touns**) or a mill (**mill touns**). Often this distinction appeared in the name of the settlement, like Kirkton of Logie Buchan and Milton of

Minnes, near Aberdeen. More common are names associated with the chief or demesne farm on an estate (known as Mains), such as Mains of Orchardtown, near the previous examples.

- The old clachans existed as rather disorderly scatters and straggles of buildings and lacked the more formally structured organisation of dwellings around greens and along lanes that one associates with English and continental villages.

- Their land was often worked on an **infield-outfield system**. The best land of the in-field, usually near the settlement, was kept in constant cultivation, mainly for oats. In order to keep its fertility high, it received all the accumulations of manure and animals were penned on it whenever possible (see Chapter Four). This land was ridged, rather like the ridge and furrow in the English lands, and was divided into strip patterns. Beyond lay the out-field, parts of which were periodically cultivated to exhaustion and then abandoned to recover during a long phase as pasture. Beyond this out-field area lay the open grazings of the moors and marshes, generally poor-quality pasture that never experienced cultivation. Damp flood-plain land in the nearby straths or glens would be mowed for hay.

- These meagre resources provided families in the Highlands with a basic diet of oat products and milk. The arrival of root crops helped a little and the introduction of potatoes underwrote an increase in population. The failure of the potato crop in the mid-nineteenth century hit hard, though not as severely as in famine-struck Ireland. Essentially the whole region was grossly overpopulated and this was as much a factor in the disaster of the Clearances as the harshness of the class of native and alien lairds.

8. HOW CAN WE RECOGNISE THE LOST CLACHANS AND FERMTOUNS?

Because their desertion was relatively recent, their houses were frequently built of stone and there has seldom been any ploughing of their sites, the evidence is usually quite obvious. In contrast to the medieval deserted village sites, at the clachans we may see buildings still standing, often right up to their roof lines.

The standing gable-end walls of single-storey cottages are frequently markers of deserted clachans and farmsteads, signalling the existence of the deserted settlement from a considerable distance away. Other remains of dwellings are likely to form loose, seemingly random, clusters, representing the rather unstructured nature of the old settlements of the Highlands. Sometimes you can

The ruins of homes such as this one in Glengairn are very frequent reminders of the Clearances that devastated society in the Scottish Highlands.

trace the outlines of little walled vegetable gardens or **kailyards** associated with the dwellings.

Traces of the damming of a nearby burn is likely to reveal a mill site, as will evidence of higher-level ponds and their mill dams. The mills concerned could be very small, often of the **click mill** type. These had tiny wheels set horizontally rather than upright in the flow and were used to grid the locally produced oats.

The date of desertion will be in the range *c.* 1750–1914, for evictions in the making of deer (shooting) forests (see Chapter One) ran through to the end of the nineteenth century. Trees sometimes grow through the rubble of deserted walls and a largish ash, for example, would suggest a clearance at the early end of the date range (as it would take a long time to grow).

By the time the Ordnance Survey maps appeared, the peak Clearance years were past. However, maps produced by British military engineers, notably General Roy's map of around 1755, depict the Scottish Highlands on the eve of disaster. Copies are held in various Scottish archives and the internet has a range of sources. They portray a tragically vanished world.

9. Did the Scottish deer forest clearances mark the end of village desertions?

Not quite; some villages failed because they were based on declining resources, while others were simply in the wrong place at the wrong time. The latest generation of village fatalities included:

- **Colliery villages** associated with doomed mines. Often their communities were very narrowly based on mining, so there were no alternative occupations available and shopkeepers depended entirely on the custom of mining families.
- A few **quarrying settlements** failed, like Porth-y-nant in North Wales, which had exported kerbstones to London. Quarrying settlements may be remote and this example had no inland road connections and exported its stone by sea.
- Villages and hamlets on Salisbury Plain, along the Dorset coast and the East Anglian Brecklands were erased in the creation of **army training ranges** in the Second World War. Though these communities were

Porth-y-nant was a Welsh quarrying village that exported its stone by sea and had no land links to the interior. Such narrowly specialised settlements were always vulnerable to the vagaries of trade.

generally promised that they would be allowed to return after the cessation of hostilities, their old homelands have remained.

- Hamlets in Cumbria, Wales and the Yorkshire Dales were inundated in the creation of **reservoirs** for the growing industrial populations of areas that were often quite far away.

10. IS THERE MORE THAN ARCHAEOLOGY TO BE LEARNED FROM THE DESERTED SETTLEMENTS?

The lost villages, hamlets and clachans provide the plainest possible lessons of the need to harmonise human populations and activities with the natural environment. There are numerous examples of communities that failed because they overstressed the local environment.

By the time the Black Death arrived and produced a ruthless solution to the problem, the countryside of England was severely overpopulated and environmentally overstretched. Valuable woodland had been surrendered and the drive to produce more calories per acre in the form of grain had caused chronic shortages of meadow and pasture. There was no environmental leeway to cope with bad seasons, so that when famines arose starvation inevitably followed, and the weakened communities were then further ravaged by epidemics.

Similarly, in the Scottish Highlands a severely inflated population was engaged in a permanent struggle for survival, and famine and epidemics were common. A much smaller and more lusty population might have found economic alternatives to the wretched Clearances. The cases of both the English villagers and the Scottish clansmen show the foolishness of blindly placing trust in superiors, whether they were members of the gentry, like the English lords of the manor, or kinsmen and hereditary chieftains, like the clan chiefs of Scotland. The case of the Tudor sheep evictions also shows that, however just the laws may be, a sectional ruling caste cannot be trusted to enforce them fairly.

There is not a single historical precedent that encourages us to believe that the natural environment can be continually abused in the quest for profits and economic growth. There are unlimited examples to show that when inconvenient concerns about excessive population, pollution and exploitation are set aside 'for the moment', the situation is likely to erupt with terrible consequences. A frightening array of diseases and traumas are waiting to take their toll of the swollen, stressed and weakened population.

— EIGHT —

Parks and Forests

1. SOME IDEAS ABOUT PARKS AND FORESTS

'Parks were invented by celebrated shapers of landscape, like 'Capability' Brown and Humphrey Repton' WRONG
'Forests were areas of wilderness that were blanketed in trees' WRONG
'The Forest was an administrative area: a royal hunting reserve that was subject to Forest Law for the conservation of game. A Forest could contain no trees whatsoever' RIGHT
'Landscape parks evolved quite directly from medieval deer parks' RIGHT
'A natural parkland type of scenery with lawns, scattered trees, groves and woods could be seen in England around 6,000 years ago and more' RIGHT

2. THE DIFFERENCES BETWEEN DEER PARKS AND FORESTS AND 'ORDINARY' COUNTRYSIDE

Deer parks and Forest-like areas where the nobility hunted existed under the Saxon kings of England, but we know little about them. William the Conqueror (1066–87), who, like most of his descendants, was an obsessive blood-sports enthusiast, formalised anti-poaching legislation and extended the area on which the Forest Law was imposed.

Forests were extensive and exclusive royal hunting areas and could cover dozens of square miles. Forests did not necessarily have extensive wooded areas. Some consisted largely of moorland, while others were well wooded or contained large areas of agricultural land but all were subject to the special Forest Law.

Deer parks, in contrast, were much more confined and were the private hunting grounds of leading churchmen and lords of the high and middle ranks. Forests had regularly patrolled boundaries but no physical barriers to contain the larger game, but the far smaller deer parks were like enormous paddocks in which game was confined by banks and ditches, palings, stone walls or combinations of these features.

Only monarchs had Forests, but leading aristocrats and churchmen had exclusive **chases**, which were similar to Forests in many ways. While modern writers insist on clear distinctions between Forests, chases and parks, documents of the Plantagenet, Tudor and Stuart eras show a more interchangeable use of the terms. It is a good idea to use a capital F for royal Forests to differentiate between them and 'forests' or tree-covered ground.

Most Forests and deer parks have lapsed and are now expanses of working countryside or suburbia (London sprawls across several former parks, as the names of some of its boroughs and localities show). However, Forests and deer parks do not vanish without any trace and we can often recognise their influence on the landscape.

3. WHAT WAS HUNTED, AND WHY?

At first aristocratic huntsmen hunted the native red deer, roe deer and wild boar. Then the Normans introduced their favourite quarry, the fallow deer, from southern Europe and it became the preferred game in deer parks. In the course of the Middle Ages wild boar became effectively extinct and deer were scarcer than today. Gifts of rare game from one aristocrat to another were highly valued.

The concept of sportsmanship seems to have played no part in the hunting rituals, and while deer were commonly coursed with greyhounds, they were also shot with arrows or bolts from hunting towers and blasted with muskets when these became available. In 1326–7 Edward II gave the Cliffords of Skipton Castle thirteen large corded nets that could be strung across thickets in wooded country to capture roe deer.

Animals of all ages were killed and the medieval hunt seems to have resembled a battlefield. In 1356 Edward Balliol, the deposed Scottish king, went hunting in Hatfield Chase, near Doncaster; after killing enough deer, both adult and young, to feed a small army, he then set upon the fishponds and slaughtered shoals of fish, including some baby pike scarcely a foot in length. Manhood seems sometimes to have been gauged by the quantity of one's kills rather than by horsemanship or forbearance.

The nobles either followed the hounds on horseback or stalked deer on foot, sometimes using animal disguises. When not terrorising the deer they were likely to have been found engaged in falconry with their falcons, goshawks and kestrels, or hunting small game, like foxes (to hunt such small game on his own estate a noble required a grant of **free warren** from the king). Different birds of prey signified different aristocratic status, while women with kestrels also participated in falconry. If an illustration of the time is to be credited, women also took pleasure in netting rabbits, using a polecat/ferret.

The perimeters of the parks were furnished with sections that functioned as **deer leaps**. Here, a deer could jump over a paling placed at the top of an inward-facing scarp to join the deer inside the park, but it could not leap both scarp and paling to get out again. However, as more deer were generally killed inside the park than would heedlessly jump into it, there was a permanent shortage of quarry. With his many Forests, the king was in a position to distribute deer as largesse. In this way he could strengthen his links with influential nobles, appease his debtors and acknowledge past favours.

Poaching is generally seen as the preserve of desperate outlaws and champions of the poor, like Robin Hood. In reality, all manner of people engaged in poaching. Some quite privileged poachers, including well-placed rectors, seem to have done so for the thrill of defying authority. **Park-breaking** was a most wounding form of insult and was done to humiliate the unfortunate park owners concerned. When Lord Latimer refused to join the Catholic earls of Northumberland and Westmorland in revolt in 1569, the earls ransacked Snape Castle and stole the horses and cattle from his park.

Red deer were the main quarry hunted in the uplands. During the last few thousand years the size of these animals has decreased dramatically, from horse- to pony-size. In the Yorkshire Dales and the Pennines a Tudor poaching war between the mighty Cliffords of Skipton Castle and their aristocratic neighbours, the Nortons and Yorkes, drove the animals there near to extinction, but they have survived in the Scottish Highlands and Islands and on the moors of south-western England.

The secretive roe deer were netted or else flushed from their woodland refuges and coursed but they survived the hunting campaigns and are now more numerous than ever. The imported fallow deer established some wild colonies after escaping from deer parks. Non-native Sika deer, Chinese water deer and muntjak deer became established in modern times. Ironically wild deer are more numerous today than they were in Robin Hood's day. The mechanisation of farming may have damaged and evicted numerous wild species, but it emptied the fields of their crowds of farmhands. Deer, quite wisely, do not like people very much, and flourish in their absence.

Remorseless hunting and the erosion of its woodland habitats finally drove the wild boar to extinction in England during the seventeenth century. Boar had been rare for many years before this, and those who still had them in their parks and woods used live boar as privileged gifts to other park owners.

In Scotland royal hunting took place on a grander scale. From the start of the seventeenth century there is a record of a far-ranging Great Hunt or **Tainchel** in the Braemar area of Upper Deeside; it lasted for twelve days and involved up to 1,500 beaters, and it accounted for some eighty deer in a two-hour spell of shooting as the beaters drove the quarry past the guns or bows of the huntsmen. Scottish medieval rulers tended to be less authoritarian than those in England, so in the Forests of Scotland the Forest Law was less rigorous and exclusive and the emphasis was more upon harmonising different Forest uses and interests.

In the latter part of Queen Victoria's reign, after the fashionable 'Balmoralism' had been established by Victoria and Albert, wealthy shooters from many parts of the world flocked to the Scottish Highlands to shoot red deer. Hundreds of families of clanspeople were evicted from their homes in order to extend the **deer forest** shooting grounds. This was the last really large-scale eviction of innocent families to take place in Britain and the upland areas of the shooting estates are littered with the rubble of abandoned dwellings. It did, however, result in the building of numerous **shooting lodges** and the establishment of many inns to cater for the shooting trade.

4. THE PARK AND ITS SETTING

The creation and regularisation of Forests were features of the Norman era and its immediate aftermath. In 1217 the child king Henry III issued the Charter of the Forest and pledged that much of the Forest land created by his grandfather, together with all his father's and uncle's Forests, should be disafforested. This marked a turning of the tide for the unpopular Forests. In contrast, deer parks tended to appear rather later. The greatest period of growth seems to have been from around 1200 to 1350, though in the north of England the peak came later, while essentially medieval examples were created there at the end of the Middle Ages and even later.

It is sometimes said that deer parks were slotted into wilderness gaps in the medieval countryside. My work in the Yorkshire Dales, perhaps the leading hunting area of medieval England, paints a very different picture. The parks were actually set in the *more productive* places, with proximity to their owners' castles and mansions being the main consideration. Lords liked to be able to walk through their gatehouses, collect their mounts from the nearby parkland pastures and begin the hunt without delay. This was a very martial society and the hunt drew heavily upon military prowess and derring-do. The coursing would often be watched by VIPs and impressionable damsels perched on battlements, gazing from lofty apartments or standing in narrow towers specially built to provide views of the coursing.

Forests were generally unpopular and people of their neighbourhoods tended to covet their wooded portions as potential farmland. Gradually they were dismantled, often having already been greatly eroded by illicit enclosures for landholdings. A few, like the enormous Forest of Knaresborough, which eventually fell to Parliamentary Enclosure, survived into the late eighteenth century and a handful, like the New Forest, Sherwood Forest and Epping Forest are still in existence today, albeit in varying forms.

5. THE IMPACT OF A PARK ON ITS SETTING

Given that nobles were inserting parks of 100, 200 or 300 acres into areas of long-settled medieval countryside, it is to be expected that much disruption would result. This was exacerbated by the fact that the parks were being introduced in such great numbers; the earls of Lancaster alone came to own almost fifty parks and the Nevilles surrounded their castle at Middleham in Wensleydale with a constellation of deer parks. Many communities must have faced eviction through the introduction of deer parks. For example, when William, Lord Conyers, improved Hornby Castle near Bedale and its setting at the end of the fifteenth century, some forty 'husbandries' or holdings are thought to have been cast down.

People who escaped eviction were obliged to look on helplessly while wild deer devoured their crops. However, one suspects that they would have been less passive when they were confident there were no foresters, parkers or 'regarders' in the vicinity.

Parks and Forests influenced the feudal roles of people in their neighbourhoods. Bondsmen might be obliged to board hunting dogs or help to set up the tented villages that sprang up during a great hunt, while woodturners could be brought in to make stacks of platters and beakers for the hunting feast. Such obligations also permeated further up the social hierarchy. The de Waltons were granted 120 acres of land in the Forest of Galtres, near York, by Edward II in return for the service of carrying a bow when the king was hunting in that Forest. So, as well as causing considerable disruption at the time of their creation, parks and Forests also created some local employment.

A medieval deer park might be managed on a day-to-day basis by the parker (giving rise to the common surname) and his servant, but Forests stood large in the landscape and had numerous officers and employees. These included the

ordinary foresters (another common surname), who were often corrupt and liable
to bully and exploit local people, and 'verderers', from two to sixteen in number,
who came mainly from the petty gentry and who, together with local
freeholders, formed the **Woodmote**. This was the court where offences against
the Forest were considered. Then there were the 'regarders', who regularly
inspected the Forest looking for illegal enclosures, thefts of timber and so on
and the 'agisters', who were rather similar but concentrated on the activities of
livestock and the collection of dues for grazing them in the Forest.

6. CAN WE PICTURE A MEDIEVAL DEER PARK?

A few medieval deer parks, like the one at Ripley in North Yorkshire, still
contain deer but most have vanished, many of them being remodelled by the
'landscapers'. However, a picture of the deer park in its heyday can be pieced
together from contemporary accounts.

Park-making or **emparking** never took place on a blank canvas. The records
show that all kinds of places were commandeered. Medieval ploughland,
commons, woods, farm clusters and even living villages were seized. The parks
were certainly not inserted into neglected and unused corners of the countryside.
Wood pasture (see Chapter One) seems particularly likely to have been seized
from the commoners. The ancient wood pasture landscape of pollards standing

A typical parkland scene at Castle Raby, Co. Durham.

in pasture is by far the most likely source of inspiration in basic medieval park-making.

However the countryside may have looked before a park was created, it was the 'wood pasture and woodland' scenery that park owners liked to create. In such a countryside of tree-dotted lawns, tree clumps and compact woods, there was fairly open, closely grazed pasture across which the deer could be coursed, but there was also cover, preventing the quarry from becoming too neurotic, and lots of well-spaced pollarded trees. These yielded leaf fronds that could be lopped down for browse as well as giving concealment to stalkers.

No owner, however rich, would neglect the commercial opportunities represented by his or her deer park. These included the following.

Agistment

This, the taking of rents from livestock owners in return for a season spent by their beasts in grazing in the lawns and thickets, was extremely important. Payment was taken at a fixed rent per animal per season. Cattle normally posed few problems, though they must have become semi-wild as they roamed the woods. Swine were a problem as they would devour new-born fawns and attack hinds that were giving birth. Thus, there was always a closed month in summer when pigs were evicted from the park.

Pannage and mast

Pigs foraged greedily for pannage (acorns) and mast (beech nuts). Sometimes these resources were agisted, but often the lord's swine or the village pigs enjoyed the feast.

Woodland products

These ranged widely and included wild honey and fruits (imagine how popular these must have been in a world without sugar cane, sugar beet and synthetic sweeteners!), but the main resources were timber products and browse. When the chronicler John Leland made an itinerary of England in the 1540s he was usually careful to comment on the woodland components of the deer parks that he passed. He clearly thought that scenic beauty and well-woodedness went together, and this was probably a widely held view then. Wood might supply the following needs:

- Fuel: normally light poles and wands from pollards or coppices that were cut up and sold as faggots.

- Timber for turning. This was purchased by a turner, who would set up his pole lathe in a clearing where he would 'turn out' platters, bowls and drinking vessels.
- Bark (preferably oak bark) was used in the tanning industry. It might be stripped off by the feudal tenants and stored in a **bark house**.
- Heavier timber was used for special purposes as necessary, such as cleft oak palings to repair the park pale.

Coppice timber

The records show that some deer park woods were sometimes worked as coppices (see Chapter One). Of course the vulnerable new growth would need to be fenced very carefully for several years after felling to protect it against incursions by deer, cattle and swine. Often a robust dead hedge of poles, wattle and thorny material was employed.

Food reserves

The park was very closely associated with its owner's castle or manor house, supplying venison for feasts. It would be quite likely to contain the manorial fishpond (see Chapter Two) in a situation that was more secure and more easily supervised than it would have been in a spot near the village. A location on a flat valley bottom or on a shelf on the valley side would be typical. Artificial rabbit warrens were also often made in parks, as at Middleham, where the cigar-shaped pillow mounds that accommodated the coneys can be seen on the skyline from the later stone castle, built near the earthworks of the first castle.

Horses

If the deer park owner was someone of social significance in the feudal world he would probably have several manors, and might have a deer park on more than one of them. Great lords could have half a dozen or more parks. The park-owning lord would progress around his manors with a large retinue, consuming his feudal dues of local production as he went. A castle or manor might be retained by a skeleton staff for most of the year. When the lord and his party arrived, all accommodation suddenly came under pressure and the park was a convenient place to pasture the retinue's horses.

Cow farms

In the South and Midlands deer parks tended to fall out of use as the medieval period progressed. Inside many of them specialised agricultural enterprises, such as cattle farms known as **vaccaries** and **horse studs**, had already been established, and sometimes these uses took over the park completely. In the north of England vaccaries often existed alongside deer parks, but the parks themselves persisted for longer.

Other uses

These were many and included quarrying and mining, as well as various industries associated with kilns, smelters and water-powered hammers and bellows.

Conclusion

The picture of the medieval deer park that emerges is of a compact area of several dozen acres that was firmly enclosed by robust palings, ditches and/or walls. Its landscape comprised rolling expanses of grazed lawn, a stipple of pollarded trees, often oaks, and groves and larger patches of woodland. From a distance one could see slowly moving specks that were deer, sheep and cattle.

This description would equally well fit the parks attributed to the great landscapers of the eighteenth century. This is no coincidence, for the landscape park was very firmly rooted in the scenic standards set by the medieval deer parks. Often just a light tweaking of the scene was necessary to convert the one into the other.

7. DISCOVERING OLD DEER PARKS

Forests had their own courts and employed far more people than did the deer parks. However, the deer parks had specially constructed boundaries, deer leaps, hunting towers and so on, and they have left clearer traces on the ground. Forests are well known and well recorded and can easily be traced. Various types of research can unearth the deer parks of a region.

In the library

A decent reference library should contain the relevant regional volumes of the *Victoria County History*. The entries for the different parishes, townships and manors are likely to pick up the documents that record the existence of a medieval park. Especially look out for any references to **licenses to empark**. In theory, any lord seeking to establish a park had to purchase a licence from the king – this was one of the ways in which kings obtained revenue. In practice the licence may not have been traced, may never have existed, or may be hidden in a grant of free warren, giving the lord concerned the right to hunt small game (foxes etc.) on his own demesne.

While in the library, check out any local parish and family histories of the area written by Victorian antiquarians and topographers. They are something of a lucky dip but may sometimes prove very helpful.

On the map

Obtain a map of the area at a scale large enough to show field boundaries (1:25,000 or larger). Deer parks were generally compact and the most popular shape was that of an egg or a pear, with the castle/manor being located at the more pointed end. When deer parks lapsed back into the working countryside, they were sub-divided into networks of fields. So we can hope for some success by looking at *shapes* and *field patterns*.

Scour the map for clusters of fields that seem to be looped around or lassoed by a continuous, curving boundary. That boundary may represent the perimeter of a lost deer park.

Study the place-names on the map – but be wary! The word 'park' derives from a word describing a paddock and it may simply be used to describe enclosed pasture or woodland. In the north it was sometimes used just to indicate good horse pasture, and now it is used there for sports grounds. However, 'park' names on maps, like the hamlet Park End in Bedfordshire, are very suggestive of former deer parks. Also look out for 'Dog' names, as these may indicate the sites of the kennels used for hunting dogs or the lanes where they were exercised.

All old maps are potentially revealing. The oldest are likely to be county maps of the sixteenth century by cartographers like William Sexton, and any good reference library should have reproductions of local examples. These sixteenth- and seventeenth-century cartographers tended to mark deer parks as little oval enclosures ringed by palings. A given map may not show all the parks then existing in a county but will give a good selection.

On the ground

As on the map, look out for continuous curving hedgerows or walls encircling packages of tidy fields that were formed when the disparking took place. Just outside Middleham in Wensleydale there is a clear distinction between the fields formed from medieval strips on one side of the former park wall and the gridwork of walls resulting from the enclosure of the Nevilles' old Sunskew park on the other.

The earthworks of deer park boundaries can be very pronounced, with deep ditches on the inner sides of the palings, hedges or walls. Inside the park make for the highest ground and examine the land surface carefully for traces of rectangular buildings. **Lodges** and **hunting towers** tended to be built on sites offering panoramic views over their park.

There could well be evidence of other medieval activities, such as fishponds, warrens, quarrying, small mill dams and other features.

Trees that were approaching middle age as the medieval period drew to a close may still be living in the former park interior. Look for oak or hornbeams showing evidence of pollarding and massive girths.

Conclusion

Landscaping did not begin with Lancelot 'Capability' Brown and his kind. It has recently been appreciated that the old deer parks were not only game reserves and economic undertakings, they were also deliberately created to enhance the aesthetic qualities of a castle or mansion and to make a striking impression on visitors (see Chapter Six). The heyday of the deer park was also the era of chivalry, when troubadours reworked the myths of King Arthur and when courtly love and feats of arms were greatly admired. This takes the medieval deer park even closer to the later landscape park, for both were rooted in romance and gentility.

8. HOW DID MEDIEVAL PEOPLE DESIGN ROMANTIC AND STRIKING LANDSCAPES?

- By introducing shallow, mirror-like **lakes**, sometimes with wooded islands, that were created by flooding the approaches to a castle, palace or great manor house. Guests would see the power centre of the dynasty towering above its shimmering reflected image.
- By carefully organising the **approach routes** for a special impact, so that the first glimpse of the seat of power came suddenly, within a thoughtfully contrived view.
- By employing **causeways**, so that the final approach to the castle was made along a narrow track raised above the surrounding water.
- By exploiting **battlements** or **detached towers** that provided sweeping prospects across the park and estate. These could also serve as vantage points during hunts.
- By developing the scenic potential of more commonplace and functional landscape elements, such as the fishponds in the park, the groves and the

lawns. The deer, flocks of sheep and roaming cattle provided eye-catchers within the idyllic scenery.

- By juxtaposing features so that the castle, palace or manor looked southwards directly over intimate flower and herb gardens, and perhaps an ornamental pond, to the tree-dotted pastures and woods of the park beyond.
- By providing other lakes for **boating** and **fishing** elsewhere in the grounds, sometimes with islands with prettily landscaped 'pleasaunces'.

The medieval ornamental landscapes have usually vanished after centuries of neglect, but one may recognise the earthworks of former dams, sluices, aqueducts, causeways and terraces and so picture how the medieval scene may have appeared.

9. THE LANDSCAPE PARK EVOLVES

We have seen that the medieval deer park was also an **ornamental landscape**. The parks created by later designers reproduced many of the landscaping motifs seen in the medieval parks. The lawns, groves, free-standing pollards and vantage points were all there in the early parks. Hunting continued after the Middle Ages and almost all the Tudor and Stuart monarchs were obsessive slayers of deer. However, various important changes were introduced.

There was a shift in the flaunting of status. The powerful Tudor monarchs with their ability to raise huge mercenary armies made the barons largely impotent in military terms. Their castles became redundant and they came to realise that, instead of living in the cold and dark behind enormously thick walls, they could be occupying splendid mansions, with vast suites of accommodation, large, light rooms and showy façades – but with only cosmetic fortification or none at all.

There were also changes in social relationships. The old castles and manors had tended to be placed beside villages or to have villages grow around them. The lord usually lived in quite close proximity to the communities that furnished him with servants and income. After the medieval period, lords tried to become rather aloof and remote from workaday communities, even if achieving this involved tearing down their villages (see Chapter Seven).

In these ways the familiar picture of the stately home standing apart from other settlements and presiding over a vast expanse of empty and carefully landscaped parkland came into being. Status could be measured in the acres/hectares of uninhabited parkland that surrounded the mansion. The new

Holkham Hall in Norfolk. Its park of 1762 reflects 'Capability' Brown's enthusiasm for great expanses of lawn that swept up to the mansion.

A grotto at Fountains Abbey.

park-makers might have been immensely rich, but they did not have access to modern earth-moving machinery or high explosives. The sculpting of the scene had to be accomplished with pick, spade and barrow, and so they were obliged to make the best use they could of the existing topography, scooping out a shallow pond here or rounding a slope or raising a hillock there.

The gardens created around 1700 were very orderly places. They embodied the Renaissance ideal of rational humanity's triumph over Nature. They often included straight avenues, perhaps with fountains at their midpoints, and equally spaced trees along their edges; geometrical ponds and canals; stepped terraces; and possibly some avenues or pathways aligned on features outside the park such as distant spires or towers. In contrast to all this unnatural symmetry, there might be an area set aside as a 'wilderness' that was approached from the garden via an imposing gate. This was one of various features anticipated by the makers of designed landscapes around medieval castles.

Water features became increasingly popular as the century evolved, and while the straight canal, circular and crescent ponds and a compact lake were being created at Fountains Abbey after 1768, at Blenheim Lancelot 'Capability' Brown had already inundated Vanbrugh's formal canal under an enormous lake. The landscaping mood had swung towards expansive curves rather than lines and angles.

The emphasis in the landscapes created by Brown and his followers was on the broad sweep rather than the detail. Formal terrace gardens beside the mansion were swept away, so that the lawns rolled up to the house, with just a sunken ditch or **ha-ha** to keep out the animals. Old streams were dammed and old mill ponds or ponded-back streams were transformed so that great lakes of serpentine rather than geometrical form could weave over the lower ground. The ancient wood pasture and deer park patterns of lawn-stippling pollards, groves and larger woods were retained, sometimes with a simplification of patterns, adjustments around their edges or new plantings to create more sweeping lines. Eye-catching features providing picnic spot places or shelter from showers, such as gazebos, fake temples and artificial hermitages, were carefully positioned, while belvederes looked out over favoured views.

By the end of the century tastes had swung more strongly away from the formal and towards the Picturesque, with landscapers like Humphrey Repton parodying what was regarded as the best of natural countryside. The lines between the different elements were blurred, so that the eye drifted freely between wood, water and lawn in a design that was more intimate and less artificial.

10. EXPLORING PARKLAND HISTORY

Parks continued to be created until the depletion of human resources by the First World War and taxation on inheritances brought the long story virtually to an end. Some Victorian parks were created, but most parks seen today are several centuries old. As such, they have experienced long histories of development and abandonment. Parks offer much interest to the landscape detectives of today. It comes in three main forms:

- What the park can tell us about life in the countryside before it was created;
- What the evidence tells us about the way the park evolved;
- How we can appraise the abandoned park as an element in the countryside today.

Features from the older countryside

Parks can be valuable archives preserving aspects of rural life dating from the periods before the park itself was created. The most important factor here is that these features were protected because the park was *never ploughed* (except during wartime shortages), ploughing being the most potent form of destruction in historical landscapes. Evidence comes mainly in the form of earthworks and includes the following main types.

- **Quarries and marlpits**. Medieval stone quarries were seldom deep. Rather, quarrymen would seek to split blocks of stone from a useful stratum, often where a near-horizontal bed outcropped at the crest of a slope (see Chapter Five). Then the stone could easily be sledged away. Limestone, for sweetening the land, was dug from **marl pits** or quarried from chalk or limestone outcrops. This work often continued after the park was created. Look for rather irregular patterns of hollows and overgrown dumps that might be heaps of chippings. Also look for the narrow rutted tracks that were used for carting the stone or marl away.
- **Lost villages**. A park could expand across a deserted village site, or one or more villages may have been demolished in its creation (see Chapter Seven). Both deer parks and landscape parks were serious assailants of Village England. Deserted village earthworks are not easy to read from ground level and it may be necessary to draw a plan in order to gain a complete picture. As described in Chapter Seven, the through-road or High Street would normally form the spine of a village, with field lanes and side lanes

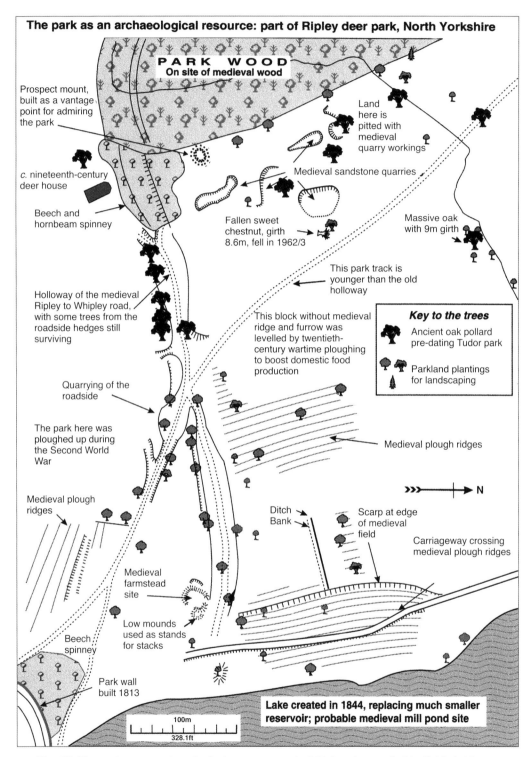

The park as an archaeological resource: part of Ripley deer park, North Yorkshire

PARK WOOD
On site of medieval wood

Prospect mount, built as a vantage point for admiring the park

Land here is pitted with medieval quarry workings

c. nineteenth-century deer house

Medieval sandstone quarries

Beech and hornbeam spinney

Fallen sweet chestnut, girth 8.6m, fell in 1962/3

Massive oak with 9m girth

This park track is younger than the old holloway

Holloway of the medieval Ripley to Whipley road, with some trees from the roadside hedges still surviving

This block without medieval ridge and furrow was levelled by twentieth-century wartime ploughing to boost domestic food production

Key to the trees

Ancient oak pollard pre-dating Tudor park

Parkland plantings for landscaping

Quarrying of the roadside

The park here was ploughed up during the Second World War

Medieval plough ridges

Medieval plough ridges

N

Ditch Bank

Scarp at edge of medieval field

Carriageway crossing medieval plough ridges

Medieval farmstead site

Low mounds used as stands for stacks

Beech spinney

Park wall built 1813

100m

328.1ft

Lake created in 1844, replacing much smaller reservoir; probable medieval mill pond site

Fig. 17. The park as an archaeological resource: part of Ripley deer park, North Yorkshire.

leading off it. Often the plot boundaries can be recognised as former hedge banks or ditches, while houses are seen as slightly raised and rather narrow rectangular platforms. If a village is located, it should be possible to find the narrow lanes and trackways that once linked it to its fields and the world beyond. Isolated house platforms, the remains of dispersed farmsteads or cottages, may also be found and most parks should display a few. Farmsteads often appear as the traces of several buildings on either side of a track or as the earthworks of a house with those of outbuildings close by. Those of **courtyard farm** type had the buildings arranged around a squarish yard, and may sometimes be recognised from earthworks. Traces of holloways merit some thought: the lanes must have been going *somewhere* and their relics may be like arrows pointing towards a deserted settlement.

- **Churches**. The isolated church is a characteristic part of the parkland scene. Usually it is the church of a village that was removed when the park was created. Such churches sometimes survived even when their congregations were rehoused outside the park, and some were converted to serve as the private chapel and mausoleum of the controlling dynasty. In both cases

Wimpole Hall in Cambridgeshire stands in a 3,000-acre (1,200ha) park landscaped by Charles Bridgeman, 'Capability' Brown and Humphrey Repton. In the course of the park's development, a village was uprooted, relocated and then moved again.

churches tend to have become packed with the tombs and memorials of that family, as described above; if the building has medieval features and architecture of different ages it is very likely to have been pinched from the village. Gentle troughs and platforms around it may signal the location of the old village. New churches, too, could occasionally be built in parks, as at Studley Royal (see below), where there is a deserted settlement but in a different place.

- **Trees**. People imagine that all the trees in a park are parts of a grand landscaping plan. In reality the oldest trees are likely to have been adopted from the pre-existing working countryside. Look out for massive old pollards; any more than five centuries old date back to the Middle Ages and any oaks more than seven or eight centuries old may well be coming to the ends of their lives but could pre-date a medieval deer park. Ages of trees can be roughly determined by applying a curve that relates age to girth (at chest height). I have found the simple Mitchell (1966) 'woodland rate' of ½in (13mm) of extra girth per year a rough and ready guide to all but the older free-standing deer park trees in the north of England, but the rate may come closer to his 'open-growing rate' of 1in (26mm) per year in the south of England.

- **Hedgerows**. Park makers wanted to enjoy the products of landscaping in their own lifetimes. The countrysides that they commandeered were usually criss-crossed by hedgerows packed with hedgerow trees. The answer was simple: pull out the shrubs and leave the mature hedgerow pollards, standards and shredded trees as landscaping trees. That this happened can be demonstrated time after time by discovering the old hedge-lines embedded in the parkland scenery. Most of the hedgerow trees were pollarded, so look for pollards, many centuries old, of native species such as oak, ash, hornbeam and so on and see if they form fragmented lines. When such lines are suspected, follow them looking for tree stumps, which tend to be quite durable, and for the saucer-like depressions (I call them **tree holes**) formed when trees have fallen and hauled out masses of earth in their roots. The lines can be plotted to reconstruct the old patterns of hedged fields. Sometimes the traces of a hedge bank and a hedge-foot ditch can be recognised.

Features of the parkland scene

The landscape that was manipulated for pleasure had its own range of features, most of them ornamental, but there were also some of a functional nature.

These trees in the park at Studley Royal seem to be part of a landscaping scheme, but in fact they are derived from a pre-existing hedgerow.

- **Buildings which enhanced the park.** These included domed **temples** in fashionable Classical styles and buildings that provided vantage points for viewing particular vistas, like **gazebos** and **belvederes**. Towers and **obelisks** often served as memorials and some carry bragging inscriptions concerning the local lord and his achievements. Little lodges for amorous assignations might be dotted round, sometimes with bizarre interiors, like shell-covered walls, and even elaborate tree houses might be built.
- **Eye-catchers.** Such buildings as those mentioned above could serve as **eye-catchers**, but the spectrum of visual conversation pieces was much broader. **Avenues** directed the gaze to noteworthy features lying outside the park, in the way that the main avenues at Studley Royal lead to Ripon Minster. **Grottoes**, the best ones being associated with artificial cascades and mock hermitages, were also popular. **Follies**, sometimes in the form of tastefully ruined 'buildings' or pinnacles, were provided inside the park or beyond it. Some follies, like the Yorke folly, a broken arch above Pateley Bridge, were

erected independent of any park, and such otherwise aimless projects could provide local employment in hard times.

- **Bridges**. Examples like Vanbrugh's bridge at Blenheim could be built in styles more monumental than their functions required, while smaller bridges were often built to an exaggeratedly rustic appearance. Sometimes the bridge served as a vantage point associated with a lake or a carefully engineered waterfall, as at Dodington Park in Gloucestershire or Ripley in North Yorkshire.

- **Functional buildings**. In addition to the more obvious examples, like stables and kennels and the **boathouses** (some of them semi-subterranean) associated with lakes, the most notable are **ice houses**. These take the form of insulated vaults that were normally situated on slopes overlooking the landscaped lakes. When the lake froze in winter, the ice was carted up to the ice house and stored; it could be used to keep food and drinks cool or could be ground up to provide cold sweets in the summer. Some ice houses had the form of caverns and the insulation of thick walls and roofing was essential. At Studley the ice house took the form of twin domes within enclosing earthworks.

Recognising abandoned parks

Scores of parks have been disparked and returned to less romantic and less privileged uses. Normally they revert to farmland but their previous identity may still be deduced. The following features are all important clues:

- The most obvious indicator of a former park is the survival of its circuit of walls, often with a lodge and gatehouse still in occupation, even though the land inside the wall is now given over to agriculture. A wall would normally be around 6ft (1.8m) high to prevent people getting in or deer jumping out. Park walls are taller than field walls and tend to be of coursed blocks rather than of dry-stone rubble.

- Even when the parkland has gone over to arable cultivation and all the diagnostic parkland features are being ploughed away, trees from the former setting may still stand. Look for park-like patterns of trees, and if these trees are of non-native types, such as the exotic specimens that Victorians delighted in collecting, then a former park is very strongly suspected.

- When both the trees and the pasture remain, even if recent fencing or barbed wire have been used to partition the whole, the old parkland ethos will survive more strongly.

Parkland landscapes may be found lingering on after the park as constituted has gone, as here at Foelallt in Wales.

11. EXAMPLE: STUDLEY ROYAL NEAR RIPON

The park here existed as working countryside until the close of the Middle Ages. The fairly narrow valley of the River Skell, dramatised by flanking troughs gouged by glacial meltwater and with Fountains Abbey close by, presented possibilities that would have been hard to ignore in an age of park-making. After the Dissolution the neighbouring estate of Fountains Abbey was bought by the Greshams and then passed into the hands of the virulently anti-Catholic Proctors. Sexton's map of 1577 shows Studley ringed by a park paling, and some sort of coexistence between hunting and farming seems to have prevailed at the end of the sixteenth century.

Studley's owner, George Aislabie, began landscaping work during the last quarter of the seventeenth century, with scores of trees, particularly oaks, being planted in the 1680s. (These can be identified by using the girth measurement described above.) His son John was a disgraced sponsor in the South Sea Bubble disaster, and subsequently had plenty of time on his hands, which he obsessively devoted to landscaping his park.

The Aislabies longed to gain control of the Fountains estates, where the presence of a *real* ruined abbey was far more exciting than any folly. William Aislabie (1700–81) eventually managed to purchase Fountains in 1768 for the staggering sum of £18,000 and work on the great water gardens began. William's work tended towards the fashionable romantic Picturesque style, which contrasted with the more formal designs of his forebears, though new styles were already being established by Brown and his admirers.

In the 1730s the gardens and parkland rose out of the River Skell valley and on to the plateau above, where the farmland of Mackershaw was readily converted into parkland by grubbing up the hedgerow shrubs and retaining their oaks as landscaping trees.

The peculiar domed ice houses at Studley Royal would have been stocked with ice from the frozen park lake in winter.

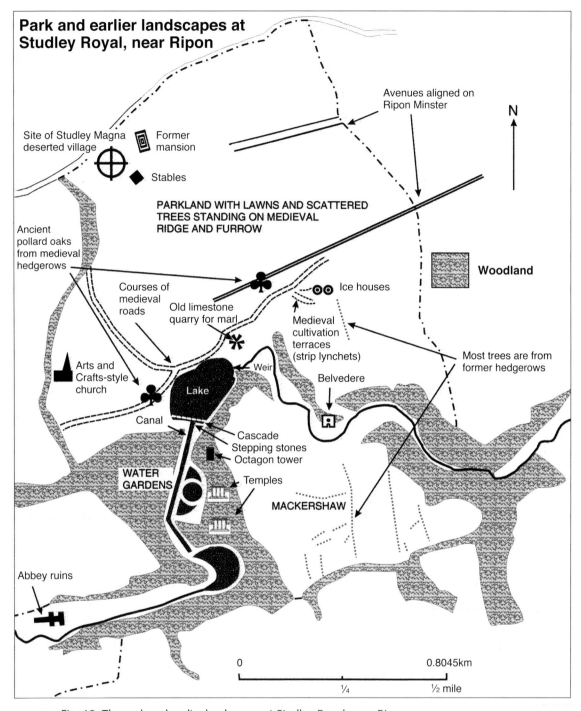

Park and earlier landscapes at Studley Royal, near Ripon

Avenues aligned on Ripon Minster

N

Site of Studley Magna deserted village

Former mansion

Stables

PARKLAND WITH LAWNS AND SCATTERED TREES STANDING ON MEDIEVAL RIDGE AND FURROW

Ancient pollard oaks from medieval hedgerows

Courses of medieval roads

Old limestone quarry for marl

Ice houses

Medieval cultivation terraces (strip lynchets)

Woodland

Most trees are from former hedgerows

Arts and Crafts-style church

Weir

Belvedere

Lake

Canal

Cascade
Stepping stones
Octagon tower

WATER GARDENS

Temples

MACKERSHAW

Abbey ruins

0   0.8045km

¼   ½ mile

Fig. 18. The park and earlier landscapes at Studley Royal, near Ripon.

A new church, dedicated to St Mary the Virgin, was designed by William Burges of London and built in an Arts and Crafts neo-Gothic style that reflected the popularity of medievalism among the upper classes. It was finished in 1871 and stands on a site rather distant both from the stables and from the mansion, which burned down in 1946.

With features ranging from medieval ridge-and-furrow ploughland to the Victorian church, Studley Royal demonstrates the range of historic landscapes that can be found in parkland.

NINE

Some Special Countrysides

The information provided in the preceding chapters can be used in many enquiries concerning historic landscapes. There are some very distinctive environments with their own particular histories and characteristics. They are explored in the following sections.

Moors and Heaths

1. SOME IDEAS ABOUT MOORS AND HEATHS

'Our heather moors are the largest of the last remaining natural wildernesses' WRONG

'One should not expect to find many archaeological traces on our moors and heaths. They are places that we humans have always avoided' WRONG

'Throughout most of England, the moors and lowland heathlands are as man-made as Piccadilly Circus or Milton Keynes' RIGHT

'In the ecology of moorlands, human beings are as important as sheep, heather and peat. Were we to ring-fence and desert all but the northernmost moors we could almost watch them vanish before our eyes' RIGHT

'Our moors are museums of life before *c*. 1000 BC' RIGHT

2. MEETING MOORS AND HEATHS

Heather moors are found on the uplands and heaths are their lowland equivalent. Extensive heather moors may be natural in Scandinavia and perhaps the north of Scotland, but further south they result from ancient human interference in the ecosystem.

One can easily put this to the test by looking at many modern moors that are experiencing crises of management. As soon as the human regulation of the environment weakens, the moors start to be colonised by bracken and trees at the expense of the heather.

The creation of upland moors seems to go back even beyond the days of farming, to the Mesolithic (Middle Stone Age) period, when hunters, seeking to open up hunting ranges and create grazing areas devoid of trees, cut and burned the natural forest. This burning reduced the removal of water by the trees (transpiration) and favoured the expansion of waterlogged areas. There vegetation could not rot in the normal way, but accumulated in beds of black, acidic peat, which gradually grew to be many feet thick. In all but the boggiest of places, the peat was colonised by heather, with its love of acid conditions and its robust ability to survive on wind-blasted plateaux.

Moor-like areas with beds of cotton grass can still be found where the bedrock is alkaline limestone if peat is able to accumulate in waterlogged basins on the plateaux. Normally, in places like the Pennines and the North York Moors the heather moors cloak the acidic sandstone rocks while the limestone supports upland grassland.

With the arrival of farming, around 6,000 years ago, the moors gradually came to be valued more as grazing than as hunting areas. Woodlands were cleared, but the severe upland climates and low fertility of the underlying sandstone must soon have led to the abandonment of much of the cropped land and its use as pasture. The shepherds discovered that by selectively burning the moors, any invading tree seedlings and saplings could be killed and the barren woody stalks of the elderly heather plants would be replaced by a regrowth of soft foliage that the sheep relished. Directly after burning, grass of the Molinia type was likely to spring up on the burned-over ground and this provided temporary pasture. Despite the benefits of burning or **swaling**, the heather grows on the very beds that produced the turf or peat used in fires, ovens and kilns, and once ignited the peat beds might smoulder for weeks. In late medieval Scotland moor burning was outlawed between April and the harvest, and in England similar legislation was produced in 1609/10.

This practice of moor burning was perpetuated by grouse-shooting enthusiasts who needed to maintain the open character of the moor and to stimulate the nutritious new heather growth that the grouse relied upon completely. From Exmoor to the Scottish Highlands swaled moors have a dappled appearance, with black patches marking the newly burned areas. Colours range from fresh green to brown as the last burning is left further behind – though the whole moor will turn mauve as the various heather species bloom in late August and September.

Heathland is the lowland equivalent of the heather moors and is generally regarded as moor lying below about 1,000ft (roughly 300m). It is found on wet ground where peat has accumulated, and above gritty sandstone beds as well as on the poorest of the sandy 'outwash' soils deposited by torrents of meltwater at the decay of the Ice Age.

3. ARCHAEOLOGY AND THE HIGH MOORS

Seen from a moving car, or even from a lofty lay-by, the moor may seem to be a desert in terms of archaeological interest or monuments. In fact, this is far from the case. Frank Elgee, a pioneering landscape archaeologist, described the North York Moors as a great living museum of the Bronze Age. The same might be said of Dartmoor, the Peak District's Dark Peak and many other moors. Heather moorland is very adept at masking its secrets; the heather growth is just high enough and dense enough to conceal a wealth of interest from the casual glance. Were it to vanish and we skimmed across the naked moors in a helicopter then we would surely see an amazing profusion of prehistoric dwellings, field walls, burial mounds, cairns, boundary banks and compounds.

The key to the richness of the moorland concerns its abandonment by settlements and ploughmen. Most of the upland moors in Britain seem to have supported quite substantial communities before becoming largely deserted. Since then, they have been able to act as museums of prehistoric life because, though they might have experienced local episodes of recolonisation during the historic period, they were never really effectively resettled.

The causes and the extent of desertion are debated, but the prime suspect is Iceland's Mt Hekla, which erupted violently at the start of the Bronze Age, around 2300 BC, and at intervals during the Bronze Age, particularly in the couple of centuries before 1000 BC. The eruptions threw unimaginable volumes of debris and ash into the air, which would have deflected sunlight and caused a cool, wet cloudiness that would have been felt most severely in the most borderline farming areas. Certainly microscopic volcanic particles (tephra) have been found on the abandoned homesteads and farmlands.

When exploring upland moors with public access provision, some care should be taken. Shorts and trainers are not advised: there may be adders basking on the rocks – they will happily to leave you alone unless you sit or stand on them – and bracken is thought to be carcinogenic, particularly its spores. One may ramble across a whole landscape (not, please, in the nesting season) and yet be little aware of the historic remains underfoot. Remains will tend, quite literally, to be stumbled upon, or to be seen in fragments, through gaps or briefly bursting though the cover. The following are the kinds of features that are likely to be lurking in the heather.

Flint scatters

Careful scouring of the moorland surface may reveal scatters of fine flint fragments. These result from the flaking of flints for arrowheads or tiny barbs for spears and may date from the Middle Stone Age, when the hunters who helped to create the moors paused to shape missiles and scrapers during their summer forays to the uplands. There is a certain thrill in finding a finely flaked arrowhead that was lost in some chase perhaps 8,000 years ago, or in seeing a pattern of flint chips lying by the boulder where their maker sat so very long ago.

Bronze Age dwellings

On the uplands these will almost invariably be **hut circles** and each will consist of a circular wall breached by a paved entrance gap flanked by small portals. Though just standing knee or waist high, such walls may well survive to their original height. The houses may be no bigger in area than a modern lounge and they were covered by a tall, conical roof of thatch and rafters that was supported by poles in a tent-like manner and rested on the low wall. While all the timbers, wattle and thatch will have gone soon after desertion, the stone walls of the hut circles may be perfectly preserved.

Settlements and compounds

Though some solitary homesteads existed, most stood within hamlets or groups of farmstead buildings. Occasionally village-sized settlements stood in upland sites, and both villages and farmsteads might be open or located within stone-walled compounds. These **pounds** probably served as overnight corrals for the livestock in a countryside where wolves loped and lynxes stalked. Just below the peak of Rough Tor on Bodmin Moor was a scatter of dwellings large enough to be a substantial and quite open village (see Chapter Four). The extra numbers were probably supported by working the tin gravels nearby. Across the (later) boundary in Devon, Grimspound on Dartmoor is a much-visited Bronze Age settlement of small dwellings guarded by a circular compound wall. The paved entrance to the pound is plainly preserved.

Barrows and cairns

The barrows of the Bronze Age resemble inverted fruit bowls. Some covered solitary burials, others groups of individuals. The rites involved varied enormously. Some people were buried along with ritual beakers or food vessels and with weapons or household items, depending on their sex, in stone boxes or *cists*, or in wooden coffins or in grave pits, while other people were cremated before having their remains interred in a barrow. The larger barrows probably marked aristocratic burials, while secondary burials, sometimes of cremated remains in urns, were often inserted later in the sides of the barrows (see Chapter Five). On the North York Moors the chains of barrows along the watersheds seem to mark territorial boundaries, while the burial mounds were often placed to be seen silhouetted on the skyline, perhaps for the same purpose. Not all bowl-shaped mounds in the moorlands were burial mounds. Many of the smaller ones are **clearance cairns** – heaps of stones gathered and dumped in great piles as the land was cleared for farming.

Ritual landscapes

Hundreds of monuments exist in moorland areas, though it is not clear how far moorlands had a special attraction for religious ceremonies and how far we see monuments surviving there simply because they escaped destruction by later agriculture. The list includes some major monuments, like the Ring of Brodgar stone circle, which stands on low ground carpeted with heather on Orkney, as well as scores of lesser ones, such as the puzzling stone rows on Dartmoor and many standing stones. If the moors always attracted disproportionate levels of ritual activity, it might be because they were often on borderlands and commons, where people from different communities would tend to meet. Ceremonies might be shared, but people may also have been anxious to establish that generations of forebears had occupied their little territory and their spirits and monuments would guard its bounds.

Human remains

Bacteria that require oxygen cannot flourish in the waterlogged, acidic environment of peat bogs. In Britain and continental Europe numerous prehistoric human bodies have been preserved in peat bogs. The reasons for their being there are debatable, but most were likely to have been 'criminals' executed for transgressing social codes or people killed as sacrifices to the gods, or both. One can only wonder if murder victims reported in the past were really corpses from the Bronze and Iron Ages. Perhaps this would explain Dead Man's Hill near Great Whernside in the Pennines, where three headless bodies unearthed from the peat were presumed to belong to murdered Scottish tinkers.

4. THE LOWLAND HEATHS

Lowland heather moors seem to have existed in England for up to 14,000 years. As the frigid ice deserts yielded to tundra landscapes of the kind that one would see today in northern Canada, heather gained a foothold. However, as the climate continued to mellow, the heather came under increasing pressure from the advancing trees and was shaded out of existence in many areas. Then humans intervened and began the remorseless removal of trees to make way for the cultivation of the land. This seems to have assisted the survival of lowland heather moors, for the land that was exhausted by cropping was soon abandoned to become grazing land. Domestic cattle and sheep combined with wild deer and cattle to prevent the trees re-establishing themselves.

The infertility of the heaths prevented them being converted into ploughlands. Beneath the heather and any surface peat, the soils tend to be leached and sandy. They do not retain water. Therefore heathland habitats experience severe droughts and are then prone to conflagrations that are fuelled by the resin-rich vegetation. However, some inches below the surface there is often contact with an impervious bedrock or a 'hard pan' – a band where nutrients flushed or leached away from the reach of plants by rain or snow are trapped. Heathlands like those around Tilford in Surrey formed upon ironstone beds and sands that were poor in nutrients and leached of minerals and humus.

Fire and human interference have helped to maintain the heaths by preventing the reinvasion by trees, notably the silver birch, which is always ready and waiting around the margin of the heath. By the controlled burning of the heath to improve grazing and by felling any trees for fuel or for craft industries, humans combined with their livestock to keep the heaths open.

Some heaths, often the ones displaying clumps of yellow-flowered gorse, burn like tinder, while others are wet. These stand upon beds of clay or have moisture trapped in a waterlogged layer above impervious bedrock. In these cases the surface is often saturated and layers of peat may accumulate; in such places the heather cover is broken by expanses of purple moor grass and squelchy sphagnum moss.

The lowland heaths were usually quite thinly peopled, yet they were greatly valued. People from the fringing villages, hamlets and farmsteads would drive in their livestock, gather bracken bedding for their hogs, dig turf (peat) for their fires and stoves, gather the tops of prickly gorse bushes for fuel, snare rabbits, rob nests and exploit many other aspects of the heathland ecology. This pattern of happy coexistence with the heath was disrupted by the population pressures

Trees advancing to colonise the moor at Brimham Rocks, near Ripon. This will happen whenever grazing pressures are lifted and burning no longer takes place.

and more 'progressive' attitudes to commons/wastes that developed after the end of the Middle Ages. Many areas of heath were reclaimed for more intensive uses. Some heaths surrendered completely to the 'improvements', while on some others the traditional practices that had long maintained the heather and gorse fell into decay.

5. TRACES OF THE OLD WAYS

Upland moors and lowland heaths may today be maintained in different ways or be declining. As well as the prehistoric remnants, all still contain the relics of the old ways of life, which may feature either prominently or subtly in the present scene. These traces include the following features.

Trackways to the moor

Like most other large commons, the moors tended to be used by different communities in the settlements ringing the moor, a practice known as **inter-commoning**. Radial systems of tracks were developed leading off the moor in all directions, like the radiating wires on a dartboard. Most were used by commoning livestock and many were used for bringing down turf cut at the peat beds. In the Anglo-Scottish Borders the hill tracks or **streets** running up to the passes or **swires** were also international routes, used for commerce, droving and warbands.

Rented pastures

In the northern uplands **agisting** (renting of grazings) could be as important as the more familiar sharing of commons. Often the streams or becks and their little valleys served as the access ways up to the expanses of agisted moorland spreading out at the head of the becks.

Moorland industries

Upland moors and lowland heaths seem unlikely venues for industry, but thin seams of coal outcrop in the Pennines, tin was worked on the Cornish moors and lead was mined in the Yorkshire Dales. The derelict buildings that one finds stranded on the high moors should not automatically be assumed to be directly related to these industries. In the lead mining areas there were kilns for burning lime or drying timber destined for fuel as well as for smelting lead. Some buildings attached to the smelt mills were actually peat stores or peat houses, where the fuel was dried. Much care is needed when exploring these places, expecially where heather masks the old shafts and gullies or **rakes**. A widespread moorland industry was that of **bracken burning**. Sometimes members of the tenant community had shares in a communal bracken bed. Some fronds might be cut in late summer for thatching or bedding, but the mowing took place after the start of autumn, after which the crop was burned to release potash for the soap and glass industries.

Standing stones

Some moors, like Exmoor, abound in upright stone pillars or **monoliths**. Some are prehistoric in age and of uncertain function, although some of these pagan symbols were later Christianised by the addition of a cross, which often takes the form of a saltire within a circle. Other stones are inscribed memorials to nobles of a lost heroic age, like the Caratacus stone on Winsford Hill, Exmoor. Like so many other ancient stones, this was redeployed and served as a Forest boundary stone. On Dartmoor a few of the standing stones are **claim markers** that were originally set up by the old tinners of the moor, though others mark the bounds of warrens. Then there are the various stones set up as way marks on the high, blizzard-prone moors. Some of these were inscribed with directions and distances to the destinations. There are also scores of crosses. Some may guard travellers or mark old preaching places, but many were erected as boundary markers, delimiting places like the sanctuary zone of a church, the estates of an abbey or the limits of a warren. Boundary stones often have simple inscriptions: (X) B, where 'X' is the initial letter of the parish, and B marks a parish boundary; (X) F marks a Forest boundary; and (X) W B is likely to mark a warren boundary.

Converging parishes

Because the resources of the heaths and moors were so valuable, communities took great pains to ensure that they had access to them. As a result township and parish boundaries (many of them doubtless much older than the Norman Conquest) formed in shapes that allowed each township a corridor of access to the moorland commons. Parishes throng around Dartmoor like suckling piglets around a sow, and the pattern is repeated throughout the uplands. A map showing parish boundaries, like the Ordnance Survey 2½in to a mile, 1:25,000 series, should reveal this for any moor one chooses to inspect.

6. RECLAIMING THE MOORS AND HEATHS

Most moors and heaths have been greatly reduced by post-medieval reclamation, and some have been improved out of existence. Up and down the country upland heather moor and lowland heath and wet heath variously posed similar challenges to would-be reclaimers, though each also had individual features.

Medieval moors and heaths had been maintained as tree-free pastures by quite heavy grazing by flocks, coupled with periodic burning. The introduction of large-scale commercial rabbit-keeping helped to maintain this pressure. In the lowland heaths of the Norfolk Brecklands overgrazing had exposed the loose soil to the winds, and severe sand-blows in the medieval centuries may have encouraged the introduction of animals that relished the sandy environment. Great warrens, like the one established by the prior of Ely around 1300, dominated the heaths. Rabbits became big business, and warreners were needed to keep poaching in check. Such men were established in defensive **warrener's lodges**, like the one surviving near Mildenhall. With the pelts valued by hatters and rabbit meat becoming a major source of protein for the poor, the warrens had a long lifespan. Some, like a few on the south-western moors, survived until after the Second World War and it was only the revolting myxomatosis rabbit disease of the 1950s that ended commercial warrening. The disappearance of the rabbit economy encouraged moor-owners to transform their moors.

The practice of nibbling away **intakes** from the moorland margins was almost as old as the hills themselves, but with the dawning of the era of fashionably improved farming some large-scale operators and entrepreneurs took an interest in moorland reclamation. John Knight, who came from an industrial background, took up the role of landowner and improver on Exmoor from 1818. He built a wall some 29 miles in length around his new estate, metalled over 20 miles of moorland tracks and broke some 2,500 acres (101ha) of moorland to agriculture. He burned off the surface peat, spread the ash as fertiliser and followed this with a heavy liming to sweeten the soil. Then oxen were harnessed to plough right down into the subsoil to break up the hard pan of clay and iron that retained the surface water. In the following spring the land was ploughed twice, the second ploughing at right angles to the first, and the initial crop was sown. Fifteen farms were created on Knight's 15,000-acre (6,070ha) Exmoor estate, and their grid-like networks of fields bounded by tall earth banks crowned with beech hedges are still characteristic features of the moorland margins.

Similar efforts were made in other moorland areas, with varying success. Around Kempswithen on the North York Moors in 1773 Sir Charles Turner had Commondale Moor scythed down to ground level and then he burned the heather. Rainwater drains were dug leading down the hillslopes and huge amounts of lime were carted up and spread on the land and then ploughed in. Several hundred acres of former moorland were then enclosed in a network of dry-stone walls and the new fields were either grazed or put to crops. In this case the immense investment was not justified and the reclaimed land became little better than rough grazing. Most of these enterprises, successful or otherwise, involved heavy liming to sweeten the naturally acidic sands and peat of the heaths and moors. Among the most numerous monuments are the **limekilns** of the limestone outcrops, where stone was burned to release the powdery lime. They are particularly numerous where limestone outcrops are juxtaposed with the peat moors of the Millstone Grit in the Pennines. Very localised occurrences of limestone in Upper Deeside were greatly valued by improving landlords for their proximity to the moors of the Grampians and Cairngorms.

In Scotland the draining of the wet heaths and mosses between the 'run-rig' ploughlands (see Chapter Two) and the reclamation of the muirs were key components of the Improvements, Scotland's equivalent of the English Agricultural Revolution. In the Scottish Highlands there was an additional use for the very high, deforested uplands and mountains. Moorland sheep grazings in the Highlands were often converted into deer 'forests' – though the only trees

Blubberhouses Moor near Skipton is still a noted grouse moor, but evidence of old incursions is visible in the rectangular fields, which may represent an attempt to increase the cultivated area during the Napoleonic Wars.

on view tended to be a zone of Scots pine and birch between the vast open tops where the deer roamed, and the intervening glens and straths which were occupied by whatever communities had survived the Clearances (see Chapter Seven). The development of deer hunting marched hand in hand with the Victorian vogue for sentimentalising a land and culture devastated in fairly recent Georgian times, and with the penetration of the Highlands by railways, notably the Highland Railway, which was completed in 1864. As the improvements in transport and the emergence of professional ghillies removed the hardships from stalking on the mountains, wealthy overseas shooters were attracted to the area and the lucrative activity encouraged the retention of the open moorland pastures. Deer forests were serious business: in 1923 some 40 per cent of the former county of Inverness-shire was given over to this use. On many estates it is still lucrative, and it has its own landscape of shooting lodges and mountain tracks. Less obvious are the deer fences, which represent attempts, not always successful, to exclude the animals from commercial conifer plantations; in bad weather, particularly, cold and starving deer will migrate down from the barren hills in search of food and shelter among the glens and hamlets.

Commercial forestry has claimed a great deal of heath and moor. Various estate plantations were established in Victorian times, while by the middle of the nineteenth century shelter belts of Scots pine, planted to stifle the winds and prevent blow-outs of the sandy soils, had become the most characteristic feature of the landscape of the Brecklands. In the First World War the potency of U-boat attacks revealed a strategic deficiency in softwood timber. After the war the Forestry Commission devoted itself to procuring a far-flung empire of moorland and heathland sites. The land was cheap but the sandy, acidic soils were well suited to growing alien firs, pines and spruce. In areas like the

The heathland landscape of the Brecklands. The planting of Scots pine shelterbelts was followed by the afforestation of large areas.

Brecklands great tracts of countryside surrendered to Corsican pine and Douglas fir, with each new acquisition in the march of monoculture causing concern to naturalists and landscape enthusiasts. Had myxomatosis not assailed the deeply rooted rabbit economy, and had the invention of bullets with percussion caps not brought the days of the flintlock and flint-knapper to an end, then the Brecklands would have had more economic strings to its bow and the advance of tree plantations into the heaths would have been less extensive.

7. GROUSE SHOOTING: THE MOORLANDS' SALVATION

The positive benefits of bloodsports to the countryside are sometimes overstated by their advocates, and the other side of the equation concerns the countless birds of prey and animal predators wantonly exterminated by gamekeepers. Grouse shooting, however, has played a vital role in preserving the integrity of moorland landscapes that have been threatened by various competing uses.

As with deer stalking, grouse shooting began as the preserve of local stalwarts who followed unfashionable and physically demanding pursuits in difficult places. So long as grouse shooting involved a long approach across rugged ground, solitary hunting and the ability to hit a fast-flying bird with a ball from a flintlock, it would remain a minority pursuit. To become popular, it had to be shown to be a suitable pursuit for a gentleman – and it also needed to be converted into an activity acceptable to the short-winded and overweight classes who could afford to indulge in it.

The development of French-designed breech-loading shotguns in the middle of the nineteenth century provided the average fop or myopic industrialist with a reasonable chance of hitting the retreating birds. It also provided such men with an opportunity to demonstrate their sporting prowess and manliness – measured in terms of the numbers of birds brought down. While the ranking of the crack-shots was jealously measured according to the carnage that these privileged gunslingers wrought, the status of the proprietors of the moors was judged by the size of the 'bag' when their moors were shot over. Immense jealousies and rivalries were involved in the contests to attract the most titled, powerful and wealthy shooting parties.

It was soon evident that the potency of the breech-loaders, reloaded in seconds by the attendant bearers, was too great for conventional shooting methods. Traditionally the guns had shot over pointers at retreating birds that the dogs had flushed. This was now too easy and on most estates a switch was made to **battue shooting**, with beaters. This involved grouse being driven by a string of beaters towards the 'guns', who were stationed, half hidden, in **butts**. The positioning of the butts and the direction of the drive had to be carefully worked out in relation to the prevailing winds, with the birds presenting challenging fast-moving targets when driven downwind.

Meanwhile, the developments in local and national transport had removed all the arduousness and uncertainty from the journey to the high moors. In Scotland, where the favoured grouse moors lay in the south-eastern sections of both the Highlands and the Southern Uplands, the railways bore aristocrats, politicians and stockbrokers alike to the stations where smart horse-drawn carriages waited to convey them to castle, mansion or shooting lodge. The English estates might be reached by grouse-shooting parties on special trains, or via trains with flat cars on which the shooter's horse carriage could travel. From the station to the lodgings and then by carriage or pony to the moor, city gents who habitually lunched well could be conveyed from their perches in Surrey or Mayfair to the windy moor having scarcely set a foot on the ground.

The railway system that bore the guns to the moor could also be used to convey their plunder back southwards to the fashionable restaurants – no small consideration in the moorland economy. Generous tips and gifts to railway staff expedited the transit. Meanwhile, resourceful poachers did their best to cater for the local hotel and butcher trade in the more fashionable towns ranged around the moors.

Grouse depend upon fresh heather shoots for food, and the swaling of the moors to encourage young growth perpetuated the traditional management practices that had created and preserved the moors. In the Highlands factors and keepers still hack down the invading Scots pines, while down south their equivalents hold the line against birch and rowan. Shooting remains very profitable on some moors. On others it has declined, and disease among the grouse is a source of concern. The keeping of hill sheep is not well subsidised by the European authorities, so moorland conservation for sheep will not make good any losses of environment caused by the contraction of grouse shooting.

On many moors the advance of trees, mainly birch, but with rowan in attendance, is obvious. A more 'natural' wooded landscape can be established across an open moor within decades, but the loss of moorland habitats would have serious consequences for a multitude of endangered birds, including black grouse, hen harriers, short-eared owls, merlins and many more, as well as for plant communities and for traditional upland landscape scenery.

Grouse moors developed their own landscapes. To help you reconstruct the picture, look for **butts**, often waist high and horseshoe shaped, but also found in

A deserted shooting lodge at Gwyffa Hiraelty, near Denbigh.

a variety of other forms. Notice how they were placed and aligned in relation to the prevailing winds and the drives. **Lodges** might be used to accommodate the overflow of a shooting party or to house the shooters and their entourage closer to the moor. They tend to be Victorian and Edwardian in age, so neo-Gothic themes are usually evident in their architecture. They earned notoriety as centres for political intrigue among the ruling class and for 'goings-on'. Lower down the hierarchy came **shooting houses** and **lunch huts**. These were places where refreshments were served between shoots. Some were specially built for the role, while others were commandeered farmsteads in vernacular styles. **Watching houses** were the preserves of the keepers, being lookout stations perched in commanding positions so that the servants of the moor could spy for poachers. Finally, **dry-stone walls** along which numbers are pecked or painted may cause some puzzles. The answer is likely to be that an existing field wall was pressed into service to act as impromptu butts, with the numerals marking the respective positions of the guns.

Downlands

1. SOME IDEAS ABOUT DOWNLANDS

'Prehistoric people all lived on the downs because everywhere else was covered in trees' WRONG
'The downs are packed with wild flowers because this is natural grassland' WRONG
'The downland pastures were created by humans and their livestock' RIGHT
'Downland is one of the most attractive and distinctive kinds of countryside to be found in Britain, but sadly it is also among the most threatened and fast-retreating of countrysides' RIGHT

2. THE NATURE OF DOWNLAND

Our image of downland is one of closely cropped, thyme-scented, emerald pastures spangled with wildflowers. We think of steep scarp faces emblazoned with white horses, of windmills on high perches and of hang-gliders launched from the crests of the scarps.

The basis of downland scenery is chalk, a form of limestone that is composed of the compacted skeletons of tiny sea organisms that were deposited on the sea floor in warm shallow seas, like today's Caribbean. The chalk dates from the latter part of the age of the dinosaurs and is younger than the north-western limestones. It is quite pure and gleams white, while the latter seem silvery-grey.

The chalk beds of the downlands have been raised and slightly domed by geological forces and then cut by rivers that wore down into the rock. Rain and frost then attacked the steep chalk river bluffs, wearing them back. They kept their steep faces as they retreated, and these form the distinctive **scarps**. These face towards the vales and the (now sometimes distant) rivers that began their formation. Behind the chalk scarps are the much more gently sloping **dipslopes**, which preserve the original, slightly dipping angle of the chalk bed and which very gradually disappear under beds of younger rock. The scarp and dipslope together form an **escarpment**.

The two key characteristics of the chalk escarpments are the **alkalinity** of the rocks and the soils formed from them and the **dryness** of the chalk countryside. The chalk underlying the downs is very pure, being about 98 per cent calcium carbonate. Chalky substances were often prescribed as indigestion cures and the alkalinity or anti-acid character of the chalk means that it is colonised by lime-loving plants – including several endangered wild orchids. Acid-loving plants,

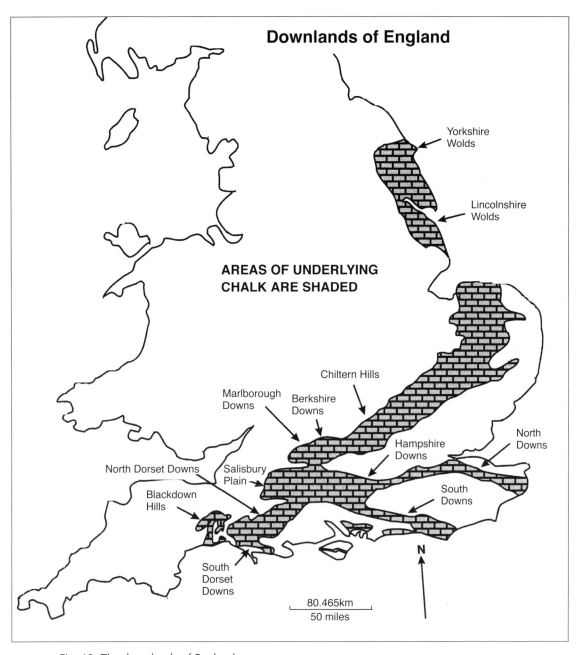

Fig. 19. The downlands of England.

like heather or bracken, will not be seen. The thin, impoverished nature of the soil makes grass less competitive, allowing scores of wildflowers to establish a foothold. Close grazing of the sward by sheep helps to prevent the grasses gaining a mastery and flowering plants are thus able to claim niches in the green mat.

Chalk is porous and will readily absorb moisture. Old school-teachers would demonstrate this by dipping a stick of blackboard chalk in a bottle of ink; soon the chalk would be blue and saturated with ink. Streams tend not to survive for long on the chalk surface and surface run-off usually drains quickly into the ground.

A striking feature of the downlands is the presence of dry valleys or **combes**. These were obviously once cut by water but are now quite dry. During the Ice Ages the chalk may have been saturated by water, which then froze. All the ice trapped in the ground would have made it impossible for the chalk to absorb surface water, and so torrents of meltwater flowing in from melting ice sheets carved out the dry valleys. Other suggestions propose formation in times of heavier rain and snowfall.

Below the chalk there lie impervious rocks, and water seeping down through the chalk is likely to encounter strata with a clay-like composition; springs/ streams or **bournes** will flow where the ground water escapes at the foot of the chalk.

In all rocks there is a water-table at the top of a saturated layer. The water-table will drop in summer, but in the winter it may rise some way into the chalk, causing springs to issue from the chalk itself. These springs are traditionally known as **winterbournes**, or streams that only flow in winter. Modern demands for water have had devastating effects on the water-table in most downland areas and many bournes only flow now because water is pumped into them from boreholes.

The nature of the chalk tends to be revealed in the countryside that we see, with the escarpments, the combes, the winterbournes, and the older farmsteads aligned along the springlines to tap a resource that could not be found further up the chalk slope.

3. PREHISTORIC PEOPLE AND THE DOWNLANDS

It used to be thought that prehistoric people congregated on the downlands because they were unable to clear or till the heavy woodland of the clay vales below. However, a meticulous search for evidence in the lowlands has shown that pottery, axes and other tools associated with day-to-day prehistoric life are also to be found there, even on some quite heavy clays.

Ancient farmers may well have been attracted to the light, well-drained soils of the downs, where the vegetation could have been more easily cleared. In fact the downland soils are shallow and poor in nutrients. Even so, the downs were wooded in their natural state, with lime-tolerant trees like beech and ash being present in great numbers. The earlier monuments of the New Stone Age, built over 5,000 years ago, must often have been created in clearings hacked through such woodland.

Flint nodules, derived from silica from fossil sponges and diatoms, occur naturally as seams within the chalk, and this indispensable tool-making resource must have drawn people to the many pits and the fewer substantial mines where top-quality flint could be found.

Another unique attraction of the downlands concerned the visual character of the chalk. The topsoil and subsoil formed only narrow zones and monuments cut into the chalk became as clearly defined as lightning in the night sky when the pure white bedrock was revealed by ditches or heaped in banks running across the emerald turf.

So why do we seem to encounter so much prehistoric life on the chalk downs? Here are the main reasons:

- The chalk was relatively easy to dig with an angled pick made from a broken antler, and it was light enough to be removed in wicker baskets. The digging of tombs, pits for sacrificial victims, processional avenues and henge ditches could be more difficult on heavier soils elsewhere, while the white chalk had the advantage of producing dramatic effects.
- If the highest and driest parts of the downs existed as open common it would have been easier for travellers to move across the country and for bordering communities to meet in places where territorial controls were looser. The fate of strangers who strayed into the settled farmlands below might have been unpleasant.
- The chalk was shaped by the plough to form fields bounded by lynchets, and many of the areas covered by these so-called Celtic fields were not ploughed again in historic times. Presumably, in terms of crop production, the soils of the downs came to be regarded as too impoverished, and too shallow and to be associated with places that were too dry and too steep to cultivate easily. Thus the distinctive ancient field patterns endured until the days of modern subsidised farming. Tragically these subsidies fuelled an

otherwise uneconomic return of ploughing, this time of a deep and highly mechanised nature. In Dorset, for example, 50 per cent of the county's traditional chalk grassland was destroyed between the mid-1950s and the early 1990s.

- Downlands became the preserve of the ambling shepherd rather than the stooped ploughman. The absence of ploughing allowed the old features and monuments to endure, while the close nibbling of the herb-rich turf by the flocks displayed them with maximum clarity, like molehills on a putting green.

- Features often mistakenly attributed to ancient humans are the narrow little parallel terraces, about a foot high, which rib the steeper slopes and are known as **terracettes**. These, too, belong to the domain of the shepherd rather than the ploughman and are (in part) sheep tracks. Over many years the little hooves of the sheep emphasised a natural process of down-slope 'soil creep', and by plodding along these little terraces they intensified the slow progress of the thin topsoil downwards.

4. DOWNLAND AND THE HISTORIC LANDSCAPE

Historic landscape features that one should look out for in downland areas include the following.

Ridgeways and trackways

The dry going underfoot and the need to bypass well-populated areas with their fields and (possible) hostility to strangers doubtless encouraged long-distance travellers to take to the lofty scarp crests and ridges. Look particularly for places where the ridgeway routes encountered steep ground. There they tended to branch into various alternative tracks, which became holloways deeply engraved into the slope (see Chapter Three).

Dewponds

With the downland being so dry, artificial watering places were needed for the flocks and herds roaming the upland pastures. Dewponds have a certain mystique, probably because people imagine that they were filled by dew, which they were not, for the run-off of rain was much more important. The oldest may date back to Roman times or even beyond. These artificial ponds were created either in dells floored with pockets of water-retentive clay or in hollows that were deepened and coated in clay or a mixture of puddled clay and straw and then coated with flints. For centuries pond-making was a distinct downland craft and it was practised within living memory. In some localities dewponds tend to be known as **shipponds** (from the old word for sheep) and fog ponds or mist ponds.

Long parishes

Like the moors, the downlands had resources that complemented those of the lowlands. Consequently parishes/townships tended to run from the rivers and bournes, with their water resources, fish and fowling, across the plump farmlands and little woods of the drained clay vales, up the scarp face and across the grazings and commons of the dipslope, to take in a broad spectrum of complementary resources. For people living at a semi-subsistance level, access to the maximum number of different resources was crucial and gave a measure of independence if any particular resource failed.

Abandoned shepherd huts

These huts, looking rather like narrow horse-boxes mounted on small iron wheels, were the abodes of shepherds entrusted with the downland flocks. Until around a century ago the shepherds would pasture the sheep on the downs during the daytime and then drive them down to be folded on the fallowing arable fields of the vale beneath in the evening, where their droppings would enrich the ploughsoil. This meant that goodness was continually being removed from the downs, though this in turn meant that wildflowers were able to compete with the grass.

Marlpits

Marlpits or **dene holes** are places where the chalk subsoil and bedrock have been excavated and carted away to be spread on sour land to sweeten it and improve its fertility. Often chalk is found in juxtaposition with 'claggy' clay, which can be broken down after mixing with lime, or with coarse, acidic sands, so its presence is particularly valued. The oldest of the pits date back to Roman times and marling was widespread in the Middle Ages and continued until factories made lime available in standard bags. **Chalkways** may be traced running down from the pits to the vales, and in the Yorkshire Wolds the pits dug into the underlying chalk are so numerous that the land beside the roads often looks as though it had been cratered by squadrons of bombers. Normally the pits take the form of bowl-shaped depressions, usually about half the area of a tennis court but sometimes larger.

5. THE DOWNLAND DICTIONARY

There are a number of words, mostly deriving from Old English, that are particular to the downland setting. When found on the map, they usually point to downland associations. These are the most common:

Bourne – a stream, often a chalk stream. The word has similarities with the burns of the north, while 'brook' seems to have taken over in the naming of streams in the bourne area during Saxon times.

Combe – a dry valley, or one that tends to dry out in summer.

Dene – this is a valley name that tends to occur in the same regions as combe names, although denes tend to be longer, narrower and steeper than combes.

Down – comes from a widespread 'hill' word that crops up in different forms throughout Britain, like the duns of the Celtic lands.

Hanger – a wood on a slope, often but not always a chalk slope, like those of the Chilterns.

Marlpit and **Chalkpit** names are quite common, but names beginning in Chal- are more likely to derive from an old 'calf' word than the Old English *calc* or 'chalk'.

6. THE WHITE HORSES

The downs offered sweeping panoramas. On the highest ground there were **beacon hills**, where bonfires were kept ready to relay warnings of invasion or news of jubilation across the kingdom. Nearby there might be windmills, gorging on the unchecked breezes, while now from the crests of the scarps one may look down on the moonlit vales and watch young farmers and post-graduates from south coast universities at work with twine, peg and board as they deftly create the latest crop circle. Soon after dawn tourists and cultists will be up on the crest to wonder at it. But from the tracks down on the vales one could also look up and see the striking hill figures rearing up the hillsides like white paper cut-outs on green baize. No other medium allowed so much show to be made for so little effort.

Extravagant claims have been made about the ages of these figures, though with little supporting evidence. The most credible candidate for great antiquity has always been the Uffington White Horse, partly because the Vale of the White Horse has been named after the figure for a very long time and partly because the horse is highly stylised, much in the manner of horses depicted on coins struck for tribal leaders near the close of the prehistoric era. Recently a surprisingly early date in the Late Bronze Age was suggested by dates obtained from silts in the features outlining the figure.

Hill figures are easily created: one simply strips off the turf and light brown soil, leaving the gleaming white bedrock exposed. However, once created, the figure needs regular attention, for if the surface is not scoured every few years, vegetation will recolonise the chalk and the figure will disappear. In order to survive through the passing centuries a figure would have to be scoured every few years regardless of invasions, plagues, famines, wars, changes in belief and changes in government. Thus any figure that endured from prehistoric, Roman or Dark Age times would have to be considered *incredibly* fortunate.

Repeated scourings can alter the outlines of a hill figure, and older ones, like the Long Man of Wilmington, are known to have changed in appearance over the years. The most recent evidence suggests that the Long Man may only date from the sixteenth or seventeenth century, and that it was outlined in brick from the outset. If the hill figures really are very old it is most surprising that the great chroniclers were silent about the great white figures in their midst. The oldest drawing of the Long Man dates only from 1710, while the famous naked Cerne Abbas giant with his cudgel might only date from the English Civil War, when clubmen formed bands of vigilantes to guard their localities against marauding troops and anarchy. The evidence of the old documents suggests a date in the middle decades of the seventeenth century.

There seems to have been a modest vogue around the Tudor to Civil War era for carving giants on chalk scarps, some of which perished. Later there was a much more pronounced enthusiasm among landowners, particularly those of Wessex, for cutting white horses in the Georgian era. There are five white horses within a 5-mile radius of Avebury and three more that do not quite fit within the radius. The Wessex horses are mostly well documented and precisely dated. In 1778 a pre-existing white horse on the slopes beneath Bratton Castle hillfort in Wiltshire was remodelled by Lord Abingdon's steward to become the famous Westbury White Horse. This in turn encouraged a fashion for such showy creations among other landowners in locations like the Marlborough Downs. In 1808 a representation of the mounted George III appeared on the downs at Osmington to proclaim his royal patronage of Weymouth nearby.

A few white horses appeared outside the Wessex paddock. The one near Strichen in North East Scotland was the whim of a Captain Fraser around 1800, who compensated for the absence of chalk by filling the figure with white quartz. The Kilburn horse on the west-facing scarp of the North York

The Westbury White Horse in Wiltshire, produced by the remodelling of an older horse in 1778.

Moors is cut in grey limestone rather than chalk and is covered in chalk pebbles for extra brightness. It was the idea of Thomas Taylor and was cut in 1857.

The habit still continues. At Litlington in Sussex, the white horse of 1838 gained a companion in about 1924. In 2002–3 a peculiar equine creation outlined in chalk slabs pinned together was created near Folkestone, having been sanctioned on a most sensitive site despite the powerful objections of the government's own nature conservation advisers. If a powerful symbol for those arriving and departing had been desired, a glance at the *Angel of the North* might have suggested more inspiring possibilities.

Old Wetlands and Salt-marsh

1. SOME IDEAS ABOUT WETLANDS AND SALT-MARSH

'The reclamation of inland fens and marshes and coastal salt-marsh took place in fairly recent times using steam and diesel pumping engines' WRONG
'Marshy wetlands were useless until they were drained' WRONG

'The reclamation of wetlands increased the area under cultivation, but involved the loss of common summer pastures for livestock, fishing, eeling, wildfowling and the relative independence of the old marshland communities' RIGHT

'Ancient attempts to recolonise wetlands must have been modest, though seawalls were built to guard land reclaimed from the Wash in Roman times. Wetlands and salt-marshes posed a bigger challenge to medieval communities than did the wooded areas. Many successful local schemes were launched, even though some coastal gains were lost in the sea storms of the fourteenth century' RIGHT

2. MEETING SOME WETLANDS

The Fens

At the end of the last Ice Age, around 12,000 years ago, the North Sea, swollen with water from the retreating ice sheets and glaciers, flooded East Anglia's Fenland basin and deposited masses of glacial debris washed in from the bed of the sea. Rivers flowing in from the south dropped their burdens of sand and silt there, too. Gradually, as the rivers continued their work, the basin was filled and the sea was nudged away northwards. Then pine, oak and yew colonised the land and a park-like setting was created, with deer, wild cattle, horses and pigs grazing and foraging in the glades and being stalked by human huntsmen. The area was still quite flat and low-lying and prone to invasion by the sea. The blackened tree trunks known as **bog oaks** that one may find hauled from the fields and dumped at their edges had been preserved for thousands of years by the Fenland peat and some date from one such inundation around 5–6,000 years ago. By this time the rising sea level had reduced the river gradients and made them more prone to flooding, with huge beds of peat forming in their badly drained valleys. Much later, around the time that Iron Age people were casting offerings to their water gods, the tides were sweeping up the fenland rivers and dropping particles of silt on their beds. With the fairly recent shrinkage of the surrounding peat, these silt-encrusted former river courses can be seen standing slightly above the surrounding black peat land as snaking, whitened ridges. They are known as **roddons**.

The Norfolk Broads

The Broads are widenings of the Norfolk rivers, like the Ant and Bure, though it was only quite recently shown, following the publication of a paper by three researchers in 1960, that they are of human rather than of natural creation. The

Prehistoric bog oaks hauled from the peat of the Fens.

Broads are, in fact, flooded medieval peat diggings. This cutting of turves was done on a phenomenal scale during the period of accelerating medieval population growth in the twelfth, thirteenth and early fourteenth centuries. The industry was spearheaded by monastic communities, with the priories of St Bene't and St Olave acquiring vast empires of peat diggings or **turbaries**. Norwich nearby was warmed and fuelled by the output of turf and bog oaks from what would become Broadland. At first the drier beds were worked and then the damper beds by the rivers, though rising sea levels were increasingly threatening and in 1287 a storm surge swept seawater over the altar of St Bene't's. For a while, in the years around 1300, contrivances of rakes and drag nets were used to scrape peat from submerged beds, but during the fourteenth century digging came to an end and the old workings were inundated and abandoned. As the centuries rolled on all memory of the turbaries was lost and the Broads were considered to be natural water features.

The windmill at Thurne in the Norfolk Broads.

The Somerset Levels

The Levels bore some similarity to the Fens but had a rather more precarious existence because the higher rainfall in the region could produce rapid flooding. At such times torrents from the hills swelled rivers like the Tone that flowed down into the peat basin around the River Parrett. Also the greater range of the tides funnelling into the Bristol Channel increased the risk of incursions by the sea. In other ways the Levels resembled the Fens, as a region where peat formed in flat, flood-prone river basins, where marine incursions threatened, and where monastic communities led the reclamation drive.

Coastal salt-marsh

Salt-marshes were found in many places along the British coast. They originated as sand flats that were exposed at low tide, and then had mud deposited on them by incoming rivers, streams and tides. As the sand flats gradually became mud banks, plants like eel grass and samphire, which are specially adapted to thrive in salty soils, colonised the banks, paving the way for other plant colonists, such as wormwood and sea lavender. The mud banks are now patterned with slightly hummocky ridges and mounds of vegetation. As the plants spread they trap more silt, and the rising tides and incoming streams cut winding patterns of creeks between them. Eventually the banks grow to heights that even the greatest tides cannot top. The old salt-marshes were malarial, secretive and uninviting to settlement and this desolation increased their appeal to smugglers. They were, however, associated with valuable common pastures and in Kent the **wicks** or huts used by medieval shepherds have given rise to some place-names. In addition, the evaporating of brine from the nearby sea in great pans produced salt, an essential agent for the preservation of meat and fish, and provided an alternative to the land-based saltworks of Cheshire. Salt-marshes experienced active colonisation during the earlier medieval centuries, though the deterioration of the climate beginning in the years around 1300 caused many retreats. Lands reclaimed from the Humber estuary by the monks of Meaux Abbey, and the coast at Cliffe in Kent, where the monks of Christchurch Priory built great sea walls, were among the many places overrun by the sea.

3. DRAINING THE WETLANDS

The drainage of wetlands and salt-marshes did not simply involve gains for agriculture. There were also losses. Fish were important sources of fresh protein

The remains of salt evaporating pans and the windmill that raised the brine at St Monans in Fife.

and the eel catch was so valued in some places that tenants might pay their entire rents in eels. Wildfowl were also important. In medieval times ducks were caught by gently shepherding the birds into the natural trap of the shallowing waters of a tapering limb of a lake, while in the early nineteenth century artificial **duck decoys** were made by creating star-shaped ponds with several narrowing arms or 'pipes' and using a fox-coloured dog to weave between wicker screens on the shore so that it seemed to appear and vanish, luring the curious and mystified ducks toward their doom. Numerous old decoys can still be found. Salt was the salt-marsh's greatest asset and was an immensely important coastal industry. Late Saxon King's Lynn was built on the remains of abandoned **salterns** and the sandy spoil from salt-making raised the ground by up to 20ft (6m), making it possible to build a town in the midst of a salt-marsh.

In exploring the fate of wetlands, the following points may be useful. First, considerable reclamation took place in the early medieval centuries, sometimes under the leadership of a local feudal lord or on the initiative of a community, but the monastic houses were especially active in the field of land reclamation.

In the Somerset Levels the abbeys of Athelney, Glastonbury and Muchelney and Wells Cathedral led the operations; in Yorkshire Meaux Abbey led the assault on the Humber wetlands; and in the Fens the abbeys of Crowland, Denney, Ramsey and Thorney and Peterborough Cathedral led the way.

Considerable reclamation work had also taken place before the Norman Conquest, though more needs to be learned about the methods used. In medieval times we know that **warping** was a widely used technique in coastal reclamation, the **warps** being embankments made of piles and brushwood. Once the land within the warp had been secured, an advance seawards would be made with the establishment of a new warp, and so the stealing of land from the sea would proceed. Earthen banks were often employed to exclude the sea from newly won areas. In Norfolk the coastal belt of natural sand dunes was fortified with posts, rails, faggots, clay and stones. A series of sea banks marked stages in the reclamation of land from the Wash, the best known being the Roman banks, which were actually constructed around AD 1250. In the internal wetlands, like the Fens and Levels, the emphasis was on improving the situation for the evacuation of water. This could involve the straightening of natural watercourses and the digging of new canals or cuts, like Bishop Morton's late fifteenth-century Leam in the Fens or the Mark Yeo cut in the Levels around 1300. In the Fens much of the reclaimed land was employed for cultivation, while in the Levels, with its wetter climate, it was mainly used for pasture.

Towards the close of the Middle Ages the magnitude of draining projects increased, but they still tended to remain localised. Because the improvements were carried out piecemeal, drainage operations in one locality often exported the problems of flooding to adjacent landowners. In the 1630s the 4th Earl of Bedford moved his operation up a notch. He employed a Dutch drainage engineer, Cornelius Vermuyden, attracted a number of entrepreneurs or 'adventurers', and began work on a regional level. A major new canal was driven right across the Fens. In the Levels the King's Sedgemoor drain was cut after 1791, and between 1797 and 1816 the King's Sedgemoor was enclosed and a series of drainage channels or **rhines** was cut to evacuate the water.

However, the fact that a scheme was grandiose did not ensure its success. Visitors to the Fens in the early eighteenth century often found the countryside flooded and wreathed in fog. Environmental problems had not been thought through. As the peat had dried, so it shrank, dried and began to be consumed by bacteria. Thus the land levels declined and flooding returned. Salvation came during the eighteenth century with the employment of windmills as pumps to raise water from one system of drains and channels into another. By the middle

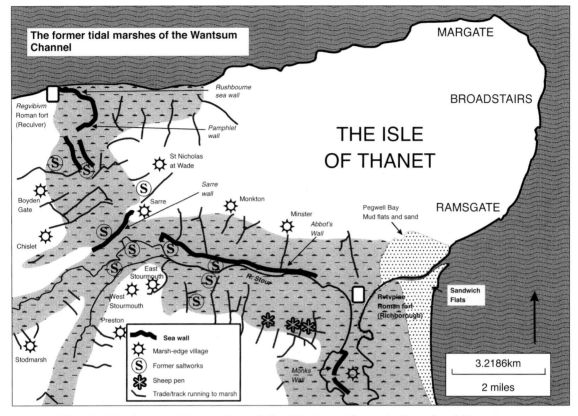

Fig. 20. The former tidal marshes of the Wantsum Channel. The Isle of Thanet was separated from Kent by the Wantsum Channel, which was guarded at each end by a Roman fort. During the Middle Ages colonists reclaimed the straits and Thanet was linked to the mainland.

of the century about 250 such mills were in operation, though after 1820 steam engines began to take over the role.

Drainage has created its own landscape. In the Fens the traces of the old roddons are overshadowed by the great waterways and canals that loom ominously above the black winter fieldscapes of ever-declining peat. In the Levels the nineteenth-century rhines are distinctive features of the moist green pastures. They were dug in 'ropes' 20ft (6m) long, and in cross-section resembled a tapering bucket, 8ft (2.4m) wide at the top, 5ft (1.5m) deep and 4ft (1.2m) wide at their flat bottoms. Once dug, they were planted with willows, the roots of which helped to stabilise their banks.

The story of drainage and land reclamation can be explored through the legacy of place-names. Table 9.1 shows some to look for during a local investigation.

One of the few surviving fenland wind pumps at Wicken Fen.

Winter visitors, including these rare whooper swans, still visit the floodable washlands beside the Fenland waterways.

When exploring landscapes of wetland and coastal reclamation, the following clues may be helpful:

- Look at the **pattern of settlement**. A string of old villages with medieval churches could formerly have stood along a seashore or on the edge of fenland. These villages could well have been the bases where the colonists lived. Places with ornate and imposing churches are likely to have enjoyed the wealth to support campaigns of colonisation.

- In drained and colonised areas, villages may be far fewer and settlers may have gravitated to **farmsteads** and **hamlets**, particularly when they took over old monastic estates.

- Check for the presence of **medieval monasteries**, **priories** and **cathedrals** in the region. These places tended to spearhead colonisation in both inland

Table 9.1. *Place-names indicating drainage and land reclamation*

Name	Language	Meaning
Adventurers	English	Land reclamation associated with entrepreneurs
Brooks	dialect	A Sussex word for salt-marsh
Carr	Old Norse	Wetland with brushwood, alder swamp
Coy	English	Place that has/had a duck decoy
Ea, yeo	Old French	River, waterway
Ey	Old English	Island, mainly one standing in marsh
Fen	Old English	Fen, low wetland
Fleet	Old English	Inlet or estuary
Gull, gullet	English	Curve in a flood bank marking an old burst or an outfall ditch
Hamm	Old English	River meadow, place surrounded by marsh
Holm	Old Norse	Island, promontory, island in marshes
Inning	English	The expanse of reclaimed land behind a sea wall
Lynne, lin, len	British	Lake or pool
Lode	Middle English	Fenland watercourse or canal associated with Roman or medieval trade
Marsh	Old English	Marsh
Mere	Old English	Large pond or small lake (but also a boundary)
Mire	Old Norse	Swamp, mire
Moor	Old English/Old Norse	Can be lowland heath and waterlogged or 'moorish' ground

Name	Language	Meaning
Moss	Old English/Old Norse	Bog
Rhine	English	Drainage cut in Somerset Levels
Trade	English	Trackway, sometimes running along a sea wall
Salt	Old English	Place associated with salt-making
Sleap	Old English	Wet, slippery place
Strode	Old English	Southern equivalent of carr
Undertakers	English	Not to do with funerals but the same as Adventurers
Waller, weller	Old English	A medieval salt boiler, marking the site of a former saltworks
Wash, was	Old English	Floodplain land
Wem	Old English	Filthy, marshy
Wick	Old English	Shepherd's hut in salt-marsh, but can also be a cheese farm, a Roman roadside village or other possibilities

wetlands and coastal regions, and to serve as pace-setters for lords and communities in adjacent areas.

- Reclamation took place within an **existing landscape**. Remember that new farmland was bought at the cost of a host of wetland resources. Fish weirs, eel traps, sheep and cattle tracks weaving through the marshes and the natural lake funnels used in wildfowling may well have vanished without trace. However, salt-making may have left traces of the places where the evaporating pans lay, perhaps in the form of spoil mounds of sand, areas of scorched ground, or 'salt' or 'waller' place-names.
- Look out for traces of **embankments**, even if they are now well inland from the sea. These could have been the sea banks employed to protect newly reclaimed land from incursions by the sea, though there is a

possibility that an example might be a small dyke or linear earthwork (see Chapter Six).

- In old fenland areas look at the **waterways**. Natural streams and rivers always sway and curve to some degree, while artificial drainage channels were dug straight. However, it was quite common for natural rivers to be straightened in order to increase their gradients, and hence their rates of flow, making it less likely that they would burst their banks. Try to piece together a picture of how the drainage system worked, from the field ditches down to the rivers.
- Look at the **field patterns** established as land was reclaimed from fen and salt-marsh. In the Fens, where the emphasis is on arable farming, modern agri-business has largely obliterated the first field patterns, but in the Levels relics of neat, rectilinear hedgerow patterns can still be seen. In places reclaimed from the sea around the coasts of Kent and Sussex the emphasis on shepherding has left the landscapes quite open.
- In the Fens and the Broads most of the **windmills** were provided to pump water rather than to mill grain. Most have gone, but the stumps of some

Field patterns created by drainage and reclamation, as seen from Burrow Mump in the Somerset Levels.

Hedged and ditched pastures on reclaimed land in the Somerset Levels.

abandoned tower mills survive, as do several better-preserved examples. There were just a few mills in coastal localities that were used to raise brine to evaporating pans, as at the quite well-preserved saltworks near St Monans in East Fife.

- Use the table above to check all the **place-names** in your locality; they can help you to re-create the old environments.

And now you are the detective and your witness, your homeland, awaits your interrogation.

Further Reading

Andrews, J. (ed.), *The Story of Where You Live* (Reader's Digest, 2005)

Aston, M., *Monasteries* (Batsford, 1993)

——, *Interpreting the Landscape from the Air* (Tempus, 2002)

Beresford, M.W., *History on the Ground*, 2nd edn (Methuen, 1971)

—— and Hurst J.G., *Deserted Medieval Villages* (Lutterworth Press, 1971)

Bettey, J.H., *Estates and the English Countryside* (Batsford, 1993)

Bowden, M. (ed.), *Unravelling the Landscape* (Tempus, 1999)

Burgess, C., *The age of Stonehenge* (Dent, 1980)

Cantor, L., *The English Medieval Landscape* (Croom Helm, 1982)

Crawford, O.G.S., *Archaeology in the Field* (Dent, 1953)

Davies, H., *Roads in Roman Britain* (Tempus, 2002)

Harvey, G., *Parkland* (National Trust, 2002)

Hawkes, J., *A Land* (Cresset Press, 1951)

Hodges, R., *Wall-to-wall History* (Duckworth, 1991)

Hoskins, W.G., *The Making of the English Landscape* (Hodder & Stoughton, 1955)

Millman, R.N., *The Making of the Scottish Landscape* (Batsford, 1975)

Parry, J., *Heathland* (National Trust, 2003)

Rackham, O., *Trees and Woodland in the Landscape* (Dent, 1976)

——, *The History of the Countryside* (Dent, 1986)

——, *Woodlands* (Harper Collins, 2006)

Smith, J. and Stevenson, D., *Fermfolk and Fisherfolk* (Mercat Press, 1992)

Smout, T.C. (ed.), *People and Woods in Scotland* (Edinburgh University Press, 2003)

Taylor, C., *Fields in the English Landscape* (Dent, 1975)

——, *Roads and Tracks of Britain* (Dent, 1979)

——, *Village and Farmstead* (George Philip, 1983)

Thirsk, J., *The English Rural Landscape* (Oxford University Press, 2000)

Winchester, A.J.L., *The Harvest of the Hills* (Edinburgh University Press, 2000)

The following books by Richard Muir may prove useful

The English Village (Thames & Hudson, 1980)

Riddles in the British Landscape (Thames & Hudson, 1981)

The Shell Guide to Reading the Landscape (Michael Joseph, 1981, repr. 1984, rev. edn 1989)

The Lost Villages of Britain (Michael Joseph, 1982, rev. edn 1985)

History from the Air (Michael Joseph, 1983)

The National Trust Guide to Prehistoric and Roman Britain, with Humphrey Welfare (George Philip, 1983)

Visions of the Past, with Christopher Taylor (Dent, 1983)

East Anglian Landscapes, with J. Ravensdale (Michael Joseph, 1984, repr. 1988)

A Traveller's History of Britain and Ireland (Michael Joseph 1984, repr. 1990)

The National Trust Guide to Dark Age and Medieval Britain (George Philip, 1985)

Reading the Celtic Landscapes (Michael Joseph, 1986)

Stones of Britain (Michael Joseph, 1986)

The National Trust Guide to Rivers of Britain, with Nina Muir (Webb & Bower, 1986, repr. 1990)

Landscape and Nature Photography (George Philip, 1987)

Old Yorkshire (Michael Joseph, 1987)

The Countryside Encyclopaedia (Macmillan, 1988)

Hedgerows, with Nina Muir (Michael Joseph, 1988)

Fields, with Nina Muir (Macmillan, 1989)

Portraits of the Past (Michael Joseph, 1989)

Castles and Strongholds (Macmillan, 1990)

The Dales of Yorkshire (Macmillan, 1991)

Villages of England (Thames & Hudson, 1992)

Coastlines of Britain (Macmillan, 1993)

The Yorkshire Countryside: A Landscape History (Edinburgh University Press, 1997)

Approaches to Landscape (Macmillan, 1998–9)

New Reading the Landscape: Fieldwork in Landscape History (Exeter University Press, 2000)

Valley of Ghosts (Northern Books, 2006)

Index